TIME
AT WAR

Fiction

Spaces of the Dark
The Rainbearers
Corruption
Meeting Place
Accident
Assassins
Impossible Object
Natalie Natalia
Catastrophe Practice
Imago Bird
Serpent
Judith
Hopeful Monsters
Children of Darkness and Light
The Hesperides Tree
Inventing God
Look at the Dark

Non-fiction

African Switchback
The Life of Raymond Raynes
Experience and Religion
The Assassination of Trotsky
Julian Grenfell
Rules of the Game
Beyond the Pale
Efforts at Truth
The Uses of Slime Mould: Essays of Four Decades

TIME
AT WAR

Nicholas Mosley

Weidenfeld & Nicolson

LONDON

First published in Great Britain in 2006
by Weidenfeld & Nicolson

1 3 5 7 9 10 8 6 4 2

A CIP catalogue record for this book
is available from the British Library.

ISBN-13 9 780 297 85240 7
ISBN-10 0 297 85240 X

Typeset at The Spartan Press Ltd,
Lymington, Hants

Printed in Great Britain by
Clays Ltd, St Ives plc

Weidenfeld & Nicolson

The Orion Publishing Group Ltd
Orion House
5 Upper Saint Martin's Lane
London, WC2H 9EA

The Orion Publishing Group's policy is to use papers that
are natural, renewable and recyclable products and made
from wood grown in sustainable forests. The logging and
manufacturing processes are expected to conform to the
environmental regulations of the country of origin.

www.orionbooks.co.uk

To
Mervyn Davies

Illustrations

All photographs used within this book have come from the author's private albums.

Foreword

When I got home from the Second World War in the autumn of 1945 I knew I wanted to be a writer but I did not know how to write about war. The books about the First World War that I had admired had been about endurance amid the horror and senselessness of war. This could be written about unequivocally. But I had come to realise that the war I had been engaged in was not senseless: it had to be fought, though the horror and impression of futility were there. So in what style could one write about something that was both necessary and futile?

In the 1980s I wrote briefly about my participation in war in my books about my father, Oswald Mosley, who spent most of the war as a security risk in jail. But these accounts were in relation to the peculiar situation of my father. It is only recently in my old age that I have felt at ease in writing fully about my experiences of war.

War is both senseless and necessary, squalid and fulfilling, terrifying and sometimes jolly. This is like life. Humans are at home in war (though they seldom admit this). They feel they know what they have to do.

It is in peace that humans for the most part feel lost: they have to find out what it is they have to do. For reassurance they find themselves dragged back to conflict and to stories of conflict. But this should be shown as unnecessary by a true story of war.

I

The Second World War got under way on 3 September 1939 when I was sixteen and staying at my father's house in Derbyshire. I heard the Prime Minister, Mr Chamberlain, announce the declaration of war; then I went out and kicked a football about on the lawn in front of the house. My old Nanny, who was at that time looking after my young brother Michael, leaned out of a window and asked if I had heard the news, and was I not concerned? I said that I did not think the declaration of war meant very much: there was something called the Maginot Line in eastern France that the Germans could not get through, and something called the Siegfried Line in western Germany that the British and French could not get through; so the politicians would just play their war games for a while, and then the whole thing would fizzle out. Surely the politicians were not mad enough for anything else to happen? My old Nanny did not seem to be impressed, and withdrew.

For most of that autumn and winter my forecast appeared to be coming true. Nothing much was happening between Germany and France. Then in May 1940 the German army went round the northern end of the Maginot Line through Belgium and Holland: apparently no one confronting the issue had paid attention to the fact that the Maginot Line did not stretch along the frontier with Belgium. I had not taken into account the possibility that politicians and generals could indeed be so mad.

In June 1940 my father, Oswald Mosley, at that time the leader of the British Union of Fascists, was arrested as a security risk and taken to Brixton Prison to be held without charge for an indefinite period under the hurriedly cobbled-up Regulation 18B(1a), which gave the Home Secretary power to detain any member of an organisation whose leaders 'have or have had associations with persons concerned in the government, or sympathetic with the system of government, of any power with which His Majesty is at war'. My father had been touring the country making speeches saying that the war was a grievous mistake and should be stopped: if we left Hitler alone he would attack Russia and leave us alone, which was what he had been saying he wanted to do. At this time I thought that my father was a politician less lunatic than most.

On the night of his arrest my housemaster came into my room at school (at Eton boys had rooms on their own) and told me that he had been telephoned by my stepmother who had asked him to break the news to me of my father's arrest. I thanked him; but he hung about as if there was something more to be said. I could not think what this might be. Then he murmured something like – Did I think there was anything to it? I realised he was asking me if I thought my father might be considered a traitor. I said – Oh no, he just thinks this war is a mistake. My housemaster seemed dubious, but left it at that.

I realised that things might be difficult, however, when I went out to attend an early morning class: a frequent anxiety had been what there might be about my father in the papers. But one of the virtues of Eton is, or was, that many boys come from families used to the ways of maverick politicians – some of whom indeed in the past might have spent time in jail on matters of principle. So in the morning there were glances, but not much was said.

It did not strike me that I myself should do anything other than volunteer to join the army before I would be due to be called up on my nineteenth birthday in June 1942. I saw what my father meant about the war being a mistake, but this did not seem to be relevant to me. Most Etonians who had not got family connections with the other services or with cavalry regiments opted to go into one of the Guards regiments; or if they wished to be slightly less conventional, into the Rifle Brigade or the King's Royal Rifle Corps. Myself and my contemporary friends planned to apply to join the Rifle Brigade, in the hope of becoming officers.

There were two grave impediments to my being accepted as a potential officer. The first was my father, who was still in jail, although now in Holloway with my stepmother (after more than a year as ordinary prisoners they had been allowed to share a double cell here at the insistence of Winston Churchill, who had once been a friend of both). But hostility against them in the country was still strong. The second snag was that from the age of about seven I had a bad stammer. Of course some kind of war work would be available to me – but an infantry officer? Lives might depend on the ability of an officer to give rapid orders.

The difficulty about my father was somewhat balanced by the influence of my formidable aunt, Irene Ravensdale, my dead mother's older sister, and a Baroness in her own right. She was acquainted with the Colonel-in-Chief of the Rifle Brigade: these were the days of the old-boy net, when people supposedly of influence could be expected to know one another. So my aunt had a word with the Colonel and explained – I have no idea what she explained, but by the time a Rifle Brigade recruiting team came down to Eton to hold interviews with potential officers, I was told that I would be accepted as a trainee, although this did not guarantee that I would graduate.

So in April 1942 I travelled with a group of mostly other ex-public schoolboys to the Rifle Brigade depot at Winchester, where for three months we were to be treated no differently from the rest of the newly recruited other ranks. I wrote to my sister of our arrival at Winchester Station –

At once of course we split up into our school cliques – Etonians rather aloof and bored and hands in pockets: the rest alternating between Rugby raucousity and grammar-school timidity. We walked crocodile-wise, Etonians at least 100 yards in the rear, until we arrived at a place which reminded me of Brixton . . . We were herded to our quarters which were like the basement of a morgue, with rows of beds constructed of steel bars, many vertical, and a few bent horizontal and arranged neatly so that the bars coincided with one's hips and the gaps with one's head and waist.

My sister, two years older than me, was at this time doing war work in London, making bits and pieces for armaments.

It was the style of Etonians to be flippant or condescending about things that might be unpleasant; thus one had managed to get through much of school life. It did not seem that the army would be very different.

A week or two later I was writing to my father –

The routine is as intense as expected; non-stop from 6.30 to 6 and very often extra fatigue after that. But there is barely time to stay depressed, and the evenings are made happy by the mere fact that we can get outside the barrack gates. We are all mixed up with the conscripts – men of 35–40 – better than younger ones who might be more aggressively hostile to us future (we hope) officers. But these are bad enough. They fuss around swearing (*always* the same drab monosyllable) spitting and interfering with everyone with hoarse belches of amusement. The sergeants are wonderful men, who give us hell on the parade ground, calling us such names as make us laugh and wonder at their power to conceive such obscenities. Off duty they do quite a lot to help us.

My sister and I had visited my father two or three times when he had been in Brixton Prison. We had been under supervision in an austere visiting room and had been amazed at our father's cheerfulness. He said he was making profitable use of his time by being taught German by some of the internees; and he then hoped to embark on a course of reading European literature and philosophy. It was as if, having made his public protests about the war, he was not outraged that he should be in prison.

At Winchester the ex-public schoolboys on the whole seemed better than others at having to shave and wash and wash up in cold water, for instance; the conscripts were better at the ritual of setting out in meticulous geometrical order their bedding and equipment ready for inspection every morning. What I remember now about the depot at Winchester is the strange mixture of bonhomie and misery – the former mostly to do with drinking beer in the evenings and making jokes; the latter often to do with my stammer. We potential officers would be taken out of our squad one by one on the parade ground and put in charge of the drill. It sometimes seemed that I, standing with my mouth open silently like an Aunt Sally at a fairground, might unwittingly become like the Emperor Christophe of Haiti who used for his amusement to march his crack troops over a cliff. Once, when my squad was proceeding at the fast trot that was the customary style of the Rifle Brigade straight towards the doorway that led from the parade ground to the NAAFI canteen, I thought there might occur some happy outcome to my predicament. But the sergeant-instructor beside me, sensing a plot, bellowed in time 'About turn! Left turn! Right turn! Knees up! At the double!' with appropriate expletives. The insults that the sergeants were accustomed to hurl at us were enjoyable, though they were usually gentle with me. I had a friend called Pollock who became something of the squad butt. When we were standing to attention the sergeant would stand very close to him and yell – 'Pollock! Spell it with a P, do you? You sack of shit!'

From Winchester I was given leave to go up to London once a week to see a stammer specialist. This was Dr Lionel Logue, who had been treating the King. I had been going to him during my last year at Eton, and I did not think he was doing me much good. I desperately wanted to get rid of my stammer, but he tried to get me speaking in lilting rhythmical cadences like a ham actor or a politician or a clergyman. While I was with him I could do this quite well; then when I got away it seemed I would rather stammer than sound like an actor or a politician or a clergyman. No one made much sense of my stammer until I was sent by the army after the war to another quite different type of specialist. He said – But has it ever struck you that you may not really want to get rid of your stammer? I was for a moment outraged: me not want to get rid of the stammer that caused me such misery? He explained how a stammer might be a form of self-protection. But the understanding of this belongs to a later part of the story.

Some of our squad had been at school at Winchester just down the hill, and they would go down on Saturdays to visit the boys they had perhaps been in love with at school. Then on Sundays we would line up for Church

Parade and march to the stunningly beautiful Winchester Cathedral where one of the popular hymns was to the tune of the German national anthem, and we would try to remember the German words. Then on our way back through the streets, proudly led by the regimental band playing the Rifle Brigade march, we would sing its time-honoured words –

> Oh the Rifle Brigade has gone away
> And they've left all the girls in the family way
> The KRRs who are coming behind
> Will have seven-and-six a week to find

– seven shillings and sixpence being the cost, in those days, of the upkeep of a child.

No one at the depot seemed much interested in my father; and I was not thinking much about the sense or ethics of the war. It seemed we were all involved in some gigantic juggernaut of fate or the grim workings of evolution. Our task was just to keep going, with as much good humour as possible. By this time both Russia and America were in the war against Hitler, so there was the sense that in the end, so long as one stayed alive, things would turn out all right.

From Winchester our group of mainly ex-public school-boys went briefly to Tidworth on Salisbury Plain, where we did training with transport. The speciality of the Rifle Brigade and the King's Royal Rifle Corps was to form motorised battalions ready for quick deployment in war. Then from Tidworth we moved to an Officer Cadet

Training Unit in York. Here we were treated more specifically as potential officers: we did tactical training at platoon and company level. But we still had to go regularly on long half-jogging marches covering ten miles in two hours, carrying heavy packs and weapons; we were tested for the dexterity with which we could take various weapons to bits and put them together again. We learned to drive trucks; we were taking on cross-country motorbike rides by a former hill-climbing champion, during which he led us up almost vertical slopes and we laughed when our machines tipped over backwards and chased us down the hill. We were lectured on current affairs and regimental history. We also felt free to indulge in some of the more traditional pastimes of officers.

I had asked my father if I could borrow his shotgun. I wrote to him from Fulford Barracks, York –

Many happy returns of the day.

Your lawyer has managed to rescue your guns from the Home Office, and they are now safely up here with me. The trouble is cartridges, which are practically unobtainable, but perhaps some of my sporting friends in the OCTU will be able to wheedle me some from their family dealers. I will be able to get in a fairly regular shoot on Saturday afternoons, and we are now being encouraged to take a gun when we go on manoeuvres on the moors. The authorities are very reasonable about all this; and if one gives a pheasant or two to the officers' mess they will let you take a gun almost anywhere.

We have now finished our mechanic's course, from which I passed as a 1st class driver-mechanic, which was really very bogus, and was granted only through systematic flattering of the instructor. Also our wireless course, which was not so successful, as I was rather over-confident and idle, spending most of the time listening to the BBC and trying to wreck the wireless schemes by sending false messages. Which displeased people, and I fear I may have got a low mark.

But we are embarking upon the most important part of our training now – endless tactics and toughening courses, horrible 5-day manoeuvres in Northumberland, sleeping open-air with one blanket and being harassed by live ammunition and artillery barrages. Then on December 18 we pass out complete with natty suiting and prominent chest and are allowed to show off to our families for a week or so. I will come and see you then just before Christmas.

The times that it seems meant most to me while I was stationed at York were those when I could get away at weekends to the home of an old school friend, Timmy, some five or six miles away; here a group of us continued enthusiastically to play the games we had played as children – a chasing-and-capture-and-escaping game called Lions; acting games; pencil-and-paper games. Then occasionally at weekends, I and others would be able to get down to London where my sister shared a flat with two girlfriends also working in her small-arms factory. We would land up in a favourite nightclub called The Nut

House where we drank and sang communal songs like *The Sheik of Araby* (to which the antiphon was *With no pants on*); or *Bell-bottom trousers coats of navy blue* (antiphon: *He'll climb the rigging like his father used to do*). These chants have stuck in my mind like strange mantras. The lady who ran The Nut House told me she had known my father, and did I know how attractive my stammer was? I said – No. This might have been a life-giving moment for me.

When the time came for me and my colleagues either to become officers or to have failed, I was interviewed by the young captain who had largely been responsible for our training and he told me that they did not usually commission cadets with a stammer as bad as mine, but . . . but I don't remember him quite being able to finish this sentence. But anyway, there I was, turning up in London for Christmas 1942 resplendent in my new Second-Lieutenant's uniform. And the battle of Alamein had by this time been won, the battle of Stalingrad was going all right, was it not? And the war seemed as distant as ancient mythology.

One of the consequences of my having become an officer was that I got permission from the Home Office to spend the best part of a day with my father and stepmother in Holloway Jail. So in the New Year I dropped in at Fortnum and Mason on the way and arrived with the inside of my huge army overcoat hung with a ham and a bottle of brandy, and under my arm a Wagner record for Diana's wind-up gramophone with a giant horn. We had a fine day – this was the first time I felt old enough to talk on anything like equal terms with my father – we did not say much about the war; we talked about ideas and books. Then towards the end of the day there was a knock on the door of the bleak cell-like room where my father and stepmother and I were sampling the brandy; my father said, 'Who is it?' and a voice said, 'The Governor.' My father said, 'Oh do come in!' and made a half-hearted attempt to hide the bottle under the table. The Governor was a pleasant man and he stayed and chatted with us for a while. Then my father said, 'Would you like a glass of brandy?' The Governor said, 'Thank you!' My stepmother went off to wash a tooth-glass. The Governor said, 'Ah, you don't often find brandy like this nowadays!'

My father still seemed extraordinarily serene in prison; it was as if prison were evidence of his disapproval of war. Then, on a later visit when we were alone together for a while, he did speak briefly of the war. He said that when I went abroad to fight, if ever it happened that I were taken prisoner, I should remember some password that he would give me in case he were able to get in touch with me. I thought this odd: surely my father could have no contacts now with Germany? He had never, unlike my stepmother, been on close personal terms with high-up Nazis. I thought – This is just a way of implying that he might still have a finger in the world of intrigue. But I did perhaps begin to wonder – Well it might not be such a bad thing after all to be taken prisoner and so survive a war which before long, surely, would be as good as won. But what a time it might still take to finish it off – for armies to slog to and fro across North Africa, and all the way back across Russia to Berlin.

2

Newly commissioned officers waiting to be sent overseas went to the Rifle Brigade Holding Battalion at Ranby, in Nottinghamshire, a rather bleak encampment of huts either side of the Retford–Worksop road. But here everything became different.

We felt ourselves liberated from institutional subservience; from the need to ingratiate and dissemble. We could begin to be what we felt we were: but most of us were only nineteen.

We were each to be in charge of the training of a platoon of thirty to thirty-five men, most of them much older than ourselves. I wrote to my Aunt Irene –

At the moment I have a platoon of 35 men all to myself who are only just starting their training, and who are ignorant and stupid beyond belief. So I have a hard and anxious job, but I believe when some of the other officers come back off leave I may have someone to help me. Unfortunately I was given the platoon which had the reputation of being the scruffiest in the Company, and now it is up to me I suppose to descruff them. They never wash, lose all their equipment and come out half dressed; but are incredibly keen when out training in the country, and good fun if you treat them right. They are so shabby and slack about their appearance and their barrack room, and yet they are so pleasant and good-natured when one chats to them. I try to be both pleasant and firm, but it is tricky.

The time is taken up with Weapon Training, which I leave to the NCOs, who are efficient, and can do that sort of thing much better than us: unending lectures on Gas, Map Reading, Tactics, and even First Aid and Topical Interest, which I give, rather shakily at first, but I am getting used to it now, and am becoming reasonably good. My sergeant is very helpful. I really do take my hat off to these old NCOs, some of whom have been in the army for years. They all play up to us junior officers, and there is no question of the jealousy which I believe you get in some regiments.

To my old school friend, Timmy, who was following in my footsteps a few months behind me and who had written asking for hints from which he could learn, I wrote –

So long as you tell your sergeant just what you want done and leave him to do it in his own way, the house on fire burns merrily. It is only when you butt in on the sergeant's pitch, and quibble with him in front of the men, that the trouble starts. When you want to take over the platoon he will step into the background and help without pestering suggestions.

With the men I have so far got on well, and we have

been able to laugh together and they do have respect. I have only had to deliver one personal rocket when I saw a man chewing gum on parade. I told him to spit it out, to which he answered that he was unable because it had stuck to the roof of his palate. I then waxed vicious and said that he either got his gum unstuck or I would get him so stuck himself that he would not be able to extricate self for weeks, at which he accordingly expectorated (is this the word?) and so we went on.

Later. Christ, am I weary this evening. My platoon is really too bloody keen for words. They led me slap through a river today, and I had to follow with pretence of enjoyment. But they are fun, and so much more worthwhile than the old sweats I was with at Winch.

When we went out on manoeuvres we were able to go to the beautiful Peak District of Derbyshire, where it seemed to make sense to do tactical training in the style of stalking-and-catching-and-rescuing games which my friends and I had played ever since childhood. My friend and colleague during these exercises was Raleigh Trevelyan, who later was to write one of the best books about fighting in the Second World War, *The Fortress*, about his experiences at the landing at Anzio. In the Peak District we would pit our platoons against each other like Cowboys and Indians; in the evenings we would all sit around campfires and sing songs under the stars. We junior officers often felt more at home with our men than we did in the officers' mess at Ranby. I wrote to my sister –

I really think that the usual life of an officer is even more narrowing and binding than that of a man. In the ranks one was admittedly restricted physically by petty regulations, but as an officer one is up against the appalling tyranny of etiquette and good manners. The mess is stuffy and staid like a Victorian clubroom; and there is no escape. One cannot even roll out and wallow in a pub. One is always under the eye of a keen and critical audience.

It seems that I was beginning to realise that in describing my men as scruffy and unruly, and yet also in important ways the salt of the earth, there was indeed a tradition in which these were likely to be aspects of the same thing.

And before long we junior officers were creating our own manner of anarchic protest by turning one of our rooms (we had rooms which two of us shared in a large hut on its own) into a fantasy nightclub which we called *The Juke Box*. Here, away from the officers' mess, we played records on a wind-up gramophone; we danced ballroom or exotic dances; some of us got hold of women's clothes. There is a tradition in armies for this sort of thing on the fringes of war – presumably as a reaction or counterbalance to the brutally macho business of killing; perhaps psychologically as a form of bonding. I do not know how many of us were at that time, or remained, in fact gay: there was no evidence then of anything overtly sexual. We had nearly all come from public schools where it seemed naturally the fashion to behave in a gay style; what better could one do with no girls in sight? I myself had been no exception to this. The word 'gay' had not been applied to homosexuality yet, but one can see how this use of it arose. Homosexuals were seen as paragons of wit and fantasy; such qualities were life-giving in wartime. In 1942 at Ranby the emphasis was on gaiety in the old sense.

Many of the denizens of *The Juke Box* went on to be killed or wounded in Italy – Timmy Lloyd, one of the occupants of *The Juke Box* room, was shot at point-blank range when leading a patrol; Charlie Morpeth had a leg blown off in a minefield. Bunny Roger, who had been famous as a fashionable milliner before the war and was old enough not to be required to do any fighting, became renowned once more in Italy for the story that he, having become impatient with his regulation officer's pistol, had seized a rifle from one of his men and, after a brief reminder from his corporal as to how it worked, had shot a German at an almost impossible range. Raleigh Trevel-yan, my companion in the cavortings in the Peak District, was grievously wounded in the hand-to-hand fighting at Anzio. Once, when he and I were out with our platoons playing our catching-and-rescuing games, I came across him in the early morning looking pleased and I said to him, 'Raleigh, you're looking very starry-eyed!' and he said 'I've been seduced by my sergeant.'

I wrote to my friend Timmy, who was following my path through the army a few months behind me –

My darling platoon is now very much to my liking. They spend most of their time on training either killing chickens or stealing eggs, of which they give me a goodly portion, so I pretend very hard not to notice, though they would steal just the same if I did. And we have riotous games of football during recreational training, when it is their sole objective to trip me up and sit on me whether I have the ball or not. Which I enjoy because some of them are rather attrac.

And later –

My flesh is being torn from my bones by the icy gales which come whipping over these bloody hills.

We were sent off to a colliery in our trucks to pick up cinders to mend a road. The colliery had cinders in plenty, but also a considerable amount of unwanted coal. The first truckload of cinders was a failure, so we were told – no more cinders. Yes but plenty more coal, we bellowed, and rushed off to load up. The platoon took the coal hopefully round to their barrack room. 'That's a good joke!' I said, and had them take it round to my room in the mess. Which they did in bulk, and filled the place with the filthy stuff. Later, of course, I found that it wasn't coal at all but slate, and would by no means burn. Thus my room is filled to overflowing with rank black rock and no hope of getting rid of it. It has also irretrievably blocked the stove in its refusal to burn. So the laugh was on me; but my platoon love me all the same.

This was the gay style. I reported to my sister that to my platoon I was known as 'Mad Mr Mosley'.

I had told my aunt that I was becoming 'reasonably good' at delivering lectures in spite of my stammer, but I do not remember this being so. What I have vivid memories of is my gallant platoon being hard pressed not to roll about in the aisles while I gagged and contorted, and my sergeant being driven eventually to bang on a table with his stick and shout – 'Don't laugh at the officer!'

In fact, perhaps my stammer was even a help to me in what is called bonding with my men, who must have dreaded the style of a gung-ho disciplinarian. The way in which a junior officer was supposed to deal with an offender was by what was called 'putting him on a charge'. This meant that he was taken up in front of a senior officer for punishment. I found I had great reluctance to put anyone on a charge: reproof could be left to the verbal pyrotechnics of the sergeants, from whom, as I had learned when in the ranks, this sort of thing was easy to accept. It seemed to suit the men if they could see their officer in some sort of predicament equivalent to their own; then they might feel some responsibility for him as well as vice versa. This was a lesson I learned that was most valuable later in the war.

The other ranks whom the junior officers came in most personal contact with were the batmen who did the chores in the officers' quarters; and they indeed seemed naturally to treat those who were nominally in charge of them like nannies with children. At the end of my time at Ranby, when I was away on some course before going on embarkation leave, my faithful batman Rifleman Baxter wrote to me –

Dear Sir, thank you for your interesting letter on life at Cawthorne, it sounds an awful place, but I am not at all surprised because it is Yorks, and you can expect something of that sort from the cold wind prevailing, which leaves its unsunny mark on the countenance of the inhabitants. At a place like that you really need a good old soldier to make you comfortable, as they can always find ways and means. I hope that you are more fortunate than many others in having a decent chap who would also have to be a B-scrounger considering the wartime scarcity of certain necessities.

One of the slightly more senior officers I remember with admiration and affection from Ranby was the Signals Officer Laurence Whistler, who would soon become famous for his beautiful engravings on glass. One of Laurence's tasks was to teach us the Morse Code. He would tap out the passages from his favourite poems, and we had to unscramble these and write them down: it was a help if one had some prior knowledge of the particular piece. Laurence was also a memorable wit. Once, when we were having dinner in the mess and a more than usually unpalatable dish was placed in front of us, someone said, 'What on earth is this?' And Laurence said, 'I think it's the Piece of Cod that passeth all understanding.'

In counterpoint to both the gaiety and the drudgery of life at Ranby, I carried on an earnest correspondence on the subject of religion with both my aunt and my father. My aunt was a fervent Christian; my father was not. My argument with my aunt had come about because she had become anxious that I was spending too many weekends perhaps pursuing 'gaiety' in London or at the homes of my friends rather than sticking to duty and commitment. I wrote –

Somebody must have been whispering some very wicked things into your ear. The idea that a Rifle Brigade officer is not allowed to venture more than 5 miles from camp is so much precious nonsense. And to take Saturday night off – well, agreed it is against the rules, but similarly it is forbidden to wear anything except army underwear, and you will not find many level-headed men, let alone an officer, keeping within the bounds of that law. Seriously, even if anyone of any importance should know – and I cannot see that they should – they would care really very little. They might make it an excuse upon which to start a row if they were dissatisfied with my work, but otherwise, Lord, they don't mind.

And the old red herring about shouldn't I suffer as my men – well really, that is a question that I settled to my own satisfaction a long time ago. Do my men mind? Heavens no. They ask me fondly after London every Monday morning. I show them that I can plunge around with them during the week, and do a great deal more work than they do too, and they judge me on my ability to handle them, and not on the amount of self-suffering I can impose upon myself when off duty. Surely this 'moan moan and let's all be miserable together' idea is horribly wrong. And thank God I truly believe that the men realise it is too.

And I had such an enjoyable weekend! A very good party on Saturday night . . .

And then later, after my aunt had sent me a copy of a speech she had made to an assemblage of bishops –

Of course I agree entirely that there is no hope for the world and the progress of our civilisation if we move and live guided merely by political or economic considerations. Thus you say that belief in religion and in a Church is essential. But you are anxious to centre this necessary Faith in the doctrine of Christianity as it is interpreted by the Church of England today, and in this I find it impossible to follow you.

Doctrine as interpreted by the C of E seems to me to be this – whether one takes the doctrine of Original Sin literally or metaphorically, it appears that God created man with a proclivity to sin, so man sinned, and continued to wallow in his sin for many gloomy centuries. Then at a given moment God sends his son down to earth in human form, and by his voluntary death the Son of God takes the sins of the world upon his shoulders, and the world is left free from sin. Thus has the ultimate purpose of the world been fulfilled by the life and death of Christ? If so, what is there here upon which we can build a faith for the future? What can we do except sit gloomily and ruminate upon the past, and wait until in the pangs of the aftermath of fulfilment we finally destroy ourselves? The early Christians clearly believed that the purpose of the world had been fulfilled in Jesus, and they hourly expected the end of the world. We were made sinful: all we can do is to pray that Christ will come a second time more swiftly to consummate us.

You will notice that all the way through this argument I have tried to use the phrases 'the doctrine of the C of E', or 'Christianity as interpreted by the Church'. I have never condemned Christianity itself, for I too believe that in the story of Christ's life and teaching there may lie the foundation of our necessary Faith.

What are the facts of Christ's life as far as we are able to ascertain them? He came into the world as a human man born of a human woman. By his personality and teaching he won a great and devoted following and performed many so-called miracles. Through his own intellectual exertions and his emotional experiences he raised his human personality to such a state of perfection that he realised that he himself might be called God. It was the agony in Gethsemane which showed him this, and it was then that he realised that if in becoming perfect man he had become God, and that it was time for him to die and to become God in form as well as in reality. Those are the facts of Christ's life. The rest is either mythical or incidental.

Now here is the foundation for a faith for the future, a hope for man as an individual. This is the message of Jesus – he shows that in man is the seed of God, and that it is through the exertions and understanding of the individual that the state of perfection can be reached. Make yourself perfect first, and then with the love that you would thereby acquire you would be able to make others perfect. He was always a supreme individualist, and the idea of absolute servility of mind to a mystical and dogmatic Church seems entirely against his nature.

These are the impressions that a somewhat irregular Church attendance and a little reading here and there have given me. My mind is not made up, and I hope it will never be, for one should never settle one's opinions, but always be seeking and searching for the Truth.

These ruminations were an attempt to escape from the wearisome routine of everyday reality. A determined effort to find a system of truth beyond the meaninglessness of anarchy. My father professed an interest in religion: he had the idea of a synthesis between Christianity and some sort of Nietzschean elitism. He had introduced me to Nietzsche when he had been reading his work in Holloway, but from the beginning of my own reading of Nietzsche I had the impression that my father was misunderstanding him; as well as, more expectedly, Christianity.

I wrote to my father from Ranby –

I believe that Christ recognises his elect just as much as Nietzsche would like us to recognise his. N's contention that the *Übermenschen* were 'beyond good and evil' is of far greater significance than 'above morality'. To be above morality is merely to be sufficiently civilised to be able to do without a conventional code of behaviour. To be 'beyond good and evil' is to see that such values (both ethical and religious) can be based on entirely different standards.

With Nietzsche's values I have very little sympathy. '*Heiterkeit*' (serenity) – yes, that is perhaps the most desirable quality that any mortal can possess. But '*Härte*' – why always the emphasis in domination and power through hardness? There is no beauty, and I would say very little nobility, in '*Härte*'. But I have wandered from the point. When I began to talk about 'beyond good and evil' I meant to go on to suggest that God is 'beyond G and E', in the sense that it is obvious that his values are based upon entirely different standards to our own. And might not this be the answer to the problem of suffering to which we are so faintly now trying to find a solution? All our ethical systems and philosophies on earth are involved so entirely within the necessary limits of our own assessments of good and evil that I do not think that we, in such an elementary state of mental development, can have any close comprehension of God's conceptions and values. The jump from 'within G and E' to 'beyond G and E' is so great that at the moment I believe it is beyond the powers of our understanding to see what lies upon the other side. When man has developed sufficiently to take this step he will be superman indeed, and close to God; but it seems that we are extremely (though not infinitely) far from it now.

I have become involved in a correspondence upon the Church with Aunty Nina. She was rather sensible about my fierce attack on the C of E, but one of her East End priests to whom she sent on my letter wrote me the most absurdly half-witted reply which only aggravated the grievance. I really do believe that these men do not understand what they say – which perhaps is best, for it is happier for them to be charged with ignorance and stupidity than with gross perversion and distortion. I'm afraid Nina thinks I have become over-influenced by Nietzsche. Which is untrue, for as I have said, with N's ethical values I have no sympathy.

Later, however, I learned that my anti-C of E diatribe had been sent by my other aunt, my mother's younger sister Baba, to her own favourite priest who happened to be a Father Talbot, Superior of the Anglican Community of the Resurrection – which, as things turned out, was to play such a large and vital part in my life years later. I wrote to my father –

Baba's priest was a very good find – far less bogus than Nina's, and very tolerant of my rather wild and woolly criticism. I seem to spend most of my spare time writing long and intricate religious letters; which does not help very much. Like GBS I ask the most searching questions, attempt far too vaguely to answer them, and finish in much the same muddle as I began. But it does keep one's mind feebly ticking over, when one might, in the circumstances, so easily be mentally dead.

In August I wrote to my aunt to say that at the end of the month I would be coming on embarkation leave before being sent abroad to heaven knows where. My aunt and my sister Vivien and my brother Michael and our old Nanny, who was now housekeeper and cook, would be staying in a small holiday house on the north Cornwall coast, and I said I would join them there. I wrote – 'Eventually one will have to look at the world objectively and to decide what is to be one's relation to it; whether to fight the horror or run from it; to search for perfection in the solitude of one's own beliefs, or in the greater struggle for external fulfilment. At the moment however everything is unkindly settled for me, and thus all I can do is sulk or giggle.'

In Cornwall we swam and surfed and picnicked and climbed about on the rocks; we played cards in the evening; we had a good time. I was among people with whom I had spent the best part of my life and whom I loved. But it seemed that we did not quite know what to say to each other about my going off to war: what can one say? My aunt wrote in her diary that I was defensive about my father and was 'shatteringly crude and offensive about Christ'. Perhaps it was not possible for me after all just to sulk or giggle.

One of the last things I did before embarking on the troopship at Liverpool was to go with my grandmother to the Home Office and put in a request to a high-up official that my father should be released from prison; he could surely, we argued, no longer be considered a security risk. And he had phlebitis, which was getting worse, and his doctor had said that without a reasonable chance of exercise he might die. Watching the Home Office official, I felt I could see the levers of his mind clicking this way and that; but whether to the unlocking of prison doors or not I could not tell. My grandmother said, 'This is his son who is going off to war.' I wondered – Could it make any difference, my going off to war?

3

The war in North Africa had been over for some months. The British and Americans had landed at Casablanca, Oran and Algiers in November 1942, and had headed east to link up with the advance of the British across the desert in the west after the victory at El Alamein in October. Hitler had declared war on America in December 1941 at the time of the Japanese attack on Pearl Harbor; for a year the Americans had concentrated on fighting the Japanese in the Pacific. They had then, however, wanted to get a foothold in the war across the Atlantic. By this time the enemy in North Africa consisted almost entirely of Germans: the Italians had faded away after defeats by the British in the two previous years and the German Afrika Korps under Rommel had taken over.

In May 1943 the Allied armies advancing from east and west met in Tunisia and the Germans surrendered en masse. In July Sicily was invaded, where the opposition was again mainly German. By the end of August Sicily had been cleared and the question was being debated among Allied leaders about whether, and how, Italy should be invaded. This was when my group of Rifle Brigade and KRRC officer reinforcements were setting out from Liverpool.

We seemed to sail far out into the Atlantic; where on earth could we be going? No one of course had told us: this was the style of wartime information. There were the inevitable rumours – we were going round the Cape of Good Hope; we were to join up with another convoy coming from America. This guess appeared to be correct, because one day there were suddenly other ships around us. Then someone said we must be in the Bay of Biscay because it was so rough; and one by one figures disappeared from the breakfast table, leaving myself and one or two other sturdy gluttons to consume their leftovers: bacon and eggs, bowls of fresh fruit that had not been seen in Britain for two or three years. Our ship, the *Vollendam*, was Dutch and had recently been to New York, where it had stocked up with provisions. I wrote to my sister 'I suffer more from being vomited against than vomiting.'

We were discouraged from working off our self-indulgence on deck after dark because it was feared we might overconfidently light cigarettes which, we were assured, could be spotted by a U-boat miles away. Down in the stiflingly hot lower decks the mass of other ranks swayed and sweated in hammocks, and were sick. On a slightly higher level, in four-berth cabins, members of the old *Juke Box* clientele lay in comatose but still decorous states of undress. Then after a few days the weather cleared, and we thought we recognised the Rock of Gibraltar on our left.

I wondered – Would we be like Aeneas who, on his way to Rome from Troy, had stopped off at Carthage, near Tunis, and had had a fine time making love to Dido? But then he had abandoned her to carry on with war, and she had committed suicide.

It turned out that the *Vollendam* was heading for Philippeville, indeed somewhere halfway between Algiers and the old Carthage. I had arranged a code with my sister whereby I might be able to tell her in letters, without too obviously breaking the censorship regulations, where we landed up. My sister's and my mythology was less Greek or Roman than 1930s films; so from Algeria I wrote to her, 'We might be able to visit Jean Gabin or Charles Boyer'.

But how little had the style of mythology changed from the time of the ancient Greeks! They had loved stories of suffering and war: we now in films loved stories of sacrifice and grief. Why were there no myths of people getting on sensibly with peace?

Near Philippeville we stayed for two months in a camp, four officers to a tent, among sand dunes. We bathed in a dangerous sea; we drank red wine and played poker and bridge. For a while we enjoyed the holiday atmosphere. I wrote to my sister – 'Yesterday we played football in a temperature equivalent to the melting-point of flesh: ten effete and flabby young officers beat eleven horny old Scotsmen who have sulked most ungraciously ever since.'

But then it seems we got homesick because I and some others volunteered for the parachute regiment. We understood that to succeed in this would get us back to England for a while; but when tested I was judged to be too tall and too myopic. We were sent on manoeuvres with armoured cars in the desert; during one scrimmage with the 'enemy' I reported to my father – 'I captured an enormous Captain in a hush-hush job whose face seemed vaguely familiar. Unfortunately I treated him with respect, for it turned out to be Randolph Churchill. If I had known earlier I would have thrown him into a dungeon.' When I was a child Randolph Churchill had been a good friend of my father's; now he was so no longer.

I began to have renewed fantasies about how, if or when I did eventually get into the fighting, it might indeed be sensible to be taken prisoner. What was this human lust for war? I had paid my respects to it, but I did not need to remain part of it for ever. And in prison camp I might be able to spend the rest of the war profitably studying and practising writing. This was to a large extent a joke – yet not totally. The war really did seem to be as good as won; and what was the point of being killed in what seemed to be everyone's insistence on unconditional surrender or destruction? And surely my father was right when he said that the only real winners would be the Russians and Americans? I wrote to my sister – 'The whole thing is so obviously absurd, so tremendously ridiculous.'

My sister became my chief correspondent when I was abroad; I had no regular girlfriend. My sister and I had always been close as children, like orphans in a storm. As I grew older I felt allegiance to my small circle of school friends, but my sister was never excluded from the style and substance of this. From Philippeville I wrote to her –

Last week I was whirled away darkly at dead of night to guard some Italian prisoners, which I found most agreeable, the Italians waiting on me hand and foot, and me eating all the rations. Unfortunately my only companions were the most granite of Scotchmen, whom I found even harder to understand than the Italians. I was followed around by a flock of interpreters. Equally suddenly and darkly I was torn away yesterday, my rule at the prison camp I suppose having been too much like an operatic burlesque for the authorities. As I returned I met Anthony, very complacent in an ambulance, suffering from infectious diarrhoea, no doubt caused by the incredible quantity of food consumed, and complete lack of strength in the muscles. He is away at the hospital now, no doubt very comfortable and keeping the complaint well supplied with material.

Anthony had been my great friend from infant school days, with whom I had volunteered for the Parachute Regiment, and with whom I had even briefly discussed the idea of being taken prisoner.

We were allowed to send home one airmail letter a week, so I wrote to my sister very small on the flimsy paper and asked her to pass on my letters to other members of the family. I added – 'I doubt if many others will get as far as this without a weary shake of the head, even if you are able to.'

For the rest, my letters were full of the pleasures of a Mediterranean summer holiday – games of rounders on the beach, swimming out to a ghostly half-sunken wreck half a mile out at sea, in the evenings more of the old acting and paper games, then getting lost in the dark on the way back to the tent from the mess. I reported that I had difficulty in communicating with the Italian waiters in the mess because the only line in Italian that I seemed easily to remember was 'Your tiny hand is frozen'. Then –

I have at last been made to do some work, which is most tiresome. I plod around for miles over the most mountainous country, trying feebly to keep up with more great strapping Scotchmen who I suppose were born and bred upon such hills. How one's thighs wobble! Anthony is still having the most blissful time in hospital. There is absolutely nothing wrong with him, but they put him into a diphtheria ward by mistake, and so he is now in quarantine. But he is allowed out briefly, so we meet for enormous teas at the café. The latest horror is a plague of toads who have completely occupied our tent and croak furiously throughout the night. We had a great hunt yesterday and found one in my spongebag. Our screams could be heard for miles.

On one trip inland I caught a glimpse of the city of Constantine, which still remains in my mind as one of the most beautiful cities I have ever seen. On a road to the desert one suddenly comes across it glowing on its vast rock surrounded by a deep gorge. It seemed to be a place that war could not touch.

By this time the Allies had landed in Italy – both in the 'heel' at Taranto, and above the 'toe' at Salerno, from which Naples was occupied on 1 October. Mussolini had resigned in July; and in September the Italian government that had taken over from him had capitulated to the Allies.

Then in October, as part of a deal with the Allies which assured it of reasonable terms, the Italian government declared war on Germany. The Allies had wondered if in this event the Germans would retreat from Italy; but instead they reinforced the troops that had withdrawn almost intact from Sicily, and they put up unexpectedly strong resistance at Salerno. They seemed, in fact, ready to fight all the way up the mountainous terrain of Italy. However the Allied landings on the east coast at Taranto had gone smoothly. I wrote to my sister –

Oh the news, the palpitations, the chaos! I am leaving here at 4 a.m. tomorrow morning, in about 7 hours' time, and I am not packed and all my fantastic amount of luggage is strewn about the place. I know not where I go. In quest of Vivien? [The *Vivien* was the name of my father's motor-boat stored in a cave near Naples.] To the place in whose beginning is the home of Scarlett O'Hara?

I will send you a new address as soon as I am at rest. I really must be off, down to the busy sea, 'but to hear the mermaids singing each to each'? Not B. likely. Down to the squelch of giant squids, to the weary bleat of whales. Give my love to all. It will not be long before, ivy-crowned, I roar through Rome on an elephant.

So in November I set out with one or two others (though leaving Anthony in his hospital) on a troopship to Taranto. As we got close to the war a raging toothache overtook me; this was a calamity that seemed worse than the prospect of war. I learned later that at times of stress it was usually my teeth that savagely objected. There was no dentist on the boat; at Taranto there was one with a drill worked by a foot pedal, and an extraction instrument like a pair of pliers. However he said there seemed nothing organically wrong with my tooth; so if pain was symbolic, should one not bear it? Perhaps thus death would be made to seem acceptable?

Myself and the group I had been travelling with had been earmarked to go to a Rifle Brigade battalion which had suffered many casualties. But now we learned that this battalion was being sent home, and there were no more Rifle Brigade battalions in Italy, so we were to be parcelled out to other regiments in need of officers. This evoked mock alarm among some of our number: what – officers of a 'rifle' or 'black-button' regiment landing up with a common-or-garden 'brass-button' regiment? One of the Rifle Brigade friends I was with had a brother at Army Group Headquarters; he got in touch with him and asked – 'Please spare us this indignity, and arrange for us to be sent to some eco-friendly "black-button" regiment.' The brother said he understood our predicament (army morale was indeed kept up by such niceties) and he said he thought he might be able to get us into the 2nd Battalion of the London Irish Rifles, to be sure a black-button regiment, and which had done much fighting in North Africa and Sicily and was in need of officers. We thanked the brother. We had at least done something to affect our fate.

We moved towards the front line through transit camps referred to by acronyms which I do not now remember: in one of these, somewhere between Taranto and Bari, we got holed up for a month while we waited for our summons to join the London Irish Rifles. One day in the 'Information Tent' (so I recorded in the diary I had been keeping) I came across a paragraph in 'Home News of November 17th' which announced that 'Sir O. Mosley is to be released from prison for reasons of health'. My diary reaction to this news was 'O frabjous day calloo callay!' And then – 'It is now imperative for me to get home as soon as possible.' Did I think in some way that with the release of my father the point of my war was over?

With nothing military to do in the transit camp, and having been encouraged now to dream about the future, I spent time in looking at and writing in my diary, which I had begun at Ranby and in which I had tried to elaborate my ideas about Christianity and the 'perfectability' of man that I had written about with such abandon in letters to my aunt and to my father. But I saw how critical and abusive I had been and was being in my diary about many of the people I came across; and in some shame I wrote to my old school friend, Timmy – 'But I also say such rude things about myself that I can hardly read back without dropping a tear or two about what a horrible person I must be.' Was this in recognition of the glibness of my ideas about perfectability?

I had carried with me from England a large canister of books in order to try to continue the task I might have pursued at a university and which I had begun at Ranby – to read everything that was considered of note in English literature. Like this I might at least not be naïve about my

NM on leave in Egypt soon after the purchase of his camera, August 1944

Above Officers and NCOs of 'E' Company in Egypt, 1944

Below Fellow officers playing volleyball, Egypt, 1944

Mervyn Davies, Egypt, 1944

Above Back in Italy and waiting to go into battle. NM and Mervyn Davies with fellow officers, September 1944

Below 'E' company resting while on the march up to the line, Italy, October 1944

NM with Anthony in the
Naples flat after NM's
hospitalisation, January
1945

Profile of Anthony in
front of the window of
NM's Naples flat,
January 1945

Top Officers of 2nd Battalion London Irish Rifles on St Patrick's Day in Forli, Northern Italy, March 1945

Above An officer celebrating on St Patrick's Day, March 1945

Opposite page NM in Capri when the authorites had lost his papers, February 1945

Overleaf 2nd Battalion London Irish Rifles on parade before the final push across the northern Italian plain, April 1945

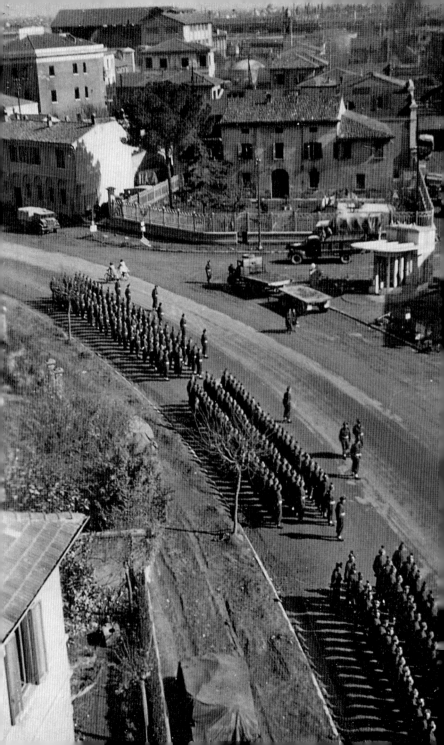

ideas. So now, in idleness in camps between Taranto and the front line, I read voraciously. I listed in my diary – *Pendennis*, *Persuasion*, *The Scarlet Letter*, *The Mill on the Floss*; also, continued from North Africa, Nietzsche and Plato. In one camp I found some of my old KRRC colleagues to argue with. I recorded – 'But I fail to dissuade them from the idea that the blind chaos of government will not end up in the ditch just because it is English. I say we are already in the ditch, and will the blind get us out of it?'

Then there appeared a further item in the *Eighth Army News* telling of crowds in London marching round Parliament Square and chanting 'We want Mosley' and 'Put him back'. So what did they want him for – to lynch him? In my diary I launched a tirade – 'People are either hollow or heavy wet sludge. What hope can there be for the world if Englishmen are thus, and one can find no one better than an Englishman?'

My toothache had gone, but I had acquired a festering raw patch on the sole of my foot which I took to be psychosomatic. Perhaps I would get gangrene and would not need to go to a prison camp after all.

A bunch of letters had caught up with me from my sister. In them she told me of the furore surrounding my father's release from prison. There were graffiti everywhere demanding 'Put Mosley back in gaol'. This must have been hard for my sister doing war work in her small-arms factory. But she was full of plans for getting the family back together again. She said that our father had gone to stay at a secret address to escape from demonstrators and the press. In order that I could write to him she would tell me where he was in code, which she hoped I would be as clever at deciphering as she had been about 'the home of Scarlett O'Hara'. He had gone to stay with 'a woman' – 'Woman' being the Mitford nickname for one of Diana's sisters. My sister also told of the night bombing of London that had started up again ('all hell is let loose when the barrage starts up'); and of a violent quarrel between our two aunts, Irene and Baba, who were now totally not on speaking terms and looked like being so for ever. 'The GREAT ROW twixt aunts goes drearily on, despite my gigantic efforts to achieve understanding. It is all so petty and futile, but neither will retract or climb down.' She told how she had taken one of her factory workmates to have coffee with my Aunt Irene ('Nina') who was now staying at the Dorchester Hotel, her house in Regent's Park having been bombed. The meeting went well – 'Auntie was superb, and Joyce came away saying "any aunt of yours would have to be a sport after all".'

I went with my would-be London Irish friend into Bari, which I said was like 'a dirty edition of Bournemouth'. But we found there a concert performance of *Tosca*, and I rhapsodised – 'You sang as I have never heard anyone sing before. It was not your voice, not the great mastery of technique: just the throbbing rise and fall of the waves, and the beat of your burning tears.' Shortly before this I had written in my diary – 'I would like to know how well I can write.' Also – 'I would like to know how original and imaginative I am compared to the very brilliant.' Well, I was only twenty.

One of our last resting places before we reached the London Irish Rifles was at Termoli, where I sat with my back against a medieval tower, and looked at the 'pale frail metallic misty hardness of the sea' and read T. S. Eliot. I wrote, 'I find him so infinitely more satisfying than the old Zephir-Lethe boys. He has a wonderful ability to make the reader's mind dance to his song, to become part of it, to think in its terms, to lose itself in his eternity of a serene and yet imminent unreality – unreality of atmosphere, while describing the very real – an artistic achievement of the very highest.' Well, I was trying.

And then: 'In even the most intelligent people I meet, or whose books I read, there is a complete lack of unity in behaviour and thought, in faith and reason.' Indeed, true enough.

So far we had travelled up through Italy by train, which I described to my sister as 'unutterable confusion – enormous pregnant Italian matrons clambering into cattle-trucks and being ejected by outraged British sergeant-majors; tiny children picking the pockets of half-witted Americans chewing gum; showers of rotten oranges hurled at any Italian soldier daring to appear in uniform. And in the middle of it all me – with an Italian girl aged 12 with tremendous breasts and false teeth on one side, and on the other an Indian who – oh God! – has begun to dribble.'

So I and my friend decided to hitch-hike the rest of the way to the front. At the last transit camp at which we stopped before reaching the London Irish Rifles, on the adjutant's desk as I clocked in there was a copy of the *Eighth Army News* with the headlines (even here!) on the continuing protests about the release from prison of my father. When I gave my name to the adjutant he said without looking up – 'Not any relation to that bastard?' I said, 'Yes, actually.' He said quickly, 'My dear fellow, I'm so frightfully sorry!' I thought – Well after all there's not much wrong with Englishmen.

But what about the London Irish?

4

The 2nd Battalion of the London Irish Rifles was part of the Irish Brigade, along with the 1st Royal Irish Fusiliers and the 6th Royal Inniskilling Fusiliers. The Brigade had come into being in January 1942 on the orders of Winston Churchill, who wanted to create a force in which men from all over Ireland could serve. The idea had come up against opposition from the government of Northern Ireland, who pointed out that there had been an Irish Brigade who had fought for the French against the English in the seventeenth century; also that the name would cause trouble now with the Irish Republic, Eire, which was neutral in the present war. Churchill insisted and the Brigade was formed.

The London Irish Rifles had been a territorial regiment before the war and at the time of the Munich crisis of 1938 the 2nd Battalion had been added to the 1st. By 1943 the 2nd LIR consisted of Irish from the North and volunteers from the South; also others from anywhere that it had picked up on the way. As part of the Irish Brigade the 2nd LIR had landed at Algiers in November 1942 and had been involved in the heavy fighting in the mountains that winter until the German surrender at Tunis in May 1943. They were then part of the army that invaded and cleared

Sicily in July. They sailed for Italy in September 1943, landing first at Taranto and then moving on by sea up the eastern coast to Termoli, which I was to find such a haven of peace a few weeks later. In October Termoli was being heavily defended at the eastern end of the German Winter Gustav Line. The 2nd London Irish joined in the fighting and Termoli was taken. From there they moved by land up the coast, overcoming strong opposition at the Trigno and the Sangro rivers. But with the success of all this the Irish Brigade as part of the Eighth Army in the east was finding itself dangerously ahead of the Allied Fifth Army on their western flank. The 2nd LIR were moved to what was supposed to be a more stable position in the central mountains. But there Allied troops were very thin on the ground and no one knew much about what the Germans were up to; though it was evident they were not simply retreating. Also it had begun to snow, was very cold, and the London Irish were equipped with no winter clothing.

I finally reached the rear echelons of the battalion on Christmas Eve 1943 in a mountain village called Pietro Montecorvino. I, aged twenty, and with no war experience, was due to take charge of a platoon of men mostly considerably older than myself who had been fighting for a year through North Africa, Sicily, and a third of the way up Italy, and were exhausted. The Rifle Brigade friend I had been travelling with was posted to a company in another village. So for the first time I was away from anyone I had been friends with.

The first thing that happened to me as I reported for duty at the adjutant's office was that my kitbag with all my own warm clothing in it was stolen; I had left it propped against an outside wall. I felt this was a calamity worse than my toothache; more desperate than my closeness to the front line. I was told that anything left lying about was pinched in a flash by the impoverished villagers. I could understand this, but could also understand for a moment the urge that must have come upon some Germans, for instance, in occupied countries to take hostages and say – 'Give us back our property or we will shoot you one by one.' It was no consolation to tell myself that at least now, with no winter clothing, I would be in the same situation as my men.

What might have been a consolation was the next day's Christmas dinner which consisted, I wrote in my diary, of 'turkey, pork, tinned plum pudding and whisky, on which everyone got drunk except me.' I was still appallingly priggish in my diary: I seemed to disapprove of anyone who was not of the type of my precious coteries from Ranby or Eton. I took refuge in admiring the beauty of the landscape; and on Boxing Day I recorded that I read the whole of *Chrome Yellow*.

(In old age I find it difficult to acknowledge the awfulness of much of my diary at this time. However, insofar as it seems to have taken the war to knock some of this out of me, this is part of the story.)

After Christmas I went to join one of the forward companies of the battalion, E Company, who were based in a village called Carpinone just behind the very sparsely held front line. Here again I found solace in the landscape – 'Three thousand feet up, we ourselves are infinitely little

45

beneath the snow-lined mountains which arise fairy-like out of the grey-green scrub twelve miles away: we understand each other, these wrinkled pyramids and I.' Well, possibly. But also there I met my company commander, Mervyn Davies, who was to play such a large part in my war, and perhaps in easing some of the pretentious stuffing out of me.

Mervyn was a Welshman, some five years older than me, who came from Carmarthen and had been to school in Swansea. He had been commissioned into the Welsh Regiment and then, when he had landed in North Africa, had found himself assigned to the London Irish Rifles through much the same chain of circumstances as me. He had fought with them in Sicily and at Termoli and at the battle of the Trigno river; he chose to stay with them, as I was to do later. When I met him in the cold stone-lined room that was the officers' quarters in Carpinone, he was tall and quiet and watchful: I thought – Rather like Gary Cooper. How does one recognise someone who is going to play an important part in one's life? By some such instinct as that by which I had claimed to recognise my 'wrinkled pyramids'? He was unlike any of the friends I had had in the army or from school. My first reference to Mervyn in my diary was, 'He has actually read *The Mill on the Floss*!'

We established a friendship through talking about books. He hoped, as I did, that the war would not totally disrupt required reading – required, that is, to try to understand what on earth humans were up to. We applied ourselves dutifully to army life, but hoped to gain a vision of what should make life valuable beyond it. In later life

Mervyn became a barrister and then a High Court judge. I used to say that he was the first good man I had known.

The two battalions of the 2nd London Irish and the 1st Royal Irish Fusiliers were given the test of holding a line in the mountains some twelve miles long with platoons dotted here and there on isolated slopes. The Germans would be able to overlook most of these from a higher ridge beyond. The Allied left flank had been halted just short of Monte Cassino. It was in the centre that the line had become seriously undermanned.

In the mountains blizzards often made visibility almost impossible. When this happened E Company remained based in the village, but even then we had to go out on patrol each day supposedly to see what the enemy were up to. We would blunder through thick snow for two or three hours and then sit huddled under the lee of a snowdrift seeing nothing, until it was time to totter back to our room in the village where, with luck, wood had been collected for a fire. In my diary I would record anything unusual that had happened in the snow: 'Big moment when given baptism of fire by a few desultory shells and mortar bombs, none closer than 300 yards but horrible whine as they drop overhead.' Then back in the comfort of the village, Mervyn and I would hazard opinions about books. I recorded, 'Mervyn began to quote T. S. Eliot's "Footsteps echo in the memory . . ." and with what delight did I carry on with ". . . towards the door we never opened into the rose garden".'

We had little contact with the local villagers, some of whom remained grimly huddled in their cellars. However to my sister I wrote that once I had 'ferreted out a famous Italian tenor who lives in the village, and we had the most glittering evening with him bellowing all the great arias too beautifully, accompanied by his brother-in-law on a watery piano.'

Then the weather cleared and the time came for the LIR to go into semi-permanent positions in the hills. It was still very cold; none of us yet had suitable clothing; some of the men were getting frostbite. I had seen comparatively little of my platoon when we were in the village; they lived and ate and slept in a different part of our building, and perhaps I was shy of them because I felt they must see me as an ignorant intruder. And when we were on patrol the snow and the wind were such that it was difficult to speak, let alone to get to know anyone. Yet had I not glimpsed at Ranby that the functioning of a good platoon depended on the nurturing of trust and affection?

Our position in the hills was on a mountain called Montenero – a wooded slope rising to higher ground on the left and falling away to a valley in front. Across the valley, on a higher ridge, was what we understood to be a stretch of the German Winter Line. But we had not yet seen any Germans; and all we knew of them was from the occasional mortar and artillery shells that came whining and whooshing as if from nowhere.

The snow was too thick and the ground was too hard to make proper trenches; the men of the three sections of my platoon – 7 Platoon – made shelters in the snow as deep as they could; and in these they had to stay during the day and while on sentry duty at night. Each section consisted of a corporal and nominally ten men but often less owing to frostbite and sickness. Two men in each section were responsible for carrying and working a Bren machine-gun, and the rest were equipped with Lee-Enfield rifles not much developed since the First World War. At platoon headquarters there were myself and the sergeant and a runner, two men with a 2-inch mortar, and an operator for the radio, which often did not work. Headquarters was in a tent with snow piled up outside it like an igloo, and inside a brazier which emitted smoke that should not be allowed to escape or it might betray our position. Here men from the sections who were not on sentry duty came to join us and try to sleep at night; the choice seemed to be between freezing and asphyxiation. Two or three times a night I would visit the sentries with a rum ration; and either my sergeant or I would try to sleep, wearing the earphones of the wireless, which was our connection to company headquarters further down the slope on the right. During the day the men in my platoon would slither down the slope two or three at a time to the company cookhouse to eat stew out of a tin with a spoon; I might manage to have a brief chat with Mervyn. Each morning the section commanders assembled in my tent to receive their daily orders. E Company was scheduled to stay in these positions for periods of three days at a time.

On the first morning of our second period, when my sergeant and section commanders were all in the tent getting their orders, an artillery shell or mortar bomb landed next to us or almost on top of us, wounding two or three and leaving us all dazed. I thought that I was wounded because I was spattered with blood; but this turned out to be from one of my corporals or my sergeant. I shouted the order to 'Stand to' – which meant that the people in the trenches would be ready to open fire. I looked out from the torn tent and saw ghostly figures coming down through the trees; they were dressed in white smocks and were making noises like wolves. I shouted an order as I had been taught – 'Enemy on the left, a hundred yards, coming through the trees, open fire!' No one fired. I did not know what to do about this: it was not a situation we had been taught how to deal with during training. The section leaders who had not been wounded were crawling back from the tent towards their trenches; my sergeant and I had a small slit trench outside the tent which was where we were to go in an emergency. My wounded sergeant had slithered to this and was lying at the bottom so that there was no room for me to get under cover except by kneeling on top of him. I shouted my order again; why had no one told us what to do if orders to fire were not obeyed? Such an event was not thought possible. My sergeant said – 'Don't tell them to shoot, sir, or we'll all be killed!' I thought this was probably true, but was not that what we were here for? However if we didn't fire, yes, we might all be taken prisoner. And wasn't this what at times I had imagined I was here for? Then I decided – or it was somehow decided for me? – no, that is not what I am here for. And my view of the world seemed abruptly to change at that moment.

As an officer used to obeying regulations, I was armed only with a pistol; officers were supposed to give orders for rifles and Bren guns to be fired, not themselves to be equipped seriously to shoot. The Germans coming down through the trees were now almost upon us: still there was no one firing. I thought I should clamber out of my useless trench and crawl to one of the forward section positions where I could myself get a Bren gun working. I had got some way when more grenades started landing; I threw myself – or was propelled – into a snowdrift. I lay there immovable for a few seconds until there was someone jerking at the lanyard of the pistol round my neck; it was a German with a sub-machine gun. I made it possible for him to remove the lanyard and pistol from round my neck; but how in God's name had I got into such a situation – and one which I had even thought desirable? The experience was unbearable. I had to get away.

My platoon were being rounded up and put in a line ready, presumably, to be marched down into the valley as prisoners and across the German lines on the further ridge. I thought I would hang back, perhaps helping one of the wounded – there were the two or three who had been in the tent – and then at the end of the line I might find a chance to dodge away. The rest of E Company should by that time have realised what was happening and Mervyn would be coming up with the reserve platoon to counter-attack. If there was firing, I could pretend to be hit by a stray bullet and then roll over down the slope. It seemed unimaginable that I had ever thought I might like to be taken prisoner! I felt deep shame. I had been mad. I should be mad no longer.

There was a wounded man who needed to be helped. I murmured to him that we should try to get away. We were at the end of the line being chivvied by a German with a rifle and bayonet bringing up the rear. There began to be bullets flying about both from the Germans on the further ridge and from some of our E Company behind. I clutched my chest and fell. The German who had been following us came and prodded me with his bayonet. I got up quickly. But I was feeling that the whole of my life hung on these moments; if I did not get away now I would never get away from being a dishonourable fraud – someone who had just wanted to get into the war for the sake of propriety and then be taken prisoner. And would it not also look as if I were under the influence of my father? There were now more mortar bombs landing and I determined to do another and more spectacular death scene, rolling over and over down the slope like a snowball or a Shakespearean actor. This I proceeded to do. I rolled on and on till it seemed I might be overdoing it; I came to rest with my head against a rock. There I thought I should stay, no matter who came after me or what happened.

I wrote later in my diary that I was not afraid; that there were some lines of T. S. Eliot going through my head – 'And I have seen the eternal Footman hold my coat and snicker, and in short I was afraid.' But I did not think I was: perhaps I was saying these lines like a mantra to stop myself being afraid – to put myself into the hands, as it were, of the eternal Footman. What has stayed in my memory is my taking careful interest in the crystalline formation of the rock an inch or two from my eyes; the taste of the ice-hard snow as I nibbled at it. How beautiful were these sensations! To be savoured as long as possible. At some distance ahead of me there was a genuinely wounded man who had dropped out from the line of prisoners and was lying in the snow; it seemed that he had been watching me and he was now calling out for me to help him. I wanted to tell him to shut up; couldn't he see I was dead? Then I could see the German who had prodded me with his bayonet coming down the slope towards me; surely this time he would not just prod me. He had been decent enough the first time; was it not justifiable to shoot escaping prisoners? He came very close with his gun pointing down at me and I remember looking up at him: he was a big, healthy man with a round face. Then there was a thump and a bang, and he fell down. It appeared that it was not I who had been shot, but the German, who lay in the snow a yard or so in front of me. He grunted for a time, then appeared to die.

What had happened, I became aware, was that Mervyn, coming up with the reserve platoon from behind, had seen the tail end of the prisoners being marched off over the hill and bringing up the rear a lone German who then branched off down the slope; so Mervyn had shot him – an extraordinary shot, I realised later, some 200 yards with a standard Lee-Enfield rifle. Behind my rock I waited till everything seemed quiet; then I stood up and waved; and after a time Mervyn, whom I had recognised, waved back. I set off towards him plunging through the snow.

I could not afterwards be sure that the German would have shot me; but he would have had either to do that or to leave me; it was too late for him to prod me into the line of prisoners again; his colleagues were disappearing into the valley. And why had he taken such trouble to come after me, except to make sure that I was dead? I had certainly put myself in a position where he would have been justified in shooting me. So it seemed that Mervyn had saved my life.

Some fifty years later, when Mervyn and I were having lunch together and talking of old times, I asked him – 'But how did it look to you? Did you see me behind that rock? Did you recognise me when I stood up?' And Mervyn said – 'No. I've never told this to you or to anyone before, but in fact when you stood up I thought you were another German, and I had you in my sights. But then, I just didn't want to do any more killing.'

So perhaps Mervyn had saved my life twice: once by doing his most remarkable shot, and then by not wanting to do any more killing.

I suppose it is inevitable that I should have come to think that by this incident my life was changed. Some half-hidden part of myself had emerged and rejected a part of the person I had been becoming – the part that had felt that war, duty, could be seen in terms of personal convenience. I had discovered shame; most unusual! And the demands of honour? Indeed, one does not talk about such things! But in my first experience of fighting almost the whole platoon for which I was responsible had been taken prisoner, and in a manner which I had once imagined desirable for myself. It was true that in the event I had gone to some pains and risk to escape; but then I had been saved by the grace of – what? – the skill, care, coincidence, of another? And so what should I learn from this? That if one risks what one feels is necessary then luck may be on one's side? But would not one day some act of restitution be demanded of me?

5

After this there is a lull, both in my memory and in my diary; also apparently in what on a larger scale was going on. I do not think we stayed in the central mountains much longer; we were told we would be moving to a base area to train for the big push north in the early spring. There were rumours, even, that we were to be sent home for a rest: soldiers keep up their spirits by such stories. Then, in the event we settled in a pleasant complex of farm buildings near Capua, north of Naples, where we were to practise river crossings and close-combat fighting among buildings.

I was aware that I was likely to be in trouble for the majority of my platoon at Montenero having been captured without firing a shot; even though I had contrived to escape. Out of a platoon of twenty-one men only six had managed to avoid capture during the original assault; the wounded man who had fallen in front of me had survived. A request for an explanation for this debacle came from Divisional Headquarters, and I wrote a report: the men had been half frozen; a mortar bomb had knocked out most of my platoon headquarters. It seemed that this was accepted, because I heard nothing more.

But I was haunted by the fact that my platoon had not

obeyed my order to open fire; although if they had, as my wounded sergeant had pointed out, we would probably most of us have been killed. So what was to be learned from this – the inadequacy of officers' training which did not countenance the possibility of orders not being obeyed? The wisdom of men who saw the futility of an order that would result in their being killed to no good purpose? But morally? Militarily? My feeling of shame had been heightened by my peculiar personal history to do with my father. What would emerge from my impression that I had been somewhat miraculously saved?

In the course of our training in the countryside near Capua I remembered what I had felt at Ranby – that for a junior officer to be on effective terms with his platoon what was required was more than a reliance upon orders; it was a two-way trust that had something of the nature of love. So I now set about fitting into the training programme of my platoon some of the stalking and catch-me-if-you-can games that I had played with Raleigh Trevelyan's platoon at Ranby – for did not war seem to be a horribly over-the-top version of a children's game? In these so-called exercises my platoon became known as being amazingly keen. In particular, we became the champion team at river crossings. I taught my crew in its flat-bottomed boat the canoeing chant from the film *Sanders of the River* – Oi ye o ko ho, or whatever – and we won most of our races. E Company, at the instigation of Mervyn, adopted a battle-cry – Woo-hoo Mahommet! – said to be the war cry of the Parachute Regiment. We evolved a private language, which replaced the ubiquitous use of the word 'fuck' with the word 'waggle'; this had to be allied to a suitably insouciant style: 'I say, just waggle over that hill, will you, and see if there are any wagglers on the other side?'

One of the highlights of this time was when the Brigade had captured from the Germans what was supposed to be an amphibious sort of jeep; this was to be given a short try-out on the river. The brigadier and the colonel and whatever other bigwig there was room for squeezed in; they proceeded in a stately manner down the bank into the water and then straight on to the bottom. To the dozens of watching and cheering men this was a great boost to morale.

My platoon was billeted in a large barn, and for the first time it was correct for me to live and eat and sleep with my men. The only concession to my supposedly superior status was that my thin mattress and blanket were set on top of a large chest like a coffin. When I was stretched out on this it could be assumed that I was asleep or no longer present; then the men could swear and grumble and carry on their ritual cross-talk. And I could listen and wonder about the nature of 'bonding'; what might be called communal love.

We were happy in our barn, but there had been difficulties in finding accommodation for the rest of the battalion. I wrote to my sister —

I was sent ahead on an advance party to choose billets for the battalion — a most unpleasant job which entails throwing Italian families out of their homes and turning a deaf ear to the calamitous ululations. One old grandam who I bounced into the street had hysterics and I had a tricky five minutes controlling her convulsions. But accustomed as I am to family hysterics in all its forms, it was not long before she was resigned to her ignoble fate. It is strange how unfeeling one becomes – I suppose it is just that one ceases to think in terms of pity and mercy; if one didn't, tears would never cease to flow down harrowed cheeks. As it was the whole business was rather frantically funny – me hammering grim and gestapo-like on the door, forcing my way through the welter of pigs and chickens which live in the best rooms on the ground floor of all these houses; up to the swarming family who live in 'orrible squalor in the attic; me ejaculating fiercely in French to an interpreter who passes on the information in even more flamboyant Italian. Then the racket really begins with the grandparents moaning in epileptic frenzy, the parents calling down all the heavens in wrath upon me, the children taking it as a good opportunity to scream and yell to their hearts' content and have a good kick at anyone they see; and finally the pigs and donkeys and turkeys etc., who blare and cackle their ridiculous animal-grab noises up the stairs in disconcerting unison. But I, the stern jack-booted I, neither flinch nor relent.

But was this funny?

There were the usual rumours about what we were waiting for: it was now mid March and the big spring advance was held up. The Monastery at Monte Cassino, on its hill some thirty miles inland from the western coast, was proving to be an insuperable barrier. The Germans were said to be occupying it in force, though this was later found to be untrue. But they were dug in on the slopes and in the town beneath it, and all attempts in the autumn and winter to take it by direct assault had failed. The Americans of the Fifth Army had tried to bypass it by crossing the Rapido and Garigliano rivers to the south, but this had resulted in such heavy casualties that they had had to withdraw. A more ambitious plan was then hatched to make a large-scale landing at Anzio, some fifty miles behind the German Gustav Line, thus cutting off Cassino and opening up the road to Rome. The landing at Anzio had gone in on 22 January, but the initial success and advantage of surprise had not been followed up owing to timid generalship, and the Germans had been able to regroup. So it was now the forces at Anzio that were in danger of being pushed back into the sea, and there were calls for renewed attacks on Monte Cassino to prevent this.

Assaults by the New Zealand Division and the 4th Indian Division were planned for February, but before one of the divisional commanders would commit his troops he insisted that the monastery should be heavily bombed. This was agreed by higher command; so the huge and beautiful eleventh-century monastery was needlessly flattened by repeated waves of heavy bombers, and the Germans, who in accordance with an agreement with the Vatican had not been within it, were now able to occupy the rubble and construct defensive positions better than any that would have been available to them before. So that when the New Zealanders and Indians did attack in February, both assaults were a complete and calamitous failure.

The London Irish, standing by in Capua ready to exploit any breakthrough, heard rumours of all this; and were ready to believe, yes, that those in command could be so stupid. And then, in March, there was renewed heavy bombing: statistics later stated that 1,100 tons of bombs were dropped by 450 heavy bombers on and around the monastery and town of Cassino for three and a half hours – after which attacks went in with as little success as ever. The bombing this time had made it impossible for Allied tanks to get over the rubble on the approaches to the town and the Rapido river.

General Fuller was later to write that the winter battle for Monte Cassino in 1943–4 was 'tactically the most absurd and strategically the most senseless of the whole war'.

The London Irish had been moved to a forward position by the river; we wondered if we were about to become the next wave of sacrificial victims. But there we stayed, because the tanks that were supposed to accompany us were stuck. Some time during this period I went back for a few days to a casualty clearing station for treatment for a bad attack of piles. This seemed symbolic. From the CCS I wrote to my old prep-school friend –

I am in hospital, or rather I am clinging to a collapsible bed and 3 thick blankets while a tempest of wind and rain fritters about me. We are supposed to be sheltered by the tent, but that gave up trying after the first icy blast, and it is now a matter between the elements and the individual.

There is one lonely figure here who has no boots. He was carried in on a stretcher weeks, months, perhaps years ago; but they carried him in with no boots. He was better within a very few days, but he had no boots, so he could not get out of bed to go away, and no one would lend him any boots. So he stays in bed and every morning the doctor comes round and says, 'What is the matter with you?' And the lonely figure says, 'I have no boots.' And the doctor clicks his tongue and takes the l.f.'s temperature and feels his pulse, and wanders sadly away. The Man With No Boots lies in bed and dreams of enormous galoshes and waders and wooden clogs, but they will never let him out because he has No Boots.

The impertinent fools who are in authority in this place have seen fit to place me on what they call a Light Diet – an amount of food so indescribably paltry as would not satisfy one of the worms that operate in my stomach. But la! Once more is the Philistine confounded, for on either side of me are men suffering most horribly from malaria, who vomit food up as fast as they put it down, and I have, by a simple process of logic, explained to them how much more satisfactory it would be if I put their food down where it will stay and feed my worms, while they will be eased of the necessity to vomit. And thus I eat 2 men's rations and my worms are surfeited (but my pile too for that matter). Unfortunately the men continue to vomit, but on an empty stomach, which is much worse, but I really can't be bothered to explain any more to them; although I am afraid that one day they may vomit themselves right away, and then I will not be able to eat their food, about which I shall be very sorry.

I recovered. I rejoined the battalion who were still waiting by the banks of the Rapido river because the tanks were still stuck. So we were sent into the mountains to the north-west of the monastery to relieve a Free French battalion who in the winter had outflanked the monastery from this side and had got as far as Monte Castellone, a rocky ridge even higher (2,500 feet) than the monastery hill and halfway round its back. But there the French had had to stop because the other attacks had failed. The higher command wanted to hold on to Castellone because from there one could look down on the monastery; but the Germans were on even higher ground beyond, so they could look down on Castellone, and any movement on it or to it could only take place at night. And even then the Germans were shelling the ridge and the approaches to it in the valley with great accuracy. And after we had crossed the valley there was a four-hour climb with mules to carry the heaviest equipment up a steep and rocky track. The shells continued but went whooshing over our heads on to the headquarters area below; but on the slippery track – it seemed always to be raining – mules were likely to slip and fall into a chasm, and if injured they had to be left with just the equipment being rescued.

When we reached the summit of Castellone the shelling intensified and the French were, understandably, in a hurry to get out. This was the chance for a usual English grumble about French volatility.

It was too rocky to dig trenches on top of Castellone, so just on the near slope the French had constructed shelters with stones known as sangers – about five foot by four by four foot high. Within each of these during daylight hours at least two men were entombed; any movement visible from outside brought on the shelling. Most of the shells hit the ridge just short of the top, sending up showers of stones, or went screeching over into the valley below. But once, I was convinced, one ricocheted horizontally off the roof of the sanger where my sergeant and I were huddled; bits of our roof collapsed, but there was no explosion.

Rations could only be distributed at night, so during the day my sergeant and I would face each other eating stew out of a tin and at some point – there was nothing else for it – we would use an empty tin to shit in. There were the inevitable jokes: Can you tell the difference?

My sergeant and I would stretch and flex our muscles, and sometimes offer our opinions about our present predicament and the meaning of life. From the small opening of our sanger we could see the destroyed monastery above which even now dive-bombers circled like lazy wasps, then swooped down for the sting. My sergeant and I agreed that it was a terrible crime to have bombed the monastery; but if we were in command of attacking forces and we thought that bombing was going to save the lives of our men including ourselves then, possibly, yes, we would order it. I had carried a vastly heavy book up the mountain in my pack – I think it was *The Brothers Karamazov*. I read its convolutions with my body contorted to catch the scarce light.

At night we had to go on night patrols, which did not seem to make sense because we could not go more than a few yards over the top of the ridge without danger of slithering into a chasm. The army had an obsession about night patrols, believing that they kept troops on their toes – which, in our cramped daytime conditions, was possibly true. So we would creep out a short distance over the ridge and find a suitable stone to sit on (I once found my 'stone' was a frozen corpse) and from there watch the firework display of tracer bullets and flares going on in the area of the town and the monastery. Then every four days we would go back down into the valley for a day's rest and sleep – though the long climb down and back up the rocky path seemed to make the short break hardly worthwhile. After a month on Castellone we were relieved by a Polish regiment (with whom we professed to communicate better than with the French) and we returned to the area where we had been waiting before behind the Rapido river, where still nothing much seemed to be happening. But we were told that we could take turns to go on a few days' leave and I chose to go to Maiori, on the southern side of the Sorrento peninsula.

I had stopped writing my diary by this time; almost my last entry was about when I had been taken prisoner at Montenero. Then I had written – 'It seems that this chronicle of an Unsentimental Journey has had its day.'

So I remember almost nothing about my days at Maiori, except that the place was beautiful, and that it was somewhere that my father and sister and stepmother and I had visited eight years earlier. So what did I think now might be a sentimental journey? Perhaps after Montenero I should try to make some reappraisal of my relationship with my father?

In my correspondence with my father about Christianity and Nietzsche when I had been at Ranby, I had written –

I see everything as a possibility, and have not the conviction to decide what is Truth and what is Right. I do not see how one can ever have this conviction, and even if one has it, why should one presume that one's convictions are right? My reason tells me what theories are the most possible, the most likely, the most desirable; but it needs more than Reason to put any theory across; it needs a great Faith. And my Reason tells me that it is dangerous to trust in Faith, for how does one know that one's Faith is Right? And so I am stuck; and am likely to remain so, I feel, until I am old and wise enough to have Faith in my Reason.

When I had reached Italy and had learned of my father's release from prison I had felt it vital that I should make my home with him after the war. But then, after I had been taken prisoner by the Germans and escaped, I felt that this in a sense was my liberation from my father; but also, strangely, that I was now able to express my gratitude to him – for having given me my taste and love for ideas;

also given me, perhaps by appreciating my outpourings, the confidence to be free of him. A few days after my experience at Montenero I had written him a letter in which I referred obliquely to the incident, then ended with a declaration so extravagantly sentimental that perhaps it could only be a farewell to what I was getting away from –

I had been wandering like Shaw's Caesar 'seeking the lost regions whence I came from which my birth into this world exiled me'. It is true that I have found many islands – immortal islands with the greatest friends that a man ever had – but I was always without home within the ocean of this spirit-world until one day I went to Holloway to visit a stranger – and then I knew that I had found the 'lost regions'; that my home was always where it had been destined to be, and that I was not alone among the waters of eternity. And now I do not believe that I can ever be entirely unhappy again: destiny has taken us thus far; it cannot be that such great promise is not to be fulfilled.

Such a feeling of gratitude can perhaps be instilled by parental approval? But what on earth its fulfilment might be will have to wait till the end of this story.

In these war years I could hardly remember my father as the person that I had indeed only caught glimpses of when I was a child – the ranting, belligerent, political figure in his black shirt or uniform; marching and strutting and roaring on platforms and on the tops of vans; what on earth was it that had got into him (rather, than, it seemed, what had he got into)? For the most part he had kept us children away from his politics. And then, in his letters to me from Holloway, he was so calm, patient, considerate. (I have published a selection of his letters to me in the second volume of my biography of him, *Beyond the Pale*.) There is one passage however that comes to my mind now when I look at the paradoxes of my father's personal life and his politics. This was when we had been discussing the nature of what might be understood as 'beyond good and evil' when one was considering the horrors and yet the apparent necessity of war. He had written −

We are therefore driven back towards a conception of suffering − of all the phenomena that are shortly called evil in the experience of man − as fulfilling some creative purpose in the design of existence: back in fact to the Faustian Riddle, usually stated with the utmost complexity but for once with curious crudity in the Prologue in Heaven [in Goethe's *Faust*] when the Lord says to Mephistopheles − 'The activity of man can all too lightly slumber; therefore I give him a companion who stimulates and works and must, as Devil, create.' *Faust* is meant to cover the whole panorama of human experience; but I believe this to be, on the whole, the main thesis of its innumerable profundities.

And indeed, from my father's inveterate cheerfulness in the calamitous failures and destruction of his politics − in his evident serenity even in prison − it does seem to me that he sometimes saw himself (as indeed others saw him) as a sort of pantomime black devil who felt he had some God-given Mephistophelean role in putting over attitudes and points of view that were not otherwise being considered; alternative proposals to an all-too-easy traditional reliance on war; other forms of discipline and endeavour. And it also perhaps explains why my father could almost always laugh − at least with me − at the ridiculousness of much of worldly goings-on, even his own; and who would wish his biography to be written after his death by someone who had known and loved him not for his politics but for what had been the wit and liveliness of his seeing his Mephistophelean role.

He hated war. His proposals to prevent it had involved, it is true, trying to turn the country into a sort of harmonious Boy Scout camp run by an impossibly benign elite. He at times even seemed to understand that this was not possible (indeed the so-called elite became very quickly malignant), though he thought it had to be tried. He used to tell the story of a conversation he had once had with Lord Beaverbrook, to whom he had said − 'You are lucky in England to have got me as a fascist leader; you might have got someone far worse!'

6

When I got back to the battalion they still had not moved, and it was now the first week in May; time was running out for the big push if there was to be any chance of it reaching the northern plain before winter. However, we were now told that it had been decided to attack direct across the Rapido river to the south and thus bypass the monastery and the town; and that the enemy's powers of observation from these would be blocked out by smoke shells. One wondered why this had not been thought of before.

We still had to wait while planes flew overhead and there was a huge artillery bombardment from guns just behind us such as there must have been, I imagined, in the First World War. Waiting with us were tanks with devices to clear mines and to bridge ditches; but the Engineers had first to go ahead to build a bridge that would carry tanks across the river. But the Germans were now returning the artillery fire, in particular on the Engineers who, while they were working, could have little protection. So bridges kept on being damaged before completion – and the waiting and shelling went on. This was the beginning of my first experience of large-scale warfare with tanks and planes and heavy artillery, and it was mind-numbing, like a tidal wave or the heart of a thunderstorm. One could not know what was happening because one's senses were cut off: there was too much noise to hear, too much violence in the air to look. One just found what shelter one could – in ditches and by hedgerows – and then stayed within oneself until the cataclysm might pass. Accounts of war are usually told from the point of view of senior officers who have made the plans and issued the orders and then try to contact one another to find out what is happening. But they have little chance of knowing this until the storm subsides, the tidal wave has retreated; then they can observe what pieces of flotsam have been washed up here, what units of men or equipment have been carried by the hurricane and landed there. And reports can be written about what plan has succeeded in the face of what determined opposition. There will be not much about what has failed. But some order will be made out of what has been a vast display of anarchy. It is the anarchy, however, that remains in the mind of an individual involved. His concern will have been to endure.

I do not know how long we waited behind the river – a single day or two – one tried to close one's mind as one closed one's eyes and ears. There came a new noise into the tumult: a ghastly wailing in the air like the cries of a celestial creature being flogged. This noise came from a German weapon that we had not come across before – a Nebelwerfer, a large-calibre multi-barrelled mortar, the noise of which when fired was said to have been specially designed to strike alarm and dismay into the hearts of the enemy. And then one could anxiously try to trace the trajectory to see where a bomb would land.

In the evening of whatever day it was the information got through that there was at last one bridge ready, so we set off to move into position to form the second wave of the attack. But so much of the ground was churned up and blocked by stuck tanks that we were forced off the track into the sodden fields, and my memory is that eventually we waded the river hanging on to ropes.

(Sixty years later, however, there was a television programme about the crossing of the Rapido river, and one of the pictures was of the only bridge – so the commentator said – which the German artillery had not destroyed; and I was sure I recognised this bridge – a slightly skew-whiff but sturdy Bailey Bridge on props, with planks or tree trunks laid crosswise, and handrails to prevent at least humans sliding off. So had we made it to this bridge after all, or just watched tanks sliding off? Memory itself slips and wobbles.)

We crossed the river one way or another, but by now it was almost dark. So we had to dig in or find a place where others had dug in previously, then try to sleep before the Irish Brigade formed the spearhead of the major break-through in the morning. My platoon found an abandoned German defensive position where there might or might not be booby traps; in one of the dugouts was a badly wounded German who had been left and was evidently dying. While my platoon settled in I tried to attend to him and understand what he was saying. He clung to me and spoke imploringly about 'Der Brief'. I found a letter that appeared to be to his wife or his sweetheart and I promised to get it posted, which I said should be possible through the Red Cross. Then he died.

In the battles for Cassino, and of the Rapido river and the Liri valley that followed, there were numerous demonstrations of the fact that in Italy at least there was no hatred between front-line troops on either side – in fact, almost the opposite. John Horsfall, who became battalion commander of the 2nd London Irish later that day when our colonel was killed, tells in his book *Fling Our Banner to the Wind* of the camaraderie between German prisoners taken by the Irish Brigade and those escorting them back across the river which was still under fire; of German medical officers and orderlies glad to help with the wounded of both sides at the casualty clearing stations; even of a motor mechanic prisoner being enrolled by the transport officer of the LIR to help repair his battered vehicles. Insofar as there was any animosity felt by front-line troops, it was likely to be directed against politicians and senior officers at the base – who made such daft and ruinous plans and seldom seemed to learn from experience. But even towards them the feeling was more that we were all caught up in this wild maelstrom of human violence and history; there was no way of altering its overall style. All the individual could do was to get on with it, and wonder whether something might be done in future to prevent this savagery. In his book John Horsfall writes of the admiration he felt for the Germans who had held on and resisted at Cassino in spite of the bombings; such a sentiment was commonplace, as was the admiration of the Germans (so it was said later) for the Allied troops who kept on attacking and being mown down almost in the manner of a First World War battle. But these views and emotions did not seem to be experienced by politicians and officers at the base.

The day after our crossing of the Rapido we were on stand-by all day to take the lead in the big push to the north. The starting time for this kept being, as usual, postponed. There were said to be not enough tanks yet across the river; the blocking-off of the monastery by smoke had to be renewed. When we had been crossing the river the smoke had often enveloped us like a low-lying fog; now, in the clearer morning air, the monastery floated like a celestial city above a fitful low-lying cloud. During the day we moved closer to our leading positions, but even with the smoke clearing it was difficult to make out anything of the larger picture. The Liri river was a tributary of the Rapido running into it from the north; the landscape of the valley was a pleasant one of low undulations and clumps of trees. All we knew of the battle was from what we heard, and endured, from what seemed to be the random violence of exploding shells and the wailing of the Nebelwerfers which we had christened Moaning Minnies. We learned that our commanding officer, Colonel Goff, had been killed by a shell from one of these while trying to see what lay ahead; also killed with him was the commanding officer of the tank regiment appointed to work with us. We had to dig new trenches to give us temporary shelter close to our starting point; the start was put back from three o'clock in the afternoon to 7.30 in the evening, and then to first light the next morning. So we stayed in our shallow trenches for another night and listened to the Moaning Minnies and watched the fireflies that seemed to exist in a different dimension from that of the flares and explosions and tracer bullets – flickering like those particles that are said to exist for a millionth of a second and then disappear – while the violence was eternal. Then, at first light, there was the monastery again like the celestial city now ready to receive us.

Throughout the night we had been given extra rum rations: now we were told there would be a hot meal to send us off. When this arrived I was standing up in my shallow trench doling out portions of stew from a canister to men of my platoon who came crawling up with their mess tins; there had been an increase of machine-gun fire at first light, but one had stopped trying to work out where it was coming from or where it was going. When I had doled out the rations there was a bit left over in the bottom of the canister so I thought, reasonably, that the least risky thing for everyone would be for me to take a second helping for myself. I had reached out my hand to do this when I was given what seemed to be a gigantic slap on the wrist – an admonition from a celestial nanny telling me not to stretch? I realised that I had been hit in the wrist by a stray bullet or piece of shrapnel. The wound did not hurt much, but it bled, and the end of my arm hung limp. It seemed that a bone must have been broken. People from my platoon headquarters came to have a look. A field dressing was applied but did not stop the bleeding; it seemed that what was required was proper bandaging and a splint. There was a brief discussion about what I should do; there was still no word or sign of the attack getting under way. I thought that at least I should go to company headquarters and let Mervyn know, and show the medical NCO what had happened. However, if I were a First World War hero, would I not tell no one and just stagger on? When Mervyn saw my wound he asked me to wait for a while because he needed me; but then, when the attack was still not ordered, he agreed that I should go to the medical officer at battalion headquarters and get the wound properly treated. So I left my sergeant, Sergeant Mayo, in charge of my platoon, and wandered off through the smoke and bits of flying metal. Then when I found the medical officer, Rhys Evans, he said there was no question of my carrying on; he gave me injections and dressed the wound and laid me on a stretcher until transport would be available to take me back across the river. The injections made me drowsy; perhaps it was then that I saw the Bailey Bridge that we crossed in my dreams. But I remember thinking – Should I be feeling grateful or guilty for that slap on the wrist as if it were from a celestial nanny? Or later – of course, both.

People who survive in battle while others die sometimes say that they feel guilty; but unless there are particular circumstances this seems senseless: the whole experience is one of it being totally out of one's control. The myth of the bullet that has one's name on it often seems appropriate, so why not an image of an unaccountable angel nanny? So long as one remembers that metaphors, however true, are not literal.

So I passed quickly through casualty clearing stations

and was ferried all the way back to a hospital near Naples, where I stayed for two weeks and had an operation to set the fractures in my wrist. And it was there that I learned, in a letter from Mervyn, that some time after I had left him the attack had finally gone in, and the battalion had taken its objective, but had sustained many casualties, including Sergeant Mayo and several of my platoon head-quarters, who had suffered a direct hit from a mortar and been killed. And this was the reality, whatever metaphor one chose. Mervyn wrote –

Dear Nick, thank you very much for your letter. I had been looking forward to hearing from you which made it all the nicer. I am glad your arm is not too frightful. After you had gone I imagined that it was much worse than my first impression, and began to calculate how you would fare with one arm and, if it were your right arm (for I could not remember which it was), whether you would ever be able to shave with your left hand. Then I thought, well, he does some things with his left arm so maybe it will not be so bad. Really, though, do let me know that it will be quite workable again. Was it very painful? Do not say that your agony was acute and intense for I shall not believe you, but I am sure it must have been trying because it probably throbbed and kept you awake for days.

I do not know whether you thought me rather intense in not telling you to go back right away as I should have done. But really it was that I relied on you to such an extent that morning when we had so few fellows who I knew would 'go'. The show went extremely well. Jock and Desmond Fay both did very well. We lost Mayo, Henshaw, O'Reilly, Keegan and Cpl Williams. All these were killed during or soon after attack. As usual one didn't think a great deal about it at the time, but later the realisation begins to appal one. Michael Clarke was killed, Geoff Searles wounded rather badly in the arm, John Culverhouse and Terry O'Connor were also wounded but not too badly. Lovatt was slightly wounded. Sorry to give you all this rather depressing news but I thought you would like to know and may not have heard. And anyway that is what has happened.

You say you will be back soon. Do come as soon as possible, for really it is not so bad, and now I have no one with whom to carry on abstruse discussions on Morality and the Cosmos. So you see your presence is necessary. I will end up now in case I become too tedious. Really I feel I could write for ages because I can write to you in a manner that is impossible in writing to folks in England. Do write again. If I am your way I will surely find out your luxurious quarters. Well there you are. Yours, Mervyn.

I grieved especially for Mayo, who was a good and beautiful man. Close comrades inscribed on the cross of his hastily dug grave 'The finest sergeant there ever was'.

When I was in hospital I began writing a poem about the battle of the Liri valley, which for some time I was quite pleased with. But reading it now I wonder if it gives as true an impression of the battle as perhaps the laconic letter from Mervyn does. What is it about poetry: it prettifies tragedy? Makes palatable that which should be objected to and changed? Perhaps some prettification is necessary for humans to bear their predicament. Such questions have become my hobby-horses in later years. But then I have never considered myself a poet. However, this is one of the only two or three decent poems I ever wrote, so I reproduce it here because, all right, poetry is an effort to make something sacramental out of the obscenity of war. And one should try to see what does or does not work.

LACRIMA LIRI

The cornfields wave toward the sky
And from above the clouds reply
With smiles of gentle sleepiness.
Below, the summer sun's caress
Lies softly on the silent plains
And deep within the sunken lanes
The trailing thorns hang down to dream
And slowly in the silver stream
The leaves of weary willows drift
And sway to lazy winds that lift
The heavy heads of drooping trees
With tenderness of silken breeze.

But Stranger, Stranger, don't you see
Behind each crimson-tinted tree
Within those hollow, haunted walls
And torn upon each thorn that falls

So gently, gently, groping down;
Beside the silent fields that crown
The sleepy summer's brittle glare
With ripples in the sun-swept air . . .

Stranger, don't you see that there
The devil's terror-laden breath
Suffuses all with taint of death?
That here one summer long ago
The silent lanes did slowly flow
With drops of dying hearts that bled
And drained the dying to the dead?
That here vain tears of frozen grief
Once trembled on each withered leaf
And hung from every tearing thorn;
And out amongst the golden corn
Blind eyes did strain in vain to see
The light that mocked their agony.

Well, does that work?
    Does battle work?

7

I was in the hospital near Naples for two weeks. Then I got ten days' convalescent leave. The world that I was finding myself in seemed to veer between the extremes of hell and heaven; to be demonstrating, if one was to understand it, the need to comprehend both possibilities.

I wrote to my father –

My wanderings have taken me into what I think is the most beautiful place I have ever seen. You remember Ischia? – the lovely island opposite Capri which we visited in the *Vivien* and where the peasants welcomed us on the beach with smiles and bottles of sweet white wine. How I got here I hardly know. Sufficient to say that my way from the hospital back to the battalion seemed about to become so tedious that faced with a delay of ten days at a dreary reinforcement centre, I stormed up to the CO and demanded leave. He complied with surprising readiness, only stipulating that I would have to find my own accommodation. From then on fate took charge. I arrived here yesterday evening from the preposterous barrel of a steamer . . . I was met by a smiling old man who took me to a clean white room with a balcony that looked out over the sea . . .

the dinner that I ate that night was such as I have not dreamed of for years except in the noble precincts of Holloway. Today I strode over the high hills that run along the centre of this island: at Forio a crowd of children and old men gathered round me at the café begging for cigarettes and hoping to humour me by saying how wonderful the English were and how they hated Mussolini. I told them I was a fanatical admirer of Mussolini, and a hundred per cent fascist, at which they stopped plaguing me for money. One little boy broke into the lusty strains of Giovanezza until he was hustled away by a policeman.

What I did not tell my father was that another small boy, about ten years old, had followed me round much of the island offering, with graphic gestures, to masturbate me – and looking surprised and hurt when I declined. In the Naples area in 1944 this was probably a profitable business; Allied soldiers were lectured regularly on the near certainty of getting venereal disease if they went with Naples prostitutes. I had given a lecture myself on the subject to my platoon, embellished with lurid illustrations of resulting physical deformities.

Back in Naples I met up with some old Rifle Brigade friends in the Officers' Club on the beautiful hill over-looking the bay. Together we enjoyed – I rhapsodised in a letter to my sister – 'exotic bathing parties in the gardens of the Winter Palace of the kings of Naples at Caserta; parties in limpid rock-bound pools surrounded by classical statues and pink champagne. We went sailing from the harbour at Posillipo; each night there was the Opera.'

It would have been impossible for me to exaggerate the joys of opera in the magnificent Naples Opera House which had reopened almost as soon as the Allies had taken over in 1943 and, so far as I know, continued in operation for the rest of the war. Anyone in uniform could get in cheaply – into the royal box if there were no other seats – and once I remember even lingering for a time in the orchestra pit. Singers were in the full-blooded Neapolitan tradition, ready to give an immediate encore of an aria if the audience demanded it. This style was a revelation; I still sometimes miss it at Covent Garden. Then from Naples I went to see the Greek Temples at Paestum. I wrote to my father –

I made the pilgrimage, some sixty miles hitch-hiking over comparatively unfrequented roads, which meant that I arrived on the scene having walked the last three miles in the heat of the day. I came across the first temple quite unexpectedly rising rather bleakly from the bushes and long grass by the side of the road. In the suddenness of the discovery I think I was a little disappointed; it was such a cold and desolate ruin; the pillars looking rather thin and forlorn under the golden heat of an Italian midday sun. But then as I wandered up beneath the grey portico I caught a glimpse of the second temple – the only temple that really matters at Paestum – a glimpse of gold more golden than the corn which shone about it; more serene and beautiful than any concentration of Italian sun. I rushed towards it in an ecstasy of wonder.

It would be impossible also to exaggerate the importance to me of being able to visit, whenever I had a break from war, the artistic treasures and beauties of Italy. They seemed to represent the efforts of humans for more than two thousand years to come to terms with their bewildering predicaments – for instance, that of claiming that they wanted peace and yet landing up in war. The large temple at Paestum was built in the sixth century BC in honour of the goddess Hera – both wife and sister of Zeus – whose chief characteristic was a jealous and vindictive rage against anyone she disapproved of, particularly any other goddess or mortal of whom Zeus was fond. She presumably provided an explanation of the rage of this kind that bedevils humans. Temples were built to placate her – monuments to order and serenity – in the hope that by this there might be a means of safeguarding loved ones and oneself, since it had not been possible to eliminate rage and jealousy altogether. Later, in Rome, I took trouble to get into the out-of-bounds Sistine Chapel and there to see Michelangelo's depiction of the expulsion of humans from the Garden of Eden – or of their preferring to risk the freedom of being able to make their own choices rather than to submit to the confines of God's laws. So was making art the means by which humans could both honour their freedom and hope to assuage its consequences? Indeed not abrogate it! Even the operas I was so excited by – I mentioned *Tosca* again in a letter home –

seemed to be trying to bind up the wounds of human tragedy and absurdity by passionate incantation and melody.

Then, on my twenty-first birthday in June, I was in a train going up to rejoin my battalion which, while I had been away, had fought all the way from Cassino up past Rome and was now by Lake Trasimeno in central Italy. I was travelling with a young volunteer officer from South Africa, Christopher Cramb, who was on his way to join the battalion. I was with him when we found we had a day free in Rome and so decided on some stratagem to get into the Sistine Chapel. We tagged on to the end of a line of Roman Catholic priests who were on their way to an audience with the Pope and, once inside the Vatican, we flaked off and had been lying on our backs for some time looking at Michelangelo's ceiling before the Swiss Guards arrived to escort us out.

One of the attractions of war is surely that it offers chances to try out one's own brand of anarchy – protected from the social disapproval and penalties that would be incurred in peace.

In Rome I heard of Rifle Brigade friends who had been killed – Timmy Lloyd, one of the landlords of *The Juke Box*; Marcus Hawkins, who had been with me on my journey to the LIR. My old school friend Anthony, who had arrived in Italy just after me, had been wounded in the foot when his sergeant had trod on one of his own anti-personnel mines, and was now temporarily back in England. My South African friend and I heard that the 2nd LIR was coming back from Trasimeno so we should wait for them in Rome: we managed some more sightseeing, then joined them at Tivoli with its beautiful fountains and gardens. There I heard of more London Irish friends who had been killed or wounded. We were then told we were all going back to have six weeks' rest in Egypt.

So one learns to accept good fortune as well as bad. We travelled down to Taranto by train and set sail across the Mediterranean to Alexandria, and went into a camp in the desert halfway between Cairo and the Suez Canal. This was a base from which we could take turns to go on leave to Cairo, but we were happy enough for a while just to hibernate in the desert. I wrote would-be amusing letters to my sister. These were my efforts, I suppose, to insist that I still thought war was something to make jokes about –

When I was in Naples I tried to buy you some silk stockings. But what the hell was Italian for silk stockings? With extraordinary presence of mind I remembered Rossini's opera *La Gazza Ladra*, which I had understood [quite erroneously, as I learned later] to mean The Silken Ladder. So without further ado I bellowed Gazza! Gazza! At a terrified youth behind a counter, and bared my elegant if slightly hairy leg. When he had recovered from the effect of this inspiring spectacle a brief but sharp discussion ensued during which he professed to understand that (a) I desired to see an orthopaedic surgeon; (b) that I wanted him to shave my legs; (c) that I was an exhibitionist; (d) that I was challenging him to show a more shapely leg himself. In the end, inevitably, he led me towards a brothel . . .

On the boat I bought a pipe, to emphasise the 'outpost of empire' pose that I envisaged. But I puffed and blew with little success. The bowl grew white hot and the spittle bubbled merrily, and the smoke burnt enough holes in my tongue to line the stomach of a carpet.

Oh dear, these jokes, how they do go on!

Could you try to get me a book by Aldous Huxley called *Point Counter Point*?

Mervyn went away to an education course in Beirut; so when it came my turn to go to Cairo I went with another company commander called Peter, who was an exuberant character with a large wavy moustache and the reputation of an experienced roué. We shared a room at Shepheard's Hotel. Cairo had for long been under no threat from war, so it was once more an exotic centre for people who were happy to be away from the austerities of Britain, whether they were working at one of the seemingly innumerable Middle Eastern headquarters, or were passing through on postings or on leave. My companion Peter was not much interested in seeing sights such as the Pyramids and the Sphinx; his idea of being on leave was to go to nightclubs and set about picking up women. For the nightclubs he found a ready companion in me; about the further part of his agenda he said – 'Don't worry, one of us can stay out of our hotel room for an hour or two, and then vice versa.' I said I'd be happy to do this for him, but I didn't think he'd need to do it for me. I don't think he quite believed me.

But we had much fun dining under the stars in the garden at Shepheard's, getting drunk and racing in carriages like chariots to the fashionable nightclubs on the Gezira racecourse; 'playing Chopsticks' (I reported to my sister) 'on the austere Grand Piano of the Club Royale Egyptian, where it was explained that I was an indefatigable piano-tuner'. Cairo was full of people enjoying the anarchy of war, and Peter soon found himself an accomplice of the sort that he required. She said she was (and from her looks even might have been) an Eastern European countess; and when I honoured my part of the bargain by assuring them I would stay out of the hotel room for whatever time they needed, she said she was sure she could fix me up with someone later. I thanked her but said I would have a look around myself. I don't think it was just squeamishness about venereal disease, or even residual homosexuality, that made me so reticent about sex: I think I felt that it was love that was being cried out for in war; the naggings of sex one could surely deal with on one's own.

But as it happened I did meet someone while my friend Peter and his companion were up to whatever. There was a girl at the Gezira nightclub called Kitty Costello; we walked hand in hand round the racecourse under the stars, caressed by the hot desert wind; we talked about love. And I must in some way have loved her, because I still remember her name. And we seemed to have got what we wanted. But about even this I had to make a joke to my sister: 'I said I was a ballet dancer and executed an intricate pas-de-quatre in the middle of a racecourse.' My new friend Kitty and I did not plan to meet again.

I had a letter from Mervyn on his education course in Beirut –

I thought I had better report on myself to you and also ask for your reassurance that you are not beating up the local clubs every day. This is a likeable place. The object of the course, so I am told, is to inspire an interest in citizenship. The chaps are earnest in the extreme, and I am sure they could not play Up Jenkins even if they tried. They like reading well-thumbed works on economics.

We had to give lectures, so for the avoidance of work I have selected two obscure legal subjects on which there are library textbooks and I give an incredibly boring half-hour.

Beyrouth is pleasant enough: the swimming is good and I am sorry to say I have been hearty enough to bathe before breakfast. The hotels are pretty empty, most people having gone up into the hills. So that any adventures that might be likely to befall me are extremely unlikely.

Have you had leave? Do let me know how it goes and who you spent it with and who you had to avoid spending it with.

There is an excellent library. All the chaps make a dive for K. Marx, which leaves the whole of the poetry section for me. Also those nice books that were coming out in England on the paintings of folks like Van Dyck

(Gogh?) So I sit reading John Donne and looking at Art photographs surrounded by scratching pens amassing copious notes on nutrition, public health, sewage and drainage. I wish you were here. We could put on a shocking prig act.

In Cairo there was trouble brewing between the troops on leave – the 78th Division of which the Irish Brigade were part – and the local population. This was August 1944 and it was felt that the war should be about to be over but was not. The party-going became more obstreperous. We were told that we might bump into King Farouk in a nightclub, so we sat around and banged our glasses on the table and sang 'King Farouk King Farouk hang your bollocks on a hook'. Out in the street the troops were angry at being pickpocketed and ripped off by traders; and it was said that boot blacks were flicking boot polish on to their uniforms. In August there was a full-scale riot by troops of the 78th Division with vehicles being overturned and windows smashed. The new commanding officer of the LIR, Bala Bredin, was reported as saying, 'There will be no peace until we have them safely back in the line.' So the rest period in Egypt for the whole Division was curtailed, and we found ourselves on our way back to Italy.

I wrote to my father, 'I'm not really sorry . . . I hope soon to be able to visit Florence and Pisa and Siena, and perhaps in a little while there will be Venice or Nice.'

In Cairo I must have managed to do some sightseeing, because I wrote home that the Sphinx had 'a pile of anti-air-raid sandbags under his chin, which gave him the appearance of having toothache'.

The news from home was that my father and step-mother, having been released from prison, were now under house arrest near Newbury, and could not travel for more than a few miles without police permission. But the family, consisting of my sister and younger brother and our two small half-brothers, were now having the chance to reassemble again. My sister wrote to me, 'We all went for a vast picnicking bicycling expedition: Daddy looks quite wonderful with a pair of clips on his trousers and an ancient cap turned back to front like a butcher's boy.' And then of a weekend to which she took my two old school friends who were temporarily back in England with wounds – 'We all sat around till 3.30 a.m. listening to Poppa discoursing fascinatingly on the theme of Will to (a) Comfort, (b) Power, (c) Achievement – Superman to the Child and so on – with a bit of Democracy v. Fascism thrown in.'

My own attitude to the war at this time was that it was just something to be got on with – no more questions about ethics or justification. And it seems that my father did not go on about the war much now either: he was thinking about what he would say or write when it was over. He had professed to be a fan of Nietzsche but he was also now a critic. His line was that what Nietzsche had seen as the 'Will to Power' was a comparatively primitive affair; what was demanded of the 'higher type' of man was rather a 'Will to Achievement'. I had not been able to read much Nietzsche yet (his books were almost unobtainable in wartime England) but it seemed to me that my father had got his own reading wrong: what Nietzsche was on about was not the ability to exercise power over other people, but a power (if this was the word) over oneself. That is, one needed the ability with part of oneself to observe and be critical of other parts of oneself: and by this possibly to reorder them. But this my father did not seem to have recognised – although he did have the capacity, sometimes, to laugh at exaggerated parts of himself. I don't think I talked much with Mervyn about Nietzsche, but Mervyn seemed to me to illustrate, with his quiet and amused irony, more of what Nietzsche meant by a 'higher' man than what had been envisaged by my father. I didn't talk much with Mervyn about my father; in later life he would say about him just – 'A man should have the courage to say what he thinks.'

In my own letters to my father during my time in Egypt I was still plunging about on difficult and not very well thought-out ground; but usually in efforts to understand the daft predicament of war in which I found myself –

I think the Hellenists of the 18th and 19th centuries shrank from the acceptance of 'horror' in nature because they did not realise what far greater potentialities for horror there are in the unnatural man. To a sensitive spirit of this generation the ruthless sense of doom in nature is not a quarter so horrifying as the miserable sense of futility when in contact with the 'unnatural' man of the present day. Anyone who has fought in the last two wars must realise this. It is incredible that there are sane men who believe that by renouncing natural life they can alter it or be immune from it. But could they not learn to make deals with it?

And then –

There is an interesting man in my Company called Desmond Fay who before the war was an active communist. He is intelligent and very reasonable; and when we feel earnest enough we talk of this and that. And the more we talk the less is the difference that I can see between the conceptions of the communist and the fascist corporate state. But then the only training I have had in the theory of Fascism was in the Pamphlets that you sent me when I was to debate on the subject at the Abinger [my prep school] Debating Society.

In one of the letters that I wrote to my father at this time there is a short passage blacked out, intriguingly, by the censor. I had been describing my often hilarious week's leave in Cairo, and the last sentence before the blackout was 'The best sport of all was being rude to the ignoble staff-officers of GHQ'.

To my sister, who had been wondering rather dolefully whether she should have a go at reading Nietzsche, I had written that my favourite line in *Also Sprach Zarathustra* was – 'I would believe only in a God who knew how to dance'.

93

8

When we arrived back at Taranto in September I found that there was now a Rifle Brigade battalion in Italy, and a formal request that I should rejoin it. I was dismayed at the prospect of having to get to know, to become trusted by, a new platoon again – and indeed, a new set of officers. And of course I did not want to lose my relationship with Mervyn. Also I had come to appreciate the anarchic style of the London Irish, and did not want to go back to what I remembered as either the 'stuffiness' or indeed the affectations of the Rifle Brigade mess at Ranby. So I told this to Mervyn, and we consulted with our CO, Bala Bredin, and he put in a formal request, backed by the brigadier and a personal plea from me, that I should stay with the London Irish. And this was granted.

The situation in Italy was now that the Germans had been pushed back to the mountains north of Florence, but still some distance short of Bologna and the northern plain. Here the Germans had planned and constructed their last-ditch defensive position, the Gothic Line. But it was not yet the end of September and there was still time, it was thought, to break through before the winter rains made movement difficult. However, the Allied armies had been seriously depleted by units being taken away for the somewhat pointless landings in the South of France in August; and the German armies in northern Italy had been reinforced – although this was not known to the Allies at the time. The Allied command thought that with one more push the German resistance might collapse. Hitler's orders were, in fact, that there should be no vestige of collapse anywhere, whatever the cost. Then, to cap all this, the rains came early. By the start of October roads and tracks in the mountains were becoming a quagmire.

The Irish Brigade made their way up the eastern coast past Termoli to Fano, and from there turned inland to Castel Del Rio on the road between Florence and Imola. The roads here were narrow mountain tracks with a cliff face on one side and a precipice on the other; these were difficult enough for trucks and heavy lorries to negotiate at the best of times; if any traffic was coming from the opposite direction, or if a vehicle broke down, then movement became impossible. Once, when the truck in which I was travelling spluttered to a halt and was holding up the huge column behind us, I got out to see what I might do to help the driver who had his head under the bonnet as if sheltering from the rain. I said, 'What's wrong?' He said, 'The fucking fucker's fucked.' This seemed a sufficient as well as poetic description.

After another hold-up in the dark, I remember clambering at the last minute unseen into the back of the truck that was carrying my platoon, among whom were some newly joined reinforcements; and one of these asked of no one in particular – 'What's the officer like then?' I was sure

I was going to hear something nice. Then after a while a voice in the dark just said – 'Greedy.'

When we finally arrived at our destination, a village by a rushing mountain stream, we heard, through a mixture of briefings and rumours, that there was a German strong-point in the Gothic Line that was holding up the Allied advance to the plain, rather as there has been at Cassino in the Gustav Line six months ago; and it was to be the task of the 78th Division to take it. This strongpoint was known as Monte Spaduro.

Spaduro was not quite the last mountain ridge before the northern plain, but it was in front of this that the Allied armies were getting held up because it dominated the valleys leading up to it. On the Allied side there had been a shuffling of divisions between the Eighth Army based on the east coast and the Fifth Army in the west, in an effort to make up for the depletion of units for the landing in the South of France. But the arrival of German reinforcements had so far made this breakthrough impossible. And now there was the rain.

When the 2nd LIR left their trucks after the long drive from the eastern coast, we were off on a three-hour slog up slippery footpaths; then into waterlogged slit trenches at our destination. We were on a ridge facing and overlooked by Spaduro. There was regular shelling. Around ruined farm buildings were dead and decomposing farmyard animals; they swelled and burst, releasing stench. And at night there was still the 'game' of going out on patrol with instructions to find out about enemy positions; in fact, going as far as seemed reasonable and then sitting beside a tree and watching shadows and listening to rustlings. And having spent enough time in what might be taken to be looking for enemy positions, we came back through our lines where there might be different people on sentry duty from those who had been there when we had gone out, and so there was a danger of their mistaking us for enemy and opening fire. Then we would report back to battalion headquarters – no sign of enemy activity – which was true enough; and we trusted that everyone would understand the rules of the game. This was a time when the most pressing threat seemed to be that of dysentery, but this was seldom serious enough for one to be carried away on a stretcher.

Other formations had been trying, and failing, to take Monte Spaduro. Now it was the turn of the Irish Brigade. It had for long been army lore that no one should move in the mountains except at night: daytime activity simply brought forth accurate machine-gun, mortar and artillery fire. But even at night in any settled position the enemy would have worked out their fixed-line fields of fire, and any attackers were likely to have become stuck in the mud of a valley and so would be sitting targets even in the dark. The rumours were that other formations who had attacked Spaduro at night had failed ruinously because of this. But it seemed that Allied headquarters did not know what else to do.

Squatting in our tiny six-foot by three slit trenches, nothing much seemed to matter to us except the shelling and the rain. The Irish Fusiliers, it was said, had been sent into a full battalion night attack on Spaduro and had had to retreat with many casualties. The Inniskillings had been called away to do a diversion elsewhere. This left the London Irish for any further attempts. But by this time the shelling on our inadequate trenches was so constant that we hardly cared. One shell landed so close to the top of my trench that the edges caved in and my backpack was riddled with shrapnel, and the book I was currently reading – I cannot now remember what it was – had a piece of metal embedded deeply in it. At least I might be able to tell the story after the war about how it had stopped my being pierced to the heart.

One night we had gone down into a valley to give support to one of the large-scale attacks; we could see nothing, we got embedded in the deep mud, we seemed to be under accurate machine-gun fire from some forward enemy position on our right. We stayed where we were for a while, then struggled back.

The machine-gun fire had appeared to come mainly from a semi-ruined farmhouse and buildings on the spur of ground that stretched for some 600 yards between the enemy and our positions. From these buildings accurate fire could be directed on fixed lines at the flanks of anyone in the valleys. We could see the farmstead in daylight if we were careful not to raise our heads too far. It began to dawn on everyone that Spaduro would never be taken unless the crossfire from this outpost was eliminated. On the map the farmhouse was called Casa Spinello. The London Irish were given the task of mounting a night attack on Casa Spinello – not head on, where there were likely to be minefields, but once again round the valley at the side.

I think everyone in Mervyn's company thought this would be useless; we would get stuck as we had got stuck before. Nevertheless, off we went the next night in the driving rain. This time we had not only to get down into the valley but supposedly up the other side and this, in the cloying mud, proved to be literally impossible. And of course, our efforts alerted the Germans in Spinello so that machine-gun and mortar fire came down on us where we were now in the open because we had been trying not to shelter but to attack. And because we were frightened and almost didn't care any more, we tended to huddle together; so we suffered a regular toll of casualties. One of them was Christopher Cramb, the young South African volunteer who had been with me in Rome. He was standing next to me and called out loudly – 'God have mercy on my soul' – and then fell and died. Mervyn was trying to get through on the radio to demand permission to withdraw, but he was told to continue with the so-called attack. Then, to his eternal credit, Mervyn decided to ignore this order and on his own initiative he led us back up the slope on our side of the valley, carrying our wounded and those we could of our dead.

When Mervyn was summoned by the colonel and the brigadier to report on his withdrawal, he said that they did not seem to understand the futility of their tactics: we would never take Spinello – nor indeed Spaduro – with cumbersome numbers of men sliding down into a mud trap at night and there remaining helpless while they were shot at from Spinello. What was necessary, he said, was for a small force of men to set off while it was still light by as direct a route as possible to Spinello, keeping as far as they could just under the shelter of the spur. Then, when they were as close to Spinello as they could get like this, they could attack running fast across open ground. This should happen shortly before the regular time of stand-to at dusk, when it was almost inconceivable that the Germans would be expecting an attack, so uncommon was any movement by day, and in fact it was possible that the Germans would be sleeping. Then if this attack on Spinello was successful there would be a chance of a major night attack on Spaduro succeeding.

The colonel and the brigadier listened to Mervyn and said – 'All right, you and your company try it.'

One of the other platoon commanders in our company was the young communist from Liverpool, Desmond Fay, with whom in Egypt I had argued amicably about communism and fascism. Desmond had been brave during the advance from Cassino, and had been awarded the Military Cross.

Now, when Mervyn gathered us to tell us of his plans, he suggested that Desmond should go out in the early afternoon with just one or two men and try to find out what was the situation in Spinello – how many Germans were there and what were their defensive positions. If possible, he should bring back a prisoner who could be questioned. Then, if Desmond's information was satisfactory, I with my platoon would lead an attack to capture the farmhouse and buildings – still in daylight, but just before the time when the Germans could be expected to be standing-to. Then if my attack was successful, the rest of the company would come up and we would hold Spinello during the night while the inevitable German counter-attacks came in, and while a large-scale Allied attack on Spaduro would go in, this time with a chance of success because the crossfire from Spinello would have been eliminated.

This scheme seemed to me both mad and yet, as it had done to Mervyn, to make some sense. But I wondered – Why has Mervyn chosen me to do the attack? Then – Oh yes, I see.

When I told my sergeant and my section commanders of this plan they too naturally thought it was mad: had we not been told never to move into the view of the enemy in daylight? I explained: Yes, but they will not believe that we could be so mad; they will not have properly woken from their daytime sleep; they will think they are dreaming. My section commanders and sergeant looked at me as if they thought they or I might be dreaming.

From a certain vantage point we could just see, by lifting our heads carefully, the farmhouse about a quarter of a mile away along the spur; some ruined farm buildings were on this side of it. We had a few hours to wait before Desmond set off on his patrol, after which it would almost certainly be our turn to go. We could pass the time by making sure that our weapons were in proper order. I had myself by this time acquired a Thompson sub-machine gun, which had the reputation at critical moments of being likely to jam. But not, surely, if one took enough trouble. There was time also to ruminate on the bizarreness of fate.

When I had been taken prisoner and had succeeded in

my decision at any cost to try to escape, I had been helped by good fortune and by Mervyn. Then later, when I had been wounded south of Cassino, Sergeant Mayo, who had taken over from me, had been killed. I had thought – All right, I am very lucky! But sooner or later there will be pay-back time. Something further will be demanded of me: either my luck will run out, or there will be some test why it should not.

So is not this now the sort of task that I have wanted, or needed, ever since most of my platoon were taken prisoner without firing a shot, even though I had managed to escape? I have needed a chance to show in a positive way a break from the cynical attitudes of my past; from the negative tendencies of my history. When Mervyn had come to tell me of his plans for my attack he had murmured, 'This is an MC job.' This was army jargon for an assignment which, if it succeeded, might result in one's being recommended for a Military Cross; if it failed one was likely to be dead.

So had Mervyn an instinct for what I might require?

(You think people don't ruminate on such things at such perilous moments? What else do they think about?)

Desmond Fay's patrol was amazingly successful. He went out with just his sergeant and came back with a German prisoner who had been half asleep in a trench by the farm buildings. The German talked: he said that Spinello was held by about thirty men during the day; at night they were in contact with troops on the hills behind who came up with more machine-guns. There was some good news in this in that it seemed the Germans might not be in good heart if the man had been taken and talked so easily; but thirty men was a lot for my depleted platoon to take on, and would not the capture of this prisoner mean that his colleagues would now have been alerted? My platoon was down to fifteen men, what with sickness and injury, and when it was time for us to form up I wondered if there would be any who would say they could not go on. There was, in fact, only one, a senior corporal who lay in the bottom of his trench and said he could not move. I talked with him for a time and then said – All right, don't. He would not have been much use in a platoon that was otherwise behaving so admirably. But I think we all felt we might be on a suicide mission.

I had two lance-corporals, Tomkinson and McClarnon, who with their sections would go with me into the attack. My sergeant would be with the Bren gun of the third section to give us covering fire. The rest of the company would be ready to give more covering fire if necessary from the hill at the back.

Desmond was to start off with us to show us the way he had reconnoitred, keeping out of sight of the farmhouse by moving under the brow of the spur. But even here we would be in full view of the Germans on the hills beyond – so was it true they would be sleeping? Then, for the last hundred yards or so, we would have to break from the cover of the spur and run to the farm buildings across open ground; if the Germans had been alerted, this is what was likely to be suicidal.

We moved off in our meagre crocodile quite openly, like people hoping not to draw attention to themselves if they show sufficient insouciance. On our right we could look across the valleys that stretched away towards Imola and the promised land of the northern plain. For the first time in weeks the rain was holding off; it was almost a beautiful evening.

We got to the place beneath the spur that seemed nearest to the farmhouse, and there we spread out and lined up. When I told the story later (I did not often do this) I used to say that I was frightened, yes, but what I was most frightened of was not being able to stand the fear – and then what would happen? The fabric of the mind would crack and I would fall through? When I had felt close to death in the snow at Montenero all I had had to do was lie still; now I had to run forward. I saw that the Bren gun was in position to give us covering fire; then I gave the order to go.

I had been a fast runner at school and now it was obviously in my interest to get into some sort of cover as soon as possible. The farm buildings were, after all, not much more than eighty yards away, which was not too bad a distance; but I was festooned with tommy-gun, spare magazines, grenades; and . . . and . . . never mind, just keep running. When I had almost reached the farm buildings I looked back and saw Corporal McClarnon's section a long way behind. I shouted, 'Come on McClarnon!' He, a sturdy man with short legs, shouted, 'I'm coming as fast as I can!' By this time Corporal Tomkinson had caught up with me; then a man with a gun popped up from the rubble of the farm buildings and Tomkinson fired at him and hit him, and I sprayed with my tommy-gun the buildings from where he had appeared. Then someone started shouting 'Don't shoot, Johnny! Play the game, Johnny!' So Tomkinson and I ran on. By this time grenades thrown from the farmhouse had started landing around us, so I called to McClarnon to take charge of any people in the buildings and Tomkinson and I got to the back wall of the farmhouse. There was now a good deal of machine-gun and rifle fire, whether from Germans on the hills beyond or our own people giving us covering fire from the back I could not tell. It was obviously urgent to get inside the cover of the house.

The farmhouse was one of those buildings on a slope which, if you go into it on the ground floor at the back, this turns out to be the first floor at the front. There did not seem to be anyone in this first floor where we came to it; the main body of Germans were evidently sheltering in the ground floor at the front. Grenades were being lobbed from round the sides of the house. I called to Tomkinson to go with his section round the right side while I went round on the left. A German had followed me from the farm building with his hands up, smiling. I told him I had no time for him, and to go and find McClarnon. Then I came to a hole in the wall of the house: this led to a room that appeared to be empty. There was also a gap in the floor just beyond the hole through which I could see to the ground floor at the front. This room appeared to be empty too. Then three Germans appeared through a door at the front; they carried automatic weapons; they saw me through the holes in the floor and wall at the same time as I saw them; I fired first and shot two of them in the legs.

The third ran out of the door at the front and one of the others hopped after him holding his leg; the other had fallen and lay where he fell. The magazine of my tommy-gun was now empty; I cursed myself for having spent so much ammunition firing blindly at the rubble of the buildings. I sheltered to one side of my hole while I fixed on a new magazine. By the time I had got back to where I could see down to the ground the second man I had hit in the legs had gone – presumably he had crawled out after the other two. So might I then be glad that I had had no more bullets in my magazine, and need not shoot him again? I called to McClarnon to leave two of his men to guard any prisoners from the buildings, then to come up with what was left of his section and go into and occupy the now empty upstairs and downstairs rooms on the left. This he did. Then I went to see how Tomkinson was doing on the right.

This side of the house was covered by German machine-guns from the hills beyond, and bullets were flying and chipping bits off the walls. Tomkinson had gone forward and taken shelter behind a well near the front of the house; his Bren gunner had been hit and two of his men were dragging him back behind the house. I joined Tomkinson by the well but we could see no door into the house except the one on the left which McClarnon was now guarding. The right front of the house seemed to have collapsed; there was just an opening like a hole to a dugout in the rubble. Bullets were chipping bits of stone around our heads, so we threw a couple of grenades at the opening and I retired in haste. Tomkinson stayed by the well, and when someone fired at him from the opening he stood up and fired what was left in his magazine back at it, before rejoining me in the shelter of the house. Then I sent him with the few men left of his section to join McClarnon who was occupying the rooms on the left.

The third section had by this time come up with my sergeant, and I went again with them to the right front corner because I thought we had to clear this – to take prisoner the Germans who seemed to have barricaded themselves into a basement through the opening in the ground-floor rubble, because surely our position would become untenable if they stayed underneath us during the night. My sergeant threw one grenade at the opening and then was hit by a stray bullet from the hills; he and his section retired to the back of the house. I was by the well, firing blindly and absurdly at the German machine-gunners on the hill who were hundreds of yards out of my tommy-gun's range. I turned to the house again to throw one last grenade and there was a German who had crawled out of the opening like a hole and was facing me holding an automatic weapon and he fired at me at point-blank range and somehow missed. My magazine was now empty again so I did a flying leap back round the side of the house (I described this later as my 'Nijinsky leap') and I determined not to go round to the front again. We would have to hold on to what we had got until morning.

It seemed that we were in occupation of most of the farmhouse except the ground floor or basement on the right, which the Germans indeed seemed to have made impregnable. Above this on the right of the first floor there was a hayloft. From the upstairs room on the left I and others crawled into this loft to see how it could be occupied and defended; then the Germans below started firing up through the floorboards. We jumped about like victims in the red-hot bull of Phalaris; we fired down through the floorboards; and then there were voices again – 'Don't shoot, Johnny!' I tried to remember my schoolboy German: 'We will not shoot at you if you will not shoot at us!' Was there not a special conditional tense? And was I not using the word for 'shit' instead of 'shoot'? But what would be the difference? I seemed anyway to have got the message through, because for the rest of the evening and night there was no more shooting up or down through the floorboards.

By this time Mervyn had arrived with the rest of the company and he insisted on going himself to have a look at the right front of the house where there was the opening to where the Germans remained; but he was almost immediately hit in the arm and leg, and was pulled back under cover. I said I would get him back on a stretcher as soon as we had one; but he insisted he was all right, he could get back on his own – and it was vital that he should do this, because he could then explain the seriousness of our situation and could get reinforcements sent up. I would be intensely sorry to see him go, because I needed both him personally and someone who would share the responsibility for defending what we had taken now that night was coming in and there were bound to be counterattacks. But Desmond had come up with Mervyn, and he was a senior lieutenant to me, so he would nominally take over. Then Mervyn went hopping back on one leg by the most direct route to our old positions; and it turned out that he had hopped unharmed straight through a minefield. We became aware of this later when the reinforcements he sent up walked into the minefield, and many were killed or wounded and the rest never got through. This was a disaster for them; but for us it seemed that there were already enough of us crammed into the farmhouse, and Desmond agreed that it would be crazy to consider digging trenches outside. So we settled down to assess our situation.

We had what was left of the three platoons of our company in the two rooms one above the other on the left of the farmhouse – some thirty men, ten of whom had wounds of some sort or other – and nine Bren guns. We arranged these on the two floors with a makeshift ladder between. Then we realised it was quite dark.

During the night three or four counter-attacks did come in from the further hills; but by this time we were experiencing a strange exhilaration. We felt invulnerable, heroic; when we heard Germans approaching we opened fire with all our weapons from every opening in all directions. I remember one man, who had lost his spectacles and could find no room at a window, firing his rifle repeatedly straight up into the air. We yelled and whooped our war cry – Woo-hoo Mahommet! – and blazed away until the attacks seemed to fade into the thin night air. It was all quite like, yes, an apotheosis of a mad apocalyptic children's game. Only once, I think, did a German get right up to the wall of the house; he shot one of our men point-blank through a window. Grenades usually bounced off the walls and exploded outside. After a time things quietened down. Our wireless was not working, so at least we were out of touch with headquarters so they could not order us to do anything different.

There was the business of tending to the wounded. Amazingly, none of my platoon seemed to have been killed. The man who had been shot through a window was suffering badly, and I and others took turns to sit with him. Eventually stretchers arrived from headquarters and we were able to send him and a few others back; also the prisoners and the wounded German who had been in the farm buildings at the back. The stretcher-bearers told us of the disaster to the reinforcements who had walked into the minefield; but extra ammunition had got through, although no food, and we had eaten nothing since sodden sandwiches the previous midday. Someone found me a bit of black German bread, which I ate ravenously.

There remained the question of what we would find outside in the morning. There had been a lot of distant firing and explosions and tracers from the hills during the night: presumably the large-scale attack on Spaduro had gone in, but to what effect we could not tell. If it had failed we would be under exposed siege for another whole day. Desmond had set about building up protective rubble in the doors and windows. I seemed to be both too tired and too triumphant to care. Whatever had been attempted, or destined, or hoped for, had come off; and I did not think anything else could really fail.

At first light we were standing-to and looking out into the cold mist like people in a Western film wondering if they would see Red Indians or the cavalry. There were figures moving on the further hills: surely they were acting too openly to be enemy? We risked a small cheer. After a while it seemed safe to step out of the front of the house into the space where only a few hours ago there had been such danger: there were some bodies of Germans lying about, one of them blocking the opening into the dugout on the right. We pulled this clear; there was still no sight or sound of anyone inside. I called in my best German again for people to come out; and then, to our surprise, there emerged, one by one like wasps from a hole, twelve men, about half of them wounded. We had not expected so many.

We sent them back under escort. The second-in-command of our company came up to take over arrangements for further defence; our battalion commander came up to congratulate us, and said that the night attack on Spaduro had been a success, thanks in large part to the success on our attack on Spinello. We hung about for the rest of the day while the situation in the hills became clearer. We were told to dig trenches outside the farmhouse in case the shelling started again, but no one paid much attention. In the evening we set about marching back – not just to our previous positions but to somewhere near Castel del Rio where we could rest. But this was a long march, and I and others were suffering both from exhaustion and a reaction of extreme other-worldliness. During a ten-minute rest on the march an officer who had not been in the battle came along the line and told us to get up and get a move on. I remember telling him to fuck off.

I wrote a long account of this battle to be sent some time later to my sister and it is from this, as well as memory, that I have taken many of the details of this account. I ended my letter by saying – 'I find it hard to believe it was I that did all those peculiar things!' and then, as if in an attempt at explanation – 'I have yet to meet a man who fought well because he believes in the cause for which he is fighting . . . it is always pride that incites and succeeds in war.'

9

The war in Europe lasted seven more months. I did not get home for almost another year. After the battle of Casa Spinello war became a matter of sticking it out, not something of which the outcome was in much doubt. Spaduro had been taken, but we still did not get through to the plain that autumn. There was too much rain; our forces were too depleted. For myself, I had done what I had wanted to do at Spinello – or what had been required, or destined. Now I wanted to get home. Pride may be required if a human feels he has to perform some task; after that it makes sense no longer.

The battalion stayed in the northern hills until well into the new year. There were more waterlogged trenches, more farmyards with rotting cattle, but no more attacks that winter. Daily existence became largely a matter of chores – weapons testing and inspection, the digging of latrines, the official inspection of feet (foot-rot had become a prevalent but preventable disease). Every so often we went down for a few days' rest to tents in the valley. I huddled under blankets and tried to read.

The canister of books I had brought with me from England had got lost somewhere on my travels in the summer; then it turned up as if miraculously on my return from Egypt. I came across an officer whom I did not know reading, of all things, a book by Richard Jefferies. I asked him how he had come across it. He said that a strange box had turned up in his luggage that looked as if it should contain ammunition, but then . . . well, he was extraordinarily grateful to me because he had been enjoying stuff that he would otherwise not have read; but of course I must have the canister back.

But now, in the mountains in the rain, I had run out of books – and anyway I did not know what I wanted to read. The world seemed so mad: did art, literature, make it any better? However, somewhere on our journey to the north we had stayed near a recently liberated prisoner-of-war camp which had a Red Cross library of English books, and we had been told we could pick out and keep any we liked. I had chosen a book by William Faulkner, of whom I had not heard, but it had an introduction by Richard Hughes, whom I admired. So I now read *The Sound and the Fury* in a bivouac tent in the pouring rain; conditions were too wet almost literally to put it down. The first third of the story is told by a mentally defective youth who hardly tries to make sense of the world around him; sense has to be looked for, hoped for, by the reader. After these are flashbacks, narrations by other members of the family, in the course of which there are glimpses of things becoming clearer. Then, about two thirds of the way through, the whole import of the story, its structure and meaning, burst upon the reader in a flash. I had never come across anything like this before. I thought – Yes this is how life

may be understood, if at all; this is the way in which I want
to write novels after the war.

Mervyn had been carried off to hospital after Spinello. I
had a letter from him from Arezzo –

Dear Nick, I have been thinking a great deal about you
lately, which goes without saying. I was so glad to see
Mann the signaller chap who said you were safe enough
and coming out of the line for a bit. I hope it is for a
long time. This letter is really to get you to write some
account of what happened after I left. I will not hold
forth in a long and boring screed myself because I
cannot write very well my left arm being in a sling. I
am well enough and I suppose will be in bed for about a
fortnight. Your performance at Casa Spinello was great.
I told the CO and the rough draft of a recommendation I sent from the hospital is with this letter. I was
very fed up with myself at the Casa. I reckon myself
pretty good in battle, but my performance there was
the worst ever. It was certainly your greatest ever
but anyway we had better not begin such a discussion
by post. Pray write. Love to Fitz, Desmond and Co.
Yours, Mervyn.

It had not seemed to anyone else that Mervyn's performance at Spinello had not been great. He too had been put
up for an award, as had Desmond; and Corporals Tomkinson and McClarnon on my recommendation. Because
the battle of Spinello had been such an important one for
the whole division, it had been watched by the brigadier

and the 78th Division general through binoculars from a vantage point on a distant hill. So its fame had spread.

We were not out of the line for as long as Mervyn had hoped; then there were night patrols again – and these were not always now an uneventful game. There was one position where we were separated from the Germans by a shallow valley along which a road ran between us and them; halfway along this road there was a bridge over a small river. It was not feasible for either us or the Germans to occupy this bridge during the day, but for some military reason it was considered crucial by both sides to be in possession of it at night. So every evening at dusk there was a race to see who would get to the bridge first: if we started too early we got shot up by the Germans in the light; if we started too late we got shot up in the dark by Germans who had got there first. At regular intervals it came to be the turn of my platoon to do this race. This was the sort of nerve-racking routine that made people break down during this long and wearying winter. There were, in fact, one or two officers who said they could not go on. This was understood by higher authority; they were not persecuted as they would have been in the First World War; they were sent back to jobs at the base. Any fear of this leading to a spate of such occurrences did not materialise. If one had not had pride, one would not have been in the front line anyway.

From one of our positions I wrote to my father –

I have constructed for myself a pleasantly secluded little dungeon in the rubble of a ruined house, about 7ft by 5ft and 3ft high, in which I hibernate for 24 hours a day, passing the time happily in communing with the less lofty Muses, concocting grotesque dishes of tinned food to fry over a tiny petrol fire, and beating off the savage assaults of many rats who share my compartment. For a limited period I am strangely content to exist thus. Unfortunately the higher Muses cannot be invoked because one has not yet achieved the degree of detachment whereby the inquiring mind can free itself from bodily squalor.

But then from the luxury of a tent in the valley –

Have been reading quite a lot of Shakespeare and Ibsen – food for interesting comparison. But it seems to me that the greatness of both as artists depends on the fact that they are neither of them profound or ardent philosophers. Thus they produce art for art's sake; even Ibsen, who is careful in his plays never to solve the problems he presents; or if he does, to contradict his first solution in a later play, thus using social, moral and spiritual problems merely as a framework for his art. This leads me to wonder if philosophy and perfect art can ever be reconciled. In Goethe, perhaps you would say? But that is a subject I know little about.

I was still dreaming about possibilities for life after the war. For so long even before the war the family had been split – with my father, my stepmother and my half-brothers in their beautiful house in Derbyshire; my sister, brother and Nanny in my mother's old home at Denham, Bucks, under the eye of my Aunt Irene; and myself happy to move between the two. Then, at the start of the war the Derbyshire house had been relinquished, the house at Denham had been requisitioned by some hush-hush scientific establishment, and my brother Micky and Nanny had gone to stay with my other aunt, Baba, in Gloucestershire. Now my father and Diana were settled into a new house and – and what? It seemed that only I thought it feasible that we should all get together again. Eventually I wrote to my sister – 'If Daddy does not want to accept the Micky guardianship of course it puts every-thing in a different light. I totally agree with you that we must not forget the old Aunt Nina–Nanny ties, and if, as you say, we cannot combine them with the Daddy ties, they must be kept separate but intact.'

And as if to assure each other of the sanctity of old childhood ties, when I came to give my sister a first intimation of the battle of Casa Spinello, in order to divert the attention of the censor I described it as if it had been one of our children's games –

I have been playing the Cornwall game with a bunch of the most energetic Germans, who defended their base with distressing determination. However, it was the long run round the kitchen garden that did it in the end, and the crafty lurk on top of the garden wall; and then we were into the swimming-pool area, too close for sight, and the poor dears are not very good when it comes to touch. But serioso, the lionesque games are an excellent training for this sort of life. We had a little skirmish around a farmhouse, the success of which I attribute very largely to my ability to leap over staircases, vanish into lavatories, and come crashing through the plaster of a roof.

Then, when we got to the place where there was the race each night to the bridge over the river –

I find that lions in the open with the Germans is not nearly so exhilarating as lions in the house. In fact it is pure hell. I am at the moment horribly war-weary and longing for a little wound in the arm again.

I was granted four days' leave in Florence. I remember little of this, my first visit to Florence, except that the museums and galleries were closed with their works of art in crates in the cellars. So the beautiful buildings had more than ever the air of fortresses, of a town fashioned by war, the home of the Medicis and Savonarola. But then, was it not true that great art had been produced in time of war when people had been in daily confrontation with danger and death, with extremes of evil and sanctity? In my memory the statues of Michelangelo's *David* and Cellini's *Perseus* were still on show in the square. Or must these have been copies? I remember absurdly bribing my way into the locked Bargello Museum and in the basement staring at a crate that was said to contain Donatello's *David*.

I had another letter from Mervyn, who was now in

hospital in Rome. He was distressed to hear that the reinforcements he had asked to be sent up to Spinello had walked into the minefield, and that their company commander, Ronnie Boyd, had been killed.

Dear Nick, I feel in a frantic letter-writing mood so I am going to set about you. I have been lying in bed (in many hospitals, in many places) and saying to myself every day – now you must do something more than reading *Esquire* and get on to reading something intense like Nietzsche; and writing copious notebooks which no one will ever read except yourself. But every day has been just the same, and I still stare weakly at *Esquire*, different copies of which appear from I don't know where.

I'm still worried over that Ronnie Boyd business for I told the CO to send 'F' Company along that way, having travelled it myself.

I met a Rifle Brigade subaltern on my way down: I forget his name, but he asked after you. Typical R.B., because he evidently regarded you as eccentric in staying away from the R.B. which to him, he made plain, was the most satisfactory regiment one could ever be in. He was very nice.

This leg of mine is getting on well, but they keep messing around with my arm, and I gather are going to do a third operation on it. Myself I think there is nothing wrong with it, I'm afraid.

I am so glad to have remembered to tell you that the Penguin Shakespeares must be avoided. I had been reading *Hamlet* off and on for months from the normal version in that American book I had. In hospital I picked up a Penguin *Hamlet* and the difference is distressing. Nearly as bad as reading the Bible R.V. after being used to the A.V.

I must try to get a few books while in this place for it was so enjoyable to argue about T. Mann and so on, and to discover that you were a Hellenist pagan and that I was a puritan more than I realised. I must get you weaving on Tolstoy – myself too, for I have not really worked him out. Did you finish *Resurrection*? It was horribly translated but the simplicity of the ideas that the chap arrived at were very impressive. Nekhlyudov I think he was called. I love these Russian names.

Good luck and learn to go carefully. *No* heroics. Yours, Mervyn.

As Christmas approached we were in a quieter part of the line and the weather cleared. There was a slope to a valley below and no sign of Germans; we could once more sit and admire the beautiful landscape. There was a farmstead in the valley that seemed deserted – except for a pig or two that snuffled about and a gaggle of strutting turkeys. We eyed these greedily. As soon as we were out of danger we were aware of hunger. It occurred to me, and I think to all my platoon, that for once a really sensible patrol would be to go down into the valley and take prisoner a few turkeys. One of my men claimed to have been in civilian life a butcher; he said that if we escorted him to the farmyard he would dispatch a few of them quickly and silently. So we set off, just before dusk, fully armed, five or six of us; and we proceeded peacefully into the valley. We surrounded the hut where we had watched the turkeys go to roost; the self-designated butcher crept in with a bayonet. After a moment the hut exploded as if a grenade had gone off inside; turkeys flew squawking and flapping in all directions, the man with the bayonet in pursuit of them vainly. Someone shouted, 'Shoot them!' I shouted, 'No!' Eventually we managed to capture a few. We carried them back in triumph and had our pre-Christmas dinner.

I had a letter from Mervyn –

It is fortunate that there is a brandy allocation in the ward as I really had to call for it after reading your demoniac denunciation of *Resurrection* and your relega-tion of it to the futile and obvious. I have certainly got over my first rapture on its account, but I really do regard it as frightfully interesting account of the work-ing of God (or what one pleases to put in place of that word) on a man's mind. It is certainly not original, as you say, but it does describe how a wrongful act worries the mind until at last you feel you have to do something to make up for it. As I understand them, Tolstoy and Dostoevsky regard this as the direct influence of God. I think (with respect) that you miss the point of the last chapter on the Sermon on the Mount. That is added as a personal reflection of the author and is not really concerned with the story at all. It was his last book and I feel he could not quite confine himself to a dissection of the mind of le bon Nekhlyudov but kept breaking into his own theological thoughts.

Really of course why we disagree is as plain to you as it is to me. You can look at the efforts of a man to convince of Christianity in a detached fashion and can be critical both of Christianity and his ways. I, on the other hand, am so desperately anxious to be convinced of Christianity's truth that I am unable to look with that critical Mosley eye. So I suppose you will call me a bigoted old puritan and smile at your own open-mindedness – with satisfaction of course.

There is just one other thing you say that I must comment on, to disagree again I am afraid. You say men will not follow the Sermon on the Mount until they are sane and merciful, and when they are that it does not matter what sermon (creed) they punch up. Apart from the fact that the second part of your conclusion implicitly denies that Jesus is of God, I reckon that the first conclusion is wrong because chaps will become sane and merciful by practising the Sermon and not, as you say, will practise the Sermon when they are S. and M. The Sermon is the means pointed out to men whereby they can better the world; and this means will end in folks being good and kind, or sane and merciful.

Then there came a day in the New Year when we were in the mountains again – somewhere close to Monte Spaduro, I think – and the weather was still fine and there was no sign of Germans; and I was standing beside my trench in the sunlight and I saw our commanding officer, Bela Bredin, and his adjutant coming along a path up the hill; and they were moving in a stately manner like a small religious procession and smiling; and I thought – So that is all right. And then Bala came up to me and said that for the battle of Casa Spinello I had been awarded the Military Cross; and so had Mervyn; and Desmond Fay had got a bar to the MC he already had; and Corporal Tomkinson had got a Military Medal and Corporal McClarnon had been Mentioned in Despatches. And so what I had not exactly hoped for nor expected but had felt I needed, this had happened; and perhaps I would not have to feel cynical again.

Mervyn wrote –

I was vastly pleased to get your letter and to read that we have both been begonged and Desmond has been bebarred. My salutations to you (and D.) and thanks for yours. I will not go on with any more mutual admiration except to say that I reckon we are all mighty fine fellows!

I knew yours was coming of course because the CO told me in a letter. Your mighty charge was terrific to see.

I wrote to my sister –

It's the full ridicule, the ultimate absurdity, but there it is – a slender little purple and white ribbon stitched upon my heaving bosom, and me in the full enjoyment of outrageous false modesty.

The MC will help, yes, for it will give authority to the anti-war, anti-patriotic preaching which I intend to deliver to one and all after the war. Even in this so-called universal war there are so very few people who have seen anything of the real fighting, that it is essential for these few to bellow their views even if it means discomforting others. I hope you won't find me too soap-boxish and bitter.

To my father I wrote –

It is the young Siegfried after all.

10

The superficial aspect of elation did not last long. We were soon back at the place we had so disliked a month or so ago – with the race to the bridge across the stream. More people were now saying they could not go on.

I had one man in my platoon – an ex-jailbird from Belfast – who was known as a troublemaker; in army jargon a barrack-room lawyer. I made him my batman/runner because I thought he would be less trouble under my eye than away from it. He was also an invigorating 'character'. Once, when we were in our perilous position by the bridge, I ordered him to take a message back to headquarters and he refused. I said, 'Obey my order or I shall shoot you!' He said, 'Then shoot me sir!' and tore open the front of his battledress. I said, 'Oh all right!'

I arranged a new nook for myself on the first floor of a hayloft; it was exposed to the shelling, but away from the attention of rats. I began to fantasise about how one might get out of this futile situation by a discreet self-inflicted accident: would this be more or less reprehensible now that I had got an MC? I imagined I might fall from my hayloft on to the concrete floor below with one leg tucked under the other in a yoga position: might this not give me a not-too-badly broken leg which would get me back to hospital?

But after a time luck was once more with me. I awoke one morning shivering and sweating with something other than fear; the Medical Officer confirmed I had a high temperature and diagnosed malaria. So off I went in an ambulance, bumping painfully over potholed roads, but how happy to be on a magical mystery tour again to – where? – Florence? Rome? Even Naples?

I wrote to my sister from Florence –

Jan 13th. I have malaria, or at least I am told I have by the learned doctors who prod my stomach. I maintain it is jaundice, and contest them every inch of the way, but they continue to pump me with quinine until I am stone deaf and sick every three minutes. I have not even the consolation of being unexpectedly out of the line – for just before I left had been offered a fearfully smart job for 2 months at the Div Training School, where I would have been a Captain and reasonably comfortable.

Jan 14th. I have triumphed over the forces of science. It is jaundice, which apparently is treated far more seriously, and I am to be evacuated back, and the further back the happier I shall be. I don't know if I shall quite make Naples, but I should drift as far as Rome.

But I did go all the way to Naples, and then on to a convalescent home in Sorrento, which as it happened was next door to the hotel in which I had stayed with my father and sister and stepmother in 1936. In hospital and on my journeys down I had been thinking – If ever in later life I come to write about all this I must try to find a style in which to express the contradictions of war – the coincidence of luck and endurance; of farce and fear; of anarchy and meaning.

From Sorrento I wrote my sister a long letter in which I tried to say what I thought I had learned from war. The direction of my arrogance had somewhat changed, but did not seem to be done away with. I wrote –

I went into this war with certain pompous opinions about my virtues and capabilities but amongst them were absolutely no pretensions that I would make a good soldier. I thought that all business-minded men would be 100 times better at organisation than myself, and I thought that all the earnest hearties who seriously believed in the righteousness of this war would be 100 times more brave. After twelve months in Italy I realised that I was wrong: I did not underestimate my own abilities; I overestimated almost everyone else's. And this startles me considerably; for I, as you know, consider this war a blasphemous stupidity, and yet in a spirit of unwilling desperation I have put more into the winning of it than most of those who say they consider it a holy crusade against the powers of the Devil.

I still do not think I have any pretensions about myself as a soldier. When things are not dangerously active I am intensely and professedly idle. Every minute I have to give to this war I grudge angrily. And when things are dangerously active I go about my business in a spirit of complete misery. And yet I have the reputation of being in action a model subaltern.

It is interesting to note that after 12 months of fighting I will forgive anyone the old failings – the boorishness, the stupidity, the dullness – if he does not possess the failings of a bad soldier. That boils down to the realisation that out here the only thing that matters tuppence in a man is his ability to be brave. That is the only standard by which one judges anyone. For if they are not brave, it is 10 to 1 that they are miserably hypocritical as well.

Now there are incredibly few people who do possess this virtue. Those who possess it least are those who preach most lustily about the holiness of the war crusade. Fortunately in my Battalion nearly everyone does possess it: they do not remain long if they don't; and that is why I am able to get on very well with them, whereas before I would have been driven into my frenzy of petulance by their shortcomings. But this breeds tolerance for people who are fundamentally worthy. The war is a head-sweller to the few who fight it, but it produces a lofty, cynical, benign swollen head – which does not rant nor strut but maintains an almost reverent humility towards anyone who knows why and whereof it is swollen. So when you see me although you may find me complacent I hope it does not take too odious a form. On the whole I think the tolerance and humility with those who understand will be far more prominent than the other feelings. But you will find out!

I tried to explain to my sister the origins of my feeling an outsider. My sister and I had been very close as children:

with both our parents so often away (my mother as well as my father had been for four years a Labour MP) we had come to depend on one another; we told each other fantasy stories in which we were literally orphans in a storm – marooned on a desert island or on a raft. My sister dealt with our situation with considerable boldness if not confidence; I was likely to get in desperate rages and try to hide myself away. Now my sister wrote to me that our brother Michael, aged twelve, was behaving in much the same way as I had done; and what should she do? In the same long letter in which I wrote to her about myself in the war, I wrote about what it seemed that such a child has to contend with –

The trouble begins when a child (or youth or what-have-you) has a constructively vivid imagination, an intolerant but quick mind, and a sensitive but intensely self-centred nature. Which is what I had and Mick has. So soon as such a child begins to think he will form certain ideas in his imagination which are made very strong and definite by the quickness and intolerance of his mind, and are very real to him owing to the virulence of his imagination. The most important of these ideas, owing to his self-centred nature, will be his ideas of himself and of how things and people ought to behave in relation to himself. Gradually as these ideas grow in clarity, and his sensitiveness and intolerance grow in intensity, he will have an increasing horror of anything that does not conform to these ideas, a horror which in some exaggerated cases becomes almost physical. Thus when he is faced with conditions which are antipathetic to his ideas, his revolt against them is spontaneous and unavoidable. In his revolt he can do one of two things. He can either try to change the conditions or he must run from them. But a child cannot change his conditions because he is neither strong enough nor has a definite enough idea what to change them to. So he sulks. He runs away. It is an almost physical reaction.

Does this explain my behaviour? I did not understand it at the time. All I knew was that in certain conditions I reacted in a way which I really could not control. I am not very clear even now as to what those conditions were, but you will remember the numerous examples as well as I. I think 'artificiality' and 'unpleasantness' were the chief characteristics of the conditions I abhorred. But these are vague terms, and it is fruitless to try to analyse them accurately. And the 'artificiality' or 'unpleasantness' was always relative only to me. Viewed dispassionately, there was very often nothing objectionable in the conditions at all. It was all a matter of how they acted on my frame of mind at the moment.

I wrote briefly and not analytically about my stammer –

On the surface I suppose it is a tragedy. Certainly without it I should have shone much more than I did at Eton. Even in the army it probably stops me from promotion. But the stammer forced me away from all superficial contacts, from all superficialities in fact. And although on the face of it this was unfortunate and forbade much material 'success', I am presumptuous enough to feel that it led to many developments in a more fundamental way. It taught me to think and to judge, to see things at more than their superficial values; to rely on more than affability to show my worth. If the stammer eventually goes, I am convinced it will have done me more good than harm. If it stays, at least it will have been of some advantage early in life, when I might so easily have become a vacant lout. I think myself it will go in time.

After Sorrento I found myself once more in what I described to my sister as 'the full gaiety of the Naples winter season'. When I had reported back this time to the transit camp to learn what arrangements would be made to get me back to the battalion they told me that they had no papers about me and would be able to do nothing with me until they had. This seemed to have something to do with the uncertainty about my being classified as either London Irish Rifles or Rifle Brigade, or neither. This situation, of course, I felt suited me very well – not just now, in Naples, but in my feeling that I was by nature an outsider – not tied to any group. So I was encouraged by the authorities again to go off on my own, with this time no indication about when I should come back. It was too cold and wet to go to Ischia or Capri, so I set about looking for a room in the old part of Naples, by the harbour, where from tall buildings washing like flags was hung across narrow streets. This was the haunt of touts who would offer soldiers their 'virgin' sisters in return for cigarettes. I soon

found a man who said he could find me a splendid apartment in return for very little money. So I was taken to a
high unprepossessing building and up bleak flights of stairs
to the home of an elderly and kind couple who showed me
two beautifully furnished rooms, which they said I could
rent. I moved in with my meagre kitbag, and sat on an
antique sofa beneath an ornate gilded mirror, and I
thought – This is the first place truly of my own that I
have ever had; it gives rise to a form of ecstasy.

I took up again my correspondence with my father that
seemed to represent a sanity-seeking journey in contrast to
that of war –

Have just read the most enthralling little book called
The Mysterious Universe by James Jeans. It appears that
the physicists have indeed done away with the old
theories of matter and energy, and have arrived by
scientific means at much the same conclusions that
Berkeley and Co hazarded in the 18th century. The
point I find fascinating is the scientific conclusion that
the universe as we know it cannot be composed of
ultimate matter and energy, but only the reflections of
ultimate reality in some Universal Mind. And we are
only able to see these reflections as reflections again in
our own mind. Now this is a very acceptable conclusion
when it is come by scientifically, for although the
Universal Mind seems to be the mind of a Pure Math-
ematician, and thus for ever somewhat beyond our
comprehension, it does at least suggest that the Universal Mind has some affinity with our own feeble

minds, thus giving us enormous significance in the universe when before it seemed as if we were of no account at all.

And later –

Before I came into contact with the physicists I had embarked on a rather dangerous heresy reasoning as follows: although we admit the hypothetical existence of God and Ultimate Reality, it appears that both are so irrevocably incomprehensible to us that there is no way by which man can approach them: Ultimate Reality is eternally indiscernible, and there is no reason to suppose that the will, intelligence or purpose of God is anywhere manifested upon earth, either in mankind or 'nature'. Why do we suppose that we have in us that which is also in God?

Reasoning thus, without the evidence of the physicists, I evolved a 'man for man's sake' religion, the only ethics of which were those imposed by the conscience of the individual – a religion close to that of the terrible Frederick [Nietzsche]! Without the physicists' evidence I think that was a reasonable view; but after my introduction to Jeans, I saw that there were very good grounds for the belief that 'we have in us that which is also in God'; also that the natural world is in some way a reflection of eternal reality. However, in either philosophy our attitude to life can be much the same – the aim being always the perfecting of man and a possible creation of a higher type of man. Whether this is the

My platoon in 'Kangaroo' armoured troop carriers, northern Italy, April 1945

Above NM's platoon on a captured German vehicle, April 1945

Opposite page from top A British tank of the 9th Lancers near Ferrara in Italy, April 1945; A tank firing near Ferrara, April 1945; A German tank on fire near Ferrara, April 1945

NM in Ossiachersee, Austria, July 1945, where he was stationed

The billets on the lake at Ossiachersee, July 1945

Left to right NM looking out of the window of the officers' billet (wearing his medal ribbon), Austria 1945; NM in the lake at Ossiachersee, July 1945

NM on leave in Florence, 1944

A fellow officer accompanying NM on his way through Italy to fight the Japanese, July 1945

NM and Mervyn Davies at the end of the war in Italy, 1945

end in itself – as it was with N – or merely the means whereby we may ultimately come in contact with Reality or Godhead, does not greatly matter. We shall doubtless know when the time comes. In the meantime to the sane man there can be only one attitude to life – to find a harmony between his consciousness and his instinct by a study of the world about him and the world that has gone before him, and an honest appreciation of the evidence thereby attained – and then to live in accordance with this harmony, always with the further purpose of increasing its range and imparting it to others. If ever a fairly universal harmony is obtained, a higher type of man will emerge. So long as the ignorant and prejudiced are in the vast majority, the harmonious man has to devote most of his energy to shielding himself from the insane clamour of the multitude; but if ever sanity is able to extend itself from the individual to society, then indeed I think there will be hope of higher creation.

This particular would-be harmonious man continued on his way through a Naples winter. My old friend Anthony, back in Italy after having been treated for his wound in England, sought me out in the convalescent home and later came to stay with me in my flat. We went to the opera – *Carmen*, *La Bohème*, *Faust*, *Turandot*, *La Traviata*. Gigli and Maria Caniglia were said to be expected from Rome. We visited Herculaneum and Pompeii; we climbed Vesuvius. In the Officers' Club we got drunk and belted out Neapolitan songs to the accompaniment of a rousing band, or swayed to sentimental yearnings about Santa Lucia or a return to Sorrento. Occasionally there were a few nurses at the club, and I remember going with one for a moonlit walk by the sea. But as I had found in Cairo, sex did not seem to have much point in war – unless, that is, one had something of the nature of a rapist.

My friend from Ranby days, Raleigh Trevelyan, who had been badly wounded at Anzio, was now working for the Military Mission to the Italian Army in Rome, where the social life was more glamorous, and he suggested I should join him. He wrote, 'I exchange pleasantries with Marchesas and dance on polished floors to the gramophone with Ambassadors' daughters; every Friday I partake of tea and scones with the Princess Doria . . . the Vestal Virgins are preparing a bullock, snow white, to sacrifice in your honour; the priests of Dionysus are already weaving garlands to adorn the pillars of the temple.' This was the old Ranby style of which I had been so fond and which I had got out of the way of with the London Irish Rifles. Later Raleigh wrote – 'How unfashionable you are supporting Gigli! You'll be a social failure in Rome.'

I still had nostalgia for the Rifle Brigade style, although I had not wanted to go back to it. When Mervyn had been convalescing in Sorrento earlier in the year and I was still laid up in Florence, he had bumped into Anthony and they had got on so well together that they had hatched a plot for Anthony to join the LIR. So when Mervyn got back to the battalion at the end of January 1945 – just as I arrived in Naples – he had spoken of this plan to our commanding officer, who had welcomed the idea, and had had a word with so-and-so who had had a word . . . and so on – and everything seemed to be in train for Anthony to join us until the Rifle Brigade got fed up and scotched the idea. In the meantime, however, Mervyn seemed to have become imbued with something of the old Ranby style and we wrote to each other about forming, with or without Anthony, a society of like-minded refugees from the earnest gung-ho spirit of war, to be known as the SDA or the Society of Decadent Anarchists. My two or three great friends and I already saw ourselves as forming what we referred to as a clique which felt itself aloof from conventional society; which made jokes about our current predicaments, and talked seriously about the meaning of life and God.

But now, owing to the non-existence of papers about me, there seemed some doubt about my getting back into the war at all. I cannot remember the details of this: it seems so unlikely. I gather what I can from Mervyn's letters. It appears that I really might have been free to go on doing as I wished – even to stay on indefinitely in my Naples flat. But then, might I not seriously be in some limbo for ever? A sort of non-person unable to get home? Mervyn wrote from the battalion who were now on the edge of the northern plain – 'What I really want you to know is that you will not be sailing up the creek if you come here under your own steam.' That is, the battalion would then sort things out. Mervyn spoke of huge St Patrick's Day parties being planned. I thought – Surely there is no point in being an outsider unless one also has the choice of being an insider?

So I set off on my own to rejoin the 2nd LIR towards the end of March. I bypassed Raleigh in Rome. I arrived at Forli on the edge of the plain, where the battalion were getting ready to celebrate a postponed St Patrick's Day because on the proper day, 17 March, they had still been in the line. The winter breakthrough had never quite been achieved, but I was regaled with hair-raising stories of the latest battles on the banks of the canals and rivers that criss-crossed the eastern end of the Po valley.

I was glad to be back in the battalion; to be with people with whom I had been through so much already. I wrote to my father –

I still wonder at my good fortune at having found my way to this battalion. The Rifle Brigade was all very jolly in the insouciant days of Winchester and York, but out here I think I would have been stifled by their so carefully posed artificiality of decency. Here the atmosphere is almost Dionysian.

When I went away in January I left behind my little translation of *Zarathustra*, with earnest instructions to one and all that they should read it before I came back. I find that they have followed my instructions to such good effect that the talk that floats around the mess at dinner time is not of obscenities or military pomposities to which one might have become resigned, but is full of erudite allusions to Will to Power, Superman, Feast of the Ass, etc.; which, although no one knows very well what he is talking about, I find most comforting. It is surely unique to find the Mess of an infantry battalion that discusses *Zarathustra*?

On the postponed St Patrick's Day we all got uproariously drunk. Anthony visited us briefly on his way to joining a battalion of the King's Royal Rifle Corps. The London Irish were due to set off in a day or two on what at last could reasonably be hoped to be the final battle of the Italian campaign. We were all lined up for inspection before setting off when my batman, the one who had invited me to shoot him for refusing to obey an order, was seen to be swaying alarmingly. The Brigadier stopped in front of him and said, 'What's wrong with you, my good man?' My batman said, 'Sir, I'm drunk.'

II

This was now the second week in April 1945. For the advance across the promised land of the Po valley and the northern plain we were for the first time since Cassino a year ago going to work with tanks and the support of heavy artillery; also now there would be fighter-bombers overhead ready to be called up to deal with opposition if it became serious. The tank regiment we were going to work with was the fashionable 9th Lancers, with two or three of whose officers I had been at school. We eyed one another warily: what on earth was I doing with the London Irish Rifles? Once I would have thought – But I'm not 'with' anyone. Now I was rather pleased to be seen as being allied to something unfashionable.

The Irish Brigade was set to advance through something called the Argenta Gap – a stretch of artificially drained land at the eastern end of the Po valley, which lay between areas that had been flooded. The Fusiliers and Inniskillings were to make the initial breakthrough across the Senio and Santerno rivers; then the London Irish were to exploit this, working in teams with tanks – one troop of tanks to each platoon. The infantry were to be carried in armoured personnel carriers known as Kangaroos – three to a platoon – consisting of the bodies of tanks or self-propelled guns with the turrets or armaments removed. When the going was straightforward the tanks would go ahead and be in charge; when they came across anti-tank opposition they would stop and give covering fire while the infantry dismounted and took charge and did a textbook attack on foot. With luck, we were told, the enemy would surrender.

This was my first experience of what might be called the heroic aspect of war – the sort of thing Germans must have experienced in Poland and France in 1939 and 1940 and in the earliest days of the Russian campaign: tanks rolling across flat country and people emerging with their hands up and what little opposition there was being dive-bombed while those in tanks could watch as if at an air show. Here in Italy people came out from villages and farmsteads with flowers and bottles of wine and the offer of kisses. In the fields there was the occasional German tank now burning and with a body perhaps hanging like a rag doll from the turret.

It was not, of course, always like this. Once a neighbouring Kangaroo was hit by an anti-tank shell and the people in my carrier were showered with bits of blood and bone. Then there were the times when we were on foot again and doing our training-ground attacks – 'One and two sections round on the right, three section give covering fire!' But more often than not, yes, when we got to our objective the enemy had disappeared. With us gaining in confidence I could even try out a more democratic form of leadership, about the feasibility of which I had wondered. Once, when the tanks had been held up by some anti-tank fire from a farmstead and I had ordered – 'Dismount! We'll go round by that ditch', a voice from my platoon piped up – 'Sir, wouldn't it be better if we went round in the carriers as far as that clump of trees and then dismounted?' And I saw the sense of this, so I shouted – 'You're absolutely right! Everyone back in the carriers!' And by the time we eventually got to our objective the enemy was indeed pulling out. My platoon seemed to appreciate this readiness to change one's mind, though it would probably only have worked in a war as good as won.

There was a constant problem with prisoners. As we advanced from Argenta towards Ferrara, more and more Germans were waiting for us with their hands up. We could not easily spare the men to escort them back, yet the time had not come when we could leave them to their own devices. On the second or third day of our advance the tank major who was nominally in command of our infantry platoon told us, when given out his daily orders, that we were taking too many prisoners. He repeated – Did we understand? We were taking too many prisoners. One of us, probably Desmond Fay, quietly spat on the ground. And we went on taking too many prisoners.

In Richard Doherty's *History of the Irish Brigade* the story of this advance is one of strategies and deployments of forces: this many regiments of field artillery here; that number of specially equipped tanks for crossing ditches and clearing mines there; such and such squadrons of planes on call overhead in what was called a 'cab-rank'. The plans and orders were precise; also what could be said to have succeeded and what could not. But there was not much need to talk of failure. Instead, there were statistics: the Irish Brigade had taken prisoner 'twenty-two officers and 2,000 other ranks'; casualties inflicted had been 'far greater'; 'seven mark IV German tanks were knocked out by the 9th Lancers for the loss of only one of their own'. From what I could see I did not think that there were many casualties on either side: certainly not on ours, apart from those in the carrier that had been hit. But what stays in my memory, as at Cassino, was the impression that no individual could know much of what was going on; one had to wait and see when it was over. But here it could indeed be felt that things were going well, and I began to think I understood something of what those ghastly Nazi armies must have felt as they bludgeoned their way smiling across Poland, France, Russia; until nemesis caught up with them and the homes they had left behind were utterly flattened, and there was no heroic ideology for them to come back to. I wrote to my father –

It is a happier form of warfare than any we have done before, but I find it exhibits the most unfortunate characteristics of one's nature. I actually find this conquest and pursuit faintly enjoyable – and at last understand the fatal temptation of aggression. But nevertheless it is for the most part tedious, and I am irked by the feeling that the end ever remains the same distance from us even as we advance.

However, there came a day early in May when we were on the outskirts of Ferrara and the crowds coming out with flowers were even more ebullient than usual, and the bangs and whooshes that could be heard were of fireworks rather than grenades or Moaning Minnies; and the German trenches we were occupying were deserted except for a litter of old love letters and a smell of stale bread. And the German radio was playing Wagner – the 'Entry of the Gods into Valhalla', I think – and it dawned on us that our war was over. Some of those I was with said later that they almost immediately began to feel strangely at a loss: for so long the war had provided a structure for their lives; a means of getting on with things in spite of doubts and fears. This feeling seemed to persist. However, I took the opportunity to borrow a jeep and drive into Ferrara to have a look at its fourteenth-century castle – a massive turreted building with reddish walls and a moat with drawbridges. This was a monument to war now to be preserved for tourists. And as an adjunct to triumphalism, there was the promise of loot.

When the Germans began to surrender en masse on 2 May, and were rounded up and carted off to prison camps, they had to leave behind . . . everything. The sides of the roads were littered with both the large-scale and the personal detritus of war – tanks, trucks, heavy guns; but also, in piles, abandoned personal weapons and possessions. We searched through these for what trophies we might pick out – in particular the prized Luger pistol. I took my fill of pistols and even a shotgun or two; and then I came cross a small and pretty piano accordion – on which quite soon I learned to play the rousing and sentimental Neapolitan songs that had seemed so much part of our war. Also one's platoon could now be fitted out with its own means of transport. I wrote to my sister –

Kennen Sie what victory means? It means I am at the moment the tempestuous possessor of three cars – a Mercedes which goes at such a horrific speed that I am terrified to take it beyond second gear; an Adler saloon which cruises at 60 without the slightest indication that it is moving; an Opel which streaks hither and thither to the desperate confusion of stray pedestrians. It means that we dine on champagne each night except when we feel leery enough to start on the brandy with the soup. It means – oh well, so much really beyond cars and wine that I suppose they are of infinitesimal significance.

The army was tolerant about such loot. Someone had to clear up the personal stuff by the road, and for a time we were allowed to keep the cars because transport was needed to get us to Austria – or to Yugoslavia, or wherever we were now heading. Rumours abounded; there were few official briefings. In Austria we might be needed to get to somewhere or other ahead of the Russians who were advancing apace from the east; for although the Russians had been our much-lauded Allies during the war, we didn't actually trust them, did we? (What – they might carry on marching west with their vast armies till they reached the Channel ports?) About Yugoslavia the briefings were as confusing as the rumours. We had been backing Marshal Tito who had been fighting a guerrilla war for years against the occupying Germans; but Tito was a communist, and he would surely now be aligning himself with the Russians. Also he was a Serbian, and might well take the opportunity to annihilate his traditional enemies the Croatians, who had tended to side with the Germans. But the Croatians were trying to surrender to us, and so should we not prevent a massacre? But this might antagonise Tito and provoke Russia. And so on. One could begin to see how the simplicities of war might be easier to deal with than the complexities of peace.

We drove north in our motley convoy bypassing Venice and going through Udine into Austria at Villach. We hardly cared where we would end up; this was the sort of uncertainty to which we had become accustomed. The rumours gathered like dark clouds: Tito might be wanting to grab a chunk of Austria, but if we moved too many troops into Austria he might grab Trieste in Italy. There was a pro-German force somewhere in the hills which consisted of Russian anti-Bolshevik Cossacks who had been fighting for the Germans; they too said they would only surrender to the British because in the hands of anyone else they would be likely to be slaughtered. In the meantime the Irish Brigade had taken over a warehouse containing tens of thousands of bottles of the Austrian liqueur Schnapps; so that the political situation assumed an air of less importance. It was even said that someone somewhere had captured a Mint which was churning out a stream of paper money. Then a new and mythical-sounding threat was said to be on the horizon – the Bulgarians! But no one seemed quite to know on which side they had been or would be fighting.

The London Irish were sent off (though my memories of this are hazy) to make some sort of contact with the Russians. We made a dash to Wolfsberg in the eastern Austrian Alps; the Russians had got as far as Graz, some thirty miles further. We sent out scouting parties; what on earth were we supposed to do if we came across Russians? Offer them some Schnapps? I have a picture in my mind of myself and my platoon arriving in some small-town square and seeing across the road some men in strange uniforms whom we took to be Russians – unsmiling and bulging out of jackets that seemed too small for them. We eyed each other warily. Then, probably because none of us understood a word of each other's language, we wandered into the middle of the square and nodded and made friends. In *The History of the Irish Brigade* it is recorded that there was a conference held at Wolfsberg in the Officers' Mess of the London Irish Rifles, at which territorial boundaries were agreed between the British and Russian forces. This was facilitated, it is suggested, not so much by Schnapps, as by alarm about the intentions of the Bulgarians.

After a week in Wolfsberg during which some of all this must have been sorted out – or must have come to be considered not really necessary to be sorted out – we withdrew to Villach, and then to villages on the northern coast of the Ossiachersee, one of the most beautiful lakes in Carinthia, the Austrian province bordering on the frontier with Italy. And there the London Irish stayed for the rest of my time with them in Austria.

What had struck us all on our entry into Austria was not only the beauty of the place and people but the orderliness, peacefulness, the lack of signs of war. The people were neither overtly friendly nor hostile; they were dignified and courteous, and paid attention to what we required. This was especially striking to the communist Desmond Fay, who on entering a recently Nazi-dominated country had expected . . . what? A people arrogant and savagely embittered? Desmond could laugh and shake his head about what he in fact found; but it was something that made us all wonder, even if we could not work out exactly what. We were at first billeted in an orphanage for children whose parents had been killed in the war: there were Germans and Poles as well as Austrians. The children all seemed to have fair hair and the most beautiful manners as well as looks. The women in charge of them herded them into outlying buildings to make room for us; we found ourselves treating the women as if they were our hostesses and we were their guests. When we first arrived there was an army rule that there should be no fraternisation with local people; later this was relaxed because it was unworkable as well as senseless. There were few men except the old left in the villages; the girls and our young soldiers began to flirt not indecorously.

We eventually had to hand over the cars we had taken as loot. Some officers came to arrangements with local farmers to keep and hide their cars until such a time as they could come and pick them up when they were out of the army.

There was still much to do with the huge number of German soldiers and officials who were keen to give themselves up – for the reason that they wanted to be fed, as well as not to fall into the hands of the Russians. From the crowds of these there had to be weeded out and interrogated those who had been Nazis in positions of responsibility who might now be prosecuted as war criminals. In the early stages of this process I was sometimes called on to act as an interpreter with my primitive German. This attempt was apt to dissolve into farce. But there were other situations that became tragically serious.

The Russian Cossack Corps that had been fighting for the Germans against what they saw as an alien Bolshevik Russia had succeeded in surrendering to the British; many had their families with them; they knew that if they were sent or taken back to Russia they would all almost certainly be shot. The Russians demanded that they should be handed over; the British prevaricated. But there had been an agreement between Churchill, Stalin and Roosevelt at the Yalta Conference earlier in the year that all such prisoners should be returned to the country they originally came from. The Cossacks could claim that they had been turned out of their country by the Bolsheviks and thus they had no country, but this carried no weight with the Russians. Orders came down from London that the Cossacks and their families, who had been camping in fields, were to be put forcibly into railway trucks and handed to the Russians. By good fortune the Irish Brigade were not required to do this. But we heard of it; and worried. What would we have done? There was a story that heartened us of a commanding officer of the 6th Armoured Division who went to the assembled Cossacks in their field and told them of the orders he had received, and that as a dutiful soldier he would have to obey them; but he would not do so until morning, and in the meantime he would remove his soldiers who were guarding the field because they were tired. And so in the morning the Cossacks and their families had gone – to mingle presumably with the hordes of displaced and often unidentifiable persons throughout Europe.

There was a similar situation with the Croatians who had been hostile to Tito's partisans and in some cases sided with the Germans. Tito was demanding that they should be handed over to him because he was now de facto ruler of Yugoslavia, but if this happened it was likely that they too would be shot. Tito gave assurances they would be treated according to conventions. They were handed over, but there is evidence that most of them were shot.

Could anything have been done to prevent this? The world of politicians and top military authorities is dependent on words and bits of paper: there have been such and such discussions and agreements; out of the boundless chaos of five years of war such people have to try to produce order. On the ground, individuals face a different kind of obligation; one should not be responsible for sending off persons to be needlessly murdered. Perhaps, indeed, the individual soldiers on the spot have a duty to try to save politicians from the sins of their terrible calling (this was a view voiced at the Nuremberg trials). The politicians may be faced with unavoidable choices of evils; soldiers may have to risk covering for them and suffering the cost.

But in the vast maelstrom that follows from the crack-up of the ice floes of war, what can any individual do with certainty, whether soldier or politician? One hopes to do one's best.

At the Ossiachersee I was made Battalion Sports Officer, whose job it was to provide occupation for those who had nothing much more militarily to do. I organised conventional games; I could pick myself for any team I liked. I had never been much good at cricket, but at this I could at least show off. Also at hockey, which I had never played before. But at football I had to deselect myself: almost anyone seemed better than me. I had been a good runner at school, so I entered myself for the 440 yards at the Army Games at Klagenfurt – and came in a long way behind the champion of the Jewish Brigade who was said to have run at the White City. After this I thought I should retire from organised sport. At Ossiachersee I watched with some admiration the flirtation games that one or two of my fellow young officers played with a very pretty young Austrian nurse at the orphanage.

It was during these days that in the course of conversation with Desmond Fay I let on that I had been to school at Eton. He had long since come to terms with me being the son of Oswald Mosley; he had said – 'Oh well, he was a serious politician.' But at the news that I was an Old Etonian he announced he was so upset that he was not sure if he could carry on with our friendship. This was not entirely a joke: it is part of Leninist theory that fascism is not the unequivocal enemy of communism – it can be a necessary stage in the collapse of capitalism. The clear-cut enemies of the communist proletariat have always been the upper classes.

I went on a week's leave to Venice and stayed on the Lido, where I had stayed with my father and mother in the summer holidays of 1930. Then, my father had spent much time flirting with my future stepmother Diana, who at that time was married to Bryan Guinness. My sister and I, I remembered, had spent much time being outraged not at my father's behaviour to my mother, which I suppose we either did not notice or took as normal upper-class behaviour, but because Randolph Churchill, one of my father's and mother's entourage, insisted on referring to us children as 'brats'. Now, on leave in Venice, I wrote to my father that I did not want to do any more sightseeing; I wanted to come home. In continuation of the letters I had written from Ranby and Naples, still in pursuit of what now increasingly obsessed me – the question of how to look for what might be an alternative to humans' propensity for war – I wrote –

I wonder if Neitzsche's final madness was really the decadent desperation that people suppose – if it were not 'tragic' in the ultimate sense – the culmination of a tragedy in the true Greek style – and therefore something to be greeted and accepted with a 'holy yea-saying'? Is anything much known of Nietzsche's final madness? It is a theory that entrances me – that it is perhaps the culmination of all 'great spirits' that they should appear to be what the rest of the world calls mad: that perhaps this one form of madness – the Dionysian madness – is really an escape into the 'eternity behind reality': neither an advance nor a regression in life but just a sidestep into something that is always beside life. Or am I slightly mad?

It seems to me that the physicists have argued themselves out of their original premises and are floating blindly . . . if all our sense-perceptions, measures, observations etc. are unreliable, indeed misleading, when it comes to interpreting the 'real' world, why do they presume that any experiment they make has any bearing on reality at all? The only thing they can be certain about is that they can never be certain of anything . . .

It seems that the infinite only makes itself known to the finite by means of selected symbols or 'emotions' (which perhaps are only the result of symbol-action): it is beyond the comprehension of the finite (human?) mind to understand the reality behind these symbols. But this does not exclude the possibility of creating – through a fuller understanding of the symbols – a higher form of consciousness which might ultimately glimpse the reality that lay behind.

I had long since seen that my father looked on Nietzsche's work mainly in political terms whereas I saw it as dealing with metaphysics – in that Nietzsche had seen that language was what humans used in their exercise of power, and that any idea of 'truth' had to recognise this and somehow overcome it. Hence Nietzsche's extraordinary elliptical, ironic, highly wrought style that had to be understood by a reader as an artwork rather than an argument. I hoped to go up to Oxford after I got out of the army in order to read philosophy and to try to get more straight my ideas about all this. (But then, when I did get to Oxford, my tutor said, 'We don't do Nietzsche' – implying that he had been a Nazi).

Mervyn had left the London Irish in Austria in order to work on the staff at Central Mediterranean Headquarters. It seemed that I might not be in a close working relationship with him again. I had a letter from him –

The chaps here are nice, but at present they seem solely interested in their work – not because they like it, because they seem to have been allowed hardly any other interests during the war. How terrible. There is also a large content of 'the affected young man' – not your sort of affectation but a far more transparent species of this sometime delectable trait.

Am READING seriously and furiously. Do you know that we have been living in ignorance (I have anyway) of *décadence* (French) as opposed to honest English decadence. The French sort is far more awful and I must define it to you as soon as I understand it so that we can practise it like mad.

Hope you have opened a branch office of the SDA; you should get many members now. I am having difficulty in extending it here of course.

PS Has your mighty epic (which we planned you would publish at the age of 80 years) taken any less amorphous shape?

For many years I forgot I had planned an epic. But here it now is, rarefied and distilled over a lifetime of not knowing quite in what style to write it.

I had been impatient to get home, not only to my family but also to my old school friends; and now when I got back to the battalion from Venice I learned that this would be possible – under the aegis of an army order that all officers and men under a certain age and with less than a certain time of serving overseas were now eligible to be sent to the Far East to continue the war against Japan – with the benefit of a month's leave in England first. So my wish to get home was granted – but rather in the manner of that ghost story in which a couple are given three wishes, the first two of which are fulfilled in such a horrific manner that the third has to be that the first two should be cancelled. However, I wrote home –

> The authorities declared I was eligible for Burma by just three weeks, and nothing that any kindly CO or brigadier out here can do can stop me. But as it happened I received the news with something like relief, and would not now alter the arrangement even if it were possible. I have been growing moribund in Austria with the harassing job of organising sports from the confines of a stuffy office. Leave, I am sure, will miraculously revive me.

I don't know how much this was bravado: it was perhaps a fatalism I had learned; and there might be a way of going east with my old clique of friends. So off I went from

Austria on the long and by now familiar journey back through Florence and Rome to Naples to wait for a boat to take me home, if only en route to tortuous approaches to Japan. I was sitting with a few fellow travelling companions on the terrace of the Officers' Club looking out across the beautiful bay at Vesuvius, which was smoking rather ominously in the distance (it had caused some consternation by half erupting the previous year: this was August 1945), and I was thinking that after all on no account did I want to go to fight Japan. Then we read in the local army newspaper that a bomb had been dropped on Japan that was a new sort of bomb – something to do with what goes on at the heart of the matter – and its effects were so horrific that countless thousands of people had been killed and the Japanese were already talking of surrender. In fact, its effects were so unknown and so uncanny that in future large-scale wars might be made impossible. So I thought – Well that's not so bad then! Good old whatever-it-is at the heart of matter!

12

Humans seem at home in war. They feel lost when among the responsibilities of peace. In war they are told what to do: they accept that they have to 'get on with it'. In peace it seems uncertain what they have to do: they have to discover what the 'it' is to get on with.

I had been keen to get home to be with my family and friends, even if it was only for a month before going out to Burma or wherever. But if the war was really about to be over, then it might be possible that I could be at peace in the Far East with my so-called clique of friends. This clique I had fantasised about in Italy was a sort of alternative family, to be enjoyed if possible in conjunction with both my father's and my sister's establishments. At school my friends and I had been, yes, in our attitudes homosexual; though only in one pairing occasionally practising. For the most part we were fantasy-gay in style, in conceits. In war this style had had to be carried on mainly by letter. But as part of occupying forces in Burma, Malaysia, might not three or four of us form an exotic home from home?

When I had gone from public school straight into the army this had seemed to be a continuation of a homosexual world in which there were no natural family ties –

no responsibilities, no chance of children. In this sense it had been like the Garden of Eden. Would it be possible to create a peacetime Eden?

In the army in Italy I had hardly thought of myself as homosexual: I had scarcely felt myself sexual at all – sex was an itch that war had pushed into the sidelines. Then, when I had been in Naples with Anthony (with whom my friendship was strictly platonic) I had written to a third member of the clique who was recovering from D-Day wounds in England – 'Anthony keeps talking paternally of the ultimate necessity of marriage and family-rearing which, he maintains, involves SETTLING DOWN at some quite early date. I do not grant him this last proposition, for I hold that it is just as preferable to be UNSETTLED in marriage as it is out of marriage.' And then – 'I WILL NOT BE RESPECTABLE.' And earlier – 'I am both ignorant and disinterested in women.'

But then, when I got home to London in September 1945, I found that the whole grandiose social whirl had started up again as if there had been only a blip since September 1939. Almost every night there were what used to be known as debutante dances, to which those thought to be socially acceptable were invited and to which I had the entrée through my sister Vivien and my Aunt Irene Ravensdale. And each of these dances seemed to consist of an enchanted garden of girls. How was it possible that I had not noticed girls before? Now, suddenly, they seemed to be everywhere and infinitely alluring; as thick on the ground as – how might it be put? – 'autumnal leaves that strew the brooks in Vallombrosa'? But had not this been

Milton's reference to fallen angels? Well, so be it. If it was love that one wanted – take one's pick!

But here was a problem: how on earth did one pick and choose? In a heterosexual world it seemed that one was expected to fall in love with just one girl, but surely with such profusion one wanted the whole lot – or at least a big bunch, an armful. But this was held to be not acceptable.

Such were the dilemmas when one was over the edge into peace. I learned that two of my old school friends were settling in to the Far East. But now, surely, it would be more pleasant and even vital for me to stay in London and explore the peacetime possibilities, however baffling, of getting to grips with women.

But with my orders to embark for Malaysia having come through, how would this be possible? After such homosexual affectations, in the heterosexual world had my luck run out?

Then, at one of these dances – at the Savoy Hotel, I think – I had retired to the bar in some exhaustion from trying to squeeze what dalliance I could into what time I had left, and there I came across a major whom I knew slightly, or perhaps he was a friend of my sister's; and he asked me what I was doing nowadays; and I said I was just off to the Far East. And he said – 'My dear fellow, why on earth do you want to do that?' And I said – 'I don't.' So he said – 'Come and see me in the War Office in the morning.' So I did, and I did not know if he would even remember me. But there he was, behind a desk even if somewhat holding his head; and he said – 'I'm afraid I can't quite manage the War Office, but would a job in

Eastern Command, Hounslow do?' And I said – 'Indeed, thank you, Eastern Command, Hounslow would do very well.' So in a day or two I received papers taking me off the draft to the Far East and instructing me to report to Hounslow Barracks – a gaunt building like a furniture depository some ten miles west of London. There, no one was expecting me, but I was given a desk and a chair, where I sat and wondered once more in what style I would one day be able to try to write about war – its luck that seemed to take the place of conventional responsibility. At intervals I played ping-pong with the man with whom I shared an office, using our desks pushed together as a table and copies of *The Manual of Military Law* as bats. Eventually work was found for me, which was to do with officers' pay and courts martial – the latter often dealing with officers caught and photographed as transvestites. And in the evening I would catch the District Line back to London, where I continued to learn the pleasure of prowling in search of – yes, this was surely a better way of putting it – the rose among the rosebud garden of girls.

So this was peace? But there remained the problem of how to make sense of responsibility.

When people said at the end of the war that they found themselves at a loss – they could no longer feel that they just had to 'get on with it' but now had to find the 'it' that they had to get on with – was this 'it' really just the evolutionary business of finding a mate, settling down, procreation? But humans had always found confusion with this; was it not a sort of war? But in so-called 'peace' there were no longer orders coming down from on high; or if religion or social custom claimed that there were, then it was still up to the judgement of individuals to respect these or reject them. Humans had to make their own dispositions to deal with the 'its' that they were finding they had to get on with – work, faith, relationship. And regarding these they felt not only at a loss, but that such a feeling was somehow reprehensible – for should not at least love, the commitment to love, the care of children (so they had an instinct to believe) be sweetness and light? And if it was not, should there really be only themselves to blame? Humans were thrown into the deep end of peace and had to learn how to swim. But why had it ever been thought that peace should be easy? If peace involved the requirement to take responsibility for oneself, then all right, yes, it could be seen how obedience in war might be easier.

I remained in the army working at Hounslow for another year. During this time I did not in fact feel that I had much responsibility. It was still ordained that I should travel on the Underground out and back each day. In the evenings, among those with whom I behaved irresponsibly it could be accepted that I was still involved in some hangover from the war.

At weekends I would go to stay with my father, who was now out of politics as well as house arrest and was leading the life of a country gentleman in Wiltshire. When I had first arrived home, landing off the troopship at Liverpool, I had gone straight to my sister Vivien who was still with her friends Rosalind and Rosie in a flat off Knightsbridge. Then, late that night we had driven down to my father and Diana, who were waiting up to welcome me with cups of tea and snacks. There was so much that might be talked about that I at least could hardly talk at all; I wondered if I would ever be able to talk about the war. This was my family and had been my home; but it did not seem, however my war ended, that I would be able to settle here again.

When I was working in Hounslow and went to stay with my father at weekends, we chatted easily enough about our shared philosophical and literary interests; but our conversation did not have the same intensity as our letters had had in war. I remained perhaps closer to my sister Vivien, who set up her own establishment in the country with our brother Micky and our old nanny. When Mervyn Davies came home shortly after me, I introduced him to Vivien and hoped they might form some relationship, but, I suppose inevitably, nothing came of this. When Mervyn got out of the army he resumed his studies in law, on his way to becoming a QC and then a judge. We still see each other at intervals to have lunch.

My friends in the Far East wrote that they were having a fine time running a local radio station through which they could broadcast their poetry. And they were sharing a mistress. Affectations of homosexuality seemed to be being blown away by peace.

I discovered that there was a way by which I could get out of the army earlier than I had expected. Shortly before I had joined up in 1942, I had taken a scholarship exam for Balliol College, Oxford; I had done little work for this knowing that I would be going off to war. But Balliol had said I had done well enough for them to keep a place for me if later I wanted it. And now it seemed that if I chose to take up this offer I could be demobilised by October 1946 rather than almost a year later. This I did. I wanted to read philosophy – to continue in a more disciplined manner my efforts to understand, among other things, why humans seemed to be at home in war, but refused to acknowledge this and thus were unable to deal with it.

When I got to Oxford, however, I was told that this was not what philosophy was about. The ancient Greek tragedians, yes, had been interested in such questions, but they came under the heading of Classics. The Existentialists? Nietzsche? They did not 'do' these at Oxford. What did they do? Descartes, Hume, Kant: Epistemology, the Theory of Knowledge: what do we mean when we say that we 'know'? But was not this what Nietzsche was on about? Was it? But I had always felt that I would have to work things out for myself.

I stayed at Oxford for just the year I would otherwise have been in the army. Then I left to write my first novel. If academic study insisted on dealing with only the bones of theory, then surely it was up to novels to portray the flesh of life. Also, I left Oxford to marry Rosemary, my eventually chosen rose from the rosebud garden of girls.

I had first noticed Rosemary at one of the innumerable fashionable dances in London. It seemed she had noticed me. But we had been wary: if one pounced conventionally, surely any quarry worth catching would have to try to get away? So how, in fact, when it came to it, *did* one pick and choose? One waited for some sign, some singularity, some jungle test like that of a smell?

I bumped into Rosemary again some months later in a coffee bar in Oxford. I said, 'Do you remember me?' She said, 'Yes.' I said, 'Good.' She said, 'I thought you were that murderer.' There was a murderer on the loose at the time who was said to chop up women and dissolve them in the bath. I thought – Well this indeed is a singular signal that one can hardly explain; but might it be what is required?

I took her out to dinner. She hardly spoke. I rattled on. After a time I said, 'What are you thinking?' She said, 'That I could send you mad in a fortnight.' I said, 'Why wait a fortnight?' I went out to where my car was parked and I gave her the keys. I lay down in the road where she could run over me. She said she did not know how to drive. I got up to show her. Then we drove back to her lodging. By the end of the evening I think we both thought we might marry.

The next weekend I suggested we go in my car for a drive in the country. She asked if we could visit her old grandmother who lived in Hertfordshire. I said – Of course. I had the impression that Rosemary's family must be hard up, for in spite of her presence at London dances she appeared to have no money for bus fares and to possess no smart clothes. On Sunday we drove through country lanes and eventually came to the gates and lodge of a drive leading to what must be a large country house. An old lady came out from the lodge to open the gates. I wondered – This is her grandmother? The old lady waved us on. We drove through what seemed to be endless acres of parkland and came to a long low house like a battleship. We went in through a back door and along stone passages where all life seemed to have stopped; then through a baize door to a small sitting room, outside which Rosemary asked me to wait for a moment. Then when I went in there was a very old lady in a wheelchair who, when her granddaughter had introduced me, said, 'And I was such a friend of your grandfather's!'

I still had no idea who this lady could be who had been a friend of my grandfather George Curzon. (I managed a bit later to glimpse an envelope lying on a desk addressed to 'Lady Desborough'.) She asked Rosemary if I would like to see what she referred to as 'the paintings'. She gave Rosemary a huge old-fashioned key and we went down a central corridor of tattered grandeur and into a long high picture gallery where, when Rosemary had opened a creaking shutter, there appeared – through cobwebs – a Van Dyck? An Italian Renaissance Holy Family? A huge portrait of a soldier on a horse that could be – surely not! – a Rembrandt? (Rosemary said – 'Yes, they say it is.') I thought it important that I should not appear to be bowled over by all this. Why should it not be as natural as anything else? But it seemed more likely than ever that we would marry.

*

So this was peace. But there still seems to me, sixty years later, to be a problem of how to write about war. From the complexities of peace you can produce an artwork. From the simplicities of war – can you portray in one breath both heroism and horror?

People are not supposed to write about their successful exploits in war: this is considered to be bad form. And about the exploits of others – well, this is easier to write when they are dead. There is a whiff of immature triumphalism in stories about successful killing – unless one has paid the price of being killed oneself. Good stories were able to be written about the First World War because then the whole absurdity could be seen as just horror, a senseless disaster. But the Second World War had not been like this – had it? It was held to be just and right. And yet there were the horrors, the disasters. There are very few good accounts of the fighting in the Second World War – one of them, as I have mentioned, is Raleigh Trevelyan's *The Fortress* about the landing at Anzio. A good story about the Second World War has to comprise a way of writing about the horror and the rightness, the misery and the satisfaction, the evil and the good, all in one. Not a problem for epistemology? No?

Perhaps more a problem for religion. The old Greeks had gods – and so did Nietzsche, although he exclaimed that his god was dead. (I later suggested in a novel that such a god might better be seen as a successful train robber retired to the Argentine.) Anyway, not much of a task here, it is true, for logical or verifiable thinking. But then what should be the style? What about my own candidate for Good Fairy: that which goes on at the heart of matter? Here, one is told, things can both be and not be at the same time; an observer affects that which is observed; reality is a function of the experimental condition. So why should not this be the style in which one might float in the deep end of peace? A lifetime's effort indeed! Or would one rather drown?

Humans seem at home in war; they do not feel at home in peace. This cannot be said often enough. So long as it is denied – so long as it is thought that peace is prevented by the actions of certain misfits – then humans cannot learn. There are few novels written about how to live in peace; they are held to be boring. People prefer to read about, and indeed many to experience, the senseless excitement of the simulation of war; the dicing with destruction and the risk of being dead. But if this is the condition on which evolution has depended and which has brought us to where we are, then it hardly makes sense to object – unless, that is, it is seen that evolution has also brought us to an awareness that this condition has become too dangerous and might be surmounted: one can be conscious, that is, of existence on another level.

Evolution has depended on carnage: some species have to be destroyed so that others survive. On the way, however, there have also evolved alliances, dependences, symbioses by which some species may help each other to survive, even if at the cost of others. It seems that humans have evolved an ability to be aware of this, even if they do not seem able to stop being at war within and among themselves. They see they have their animal nature; and, somewhat at odds with this, their human nature which sees the possibility of something different. But they do not seem to have evolved a strategy by which to be at ease with this – except perhaps through religion or the creation of works of art. In the course of evolution, that is, they have experienced an order beyond that of animal or even human nature – an order which seems to be outside evolution because it sees how evolution can be assessed and even reorganised. This order seems to manifest itself as infinite, eternal. Humans have called it the supernatural or spiritual; and it can naturally, of course, be said not to exist. But it seems to have arisen from a tendency of humans to try to make sense of their situation – that of being confined in an evolutionary process and yet also experiencing that a part of them is free of this, and even at times can influence it. They may attempt this by art; or perhaps try to do it by seeing their situation as funny.

Even in formal war there had seemed to be some spiritual ordering as well as orders coming down through chains of command – how else did I stay alive? You get on with things as best you can – but then what does 'best' involve? You keep your eyes and ears open; you learn the limitations of orders; you become aware of an ability within yourself to know what further is required. And then, when necessary, you are ready to jump in at a deep end. But I have told my story.

My last letter to my friend Timmy before he went out to Burma still hoping, perhaps, to 'prove' himself in war, was –

I feel that you were right in your decision to issue Burmawards. Not, however, for the reason you give. Life in battle is the most futile thing in the world, for it is the only futility about which one is forced to care desperately. And for this reason it is the most unreal thing in the world. Indeed, its most potent effect upon me was to suggest that there was no reality in anything;

that all was the wild imagination of an aimless mind. I now think nothing; I am too weary to wonder about the unreality of reality; I have reached the stage where everything must be accepted or rejected without inquiry. All that I have learned of men is that they are composed of such a mixture of perfidy and nobility as I cannot hope to unravel; and all I have learned of life is that there is nothing more to be known about it save that which is observable at the end of one's nose.

But then I had come home – to the garden of fallen angels; to the chance of a lifetime's learning about the paradoxes of peace?

Rosemary and I married: we got away from our families for a time by going to live on a small hill farm in North Wales – me to run the farm and to write my first novel; Rosemary to paint. Writers and painters should have one foot on the earth, should they not, as well as their heads in the clouds? But then children arrived; and we had no piped water, and in winter the stream that ran past the house froze, and roads became blocked. So after a few years Rosemary's mother suggested that for our family's sake she should hand over to us her commodious house in Sussex, which was now too big for her, and this seemed an offer we could not refuse. This story and others that follow I have told in my autobiography *Efforts at Truth*.

My friend Anthony, after a year or two in the wilderness of peace, announced that he was intending to become an Anglican monk. Then a few years later my other great friend, Timmy, went to train to be a priest; and I myself was struggling to learn to be a Christian. All this was a consequence of our coming across, in turn, a holy man, Father Raynes (I have told this story more than once); but it was also, it seems to me now, of our having, in our formative years, put everything up to question even if in our fanciful style, of our having treated nothing as sacrosanct except that one should be ready, when the time seems to have come, to jump in at a deep end. We needed for a time to put our trust in orders that might seem to come from above; then, later, I at least (and this was what I became convinced Christ and Christianity were saying) believed that whatever was necessary could be known less through commands from outside than from a faculty for being aware of an ordering that grew within oneself.

About my relationship with my father – I stayed on good terms with him so long as he remained a gentleman farmer. But by 1948 he was being enticed back into politics and I did not see so much of him; and anyway, Rosemary and I had married and were escaping to North Wales. Then, at the end of the 1950s he was standing as a parliamentary candidate for North Kensington, hoping apparently to attract the anti-black vote, and I became determined to have a decisively antagonistic confrontation with him. I managed this; and in the course of it he said he would never speak to me again. This situation lasted for several years. Then at the end of his life when he had Parkinson's disease and was finally out of politics, I became close to him again. He was, as he had been in prison, resigned and benign, and trying to look back on what had gone wrong in his life and what might have gone right.

We talked in our old freewheeling style; and just a week before he died he announced that he wished me to have all his papers so that I could write his story. He knew how much I had disapproved of his politics; he also knew I would try to tell the truth as I saw it because that had been our style.

About my loves – my marriages to my first wife Rosemary and to my second wife Verity – I have tried to tell of these in my novels. The style is one which tries to portray the hope of peace but the near impossibility of achieving it: a condition in which there seem to be no orders but only paradoxical demands for self-ordering. Love has to be self-giving yet you have to make of yourself something to give; marriage should purvey not only possession but enablement. This is what seems impossible; but also what, if admitted, seems possible through grace. Peace can be found in the mind and in the heart. War, evolution, can go on elsewhere.

Index

Royal Irish Fusiliers, 43, 47, 97, 140
Russia, 2, 8, 13, 141, 143, 146, 149
Russians, 33, 145–7, 149

Salerno, 35–6
Salisbury Plain, 8
Sanders of the River (film), 57
sangers, 64
Sangro river, 44
Santerno river, 140
Scarlet Letter, The (Hawthorne), 39
Schnapps, 146–7
Searles, Geoff, 78
Second World War, 1, 166
Senio river, 140
sergeants, 5–7, 15, 18, 20, 78
sex, 88, 136, 158
Shakespeare, William, 117; Penguin
    editions of, 120–1
Shaw, George Bernard, 27, 67
Sicily, 30, 36–7, 44, 46
Siegfried Line, 1
Siena, 90
Sorrento, 65, 127–8, 132, 136
Sound and the Fury, The (Faulkner),
    114
South Africa, 85
South of France landings, 95–6
Sphinx, 87, 90
Stalin, Joseph, 149
Stalingrad, battle of, 11
Suez Canal, 86
Sussex, 169
Swansea, 46

Talbot, Father, 27
Taranto, 35–9, 44, 86, 94

Termoli, 41, 44, 46, 95
Thompson sub-machine guns, 101,
    104, 106–7
Tidworth, 8
Timmy (school friend), 10, 15, 18, 38,
    168–9
Tito, Marshal, 145–6, 150
Tolstoy, Leo, 121–2; *Resurrection*,
    121–3
Tomkinson, Corporal, 103–6, 115,
    124
Tosca, 40, 84
transvestites, 160
Trevelyan, Raleigh, 16, 18, 57, 136,
    138, 166
Trieste, 146
Trigno river, 44, 46
Tunis, 43
Tunisia, 30
Turandot, 135
turkeys, 121–2

U-boats, 31
Udine, 146

Vatican, 60, 85
venereal disease, 82, 88
Venice, 90, 146, 152, 155
Vesuvius, Mount, 135, 156
Villach, 146–7
Vivien (motor-boat), 36, 81
Vollendam (ship), 31–2

Wagner, Richard, 11, 144
war criminals, 149
Welsh Regiment, 46
Whistler, Signals Officer Laurence,
    21

DEATH IS HARD WORK

DEATH
IS
HARD
WORK

KHALED KHALIFA

Translated from the Arabic by Leri Price

FARRAR, STRAUS AND GIROUX · NEW YORK

Farrar, Straus and Giroux
175 Varick Street, New York 10014

Library of Congress Cataloging-in-Publication Data
Names: Khalīfah, Khālid , 1964– author. | Price, Leri, editor.
Title: Death is hard work / Khaled Khalifa ; translated from the Arabic by
Leri Price.
Other titles: Mawt amal shâaq. English
Description: First American edition. | New York : Farrar, Straus and Giroux,
2019.
Identifiers: LCCN 2018033289 | ISBN 9780374135737 (hardcover)
Subjects: LCSH: Families—Syria—Fiction. | Syria—History—Civil War,
2011—Fiction. | GSAFD: War stories.
Classification: LCC PJ7942.H343 M3913 2019 | DDC 892.7/37—dc23
LC record available at https://lccn.loc.gov/2018033289

Designed by Richard Oriolo

www.fsgbooks.com
www.twitter.com/fsgbooks • www.facebook.com/fsgbooks

1 3 5 7 9 10 8 6 4 2

CONTENTS

DEATH IS HARD WORK

IF YOU WERE
A SACK OF CUMIN

Two hours before he died, Abdel Latif al-Salim looked his son
Bolbol straight in the eye with as much of his remaining strength
as he could muster and repeated his request to be buried in the
cemetery of Anabiya. After all this time, he said, his bones would
rest in his hometown beside his sister Layla; he almost added,
Beside her scent, but he wasn't sure that the dead would smell the
same after four decades. He considered these few words his last
wish and added nothing that might render them the least bit
ambiguous. Resolved to be silent in his last hours, he closed his
eyes, ignoring the people around him, and sank into solitude
with a smile. He thought of Nevine: her smile, her scent, her

naked body wrapped in a black abaya as she tried to float like the butterflies they were collecting. He remembered how his eyes shone at that moment, how his heart had thudded, how his knees trembled, how he carried her to the bed and kissed her greedily, but before he could recall every moment of that "night of immortal secrets," as they'd secretly dubbed that particular evening, he died.

Bolbol, in a rare moment of courage, under the influence of his father's parting words and sad, misted eyes, acted firmly and without fear. He promised his father he would carry out his instructions, which—despite their clarity and simplicity—would hardly be easy work. It's only natural for a man, full of regrets and knowing he'll die within hours, to be weak and make impossible requests. And then it's equally natural for the person tending to that man to put on a cheerful front, as Bolbol was doing, so as not to let the dying man feel that he has been abandoned. Our final moments in this life aren't generally an appropriate time for clear-eyed reflection; indeed, they always find us at our most sentimental. There's no room left in them for rational thought, because time itself has solidified and expanded inside them like water becoming ice. Peace and deliberation are required for reviewing the past and settling our accounts—and these are practices that those approaching death rarely take the time to do. The dying can't wait to fling aside their burdens, the better to cross the *barzakh*—to the other side, where time has no value.

Bolbol, later, regretted not having stood up to his father. He should have reminded his father how difficult it would be to carry out his instructions given the current situation. There were mass graves everywhere filled with casualties who'd never even been identified. No *'aza* lasted more than a few hours now, even for the rich: death was no longer a carnival people threw in order to demonstrate their wealth and prestige. A few roses, a few mourners yawning in a half-empty living room for a couple of hours, someone reciting a sura or two from the Qur'an in a low voice . . . that was all anybody got.

A silent funeral is a funeral stripped of all its awe, Bolbol thought. Rites and rituals meant nothing now. For the first time, everyone was truly equal in death. The poor and the rich, officers and infantry in the regime's army, armed squadron commanders, regular soldiers, random passersby, and those who would remain forever anonymous: all were buried with the same pitiful processions. Death wasn't even a source of distress anymore: it had become an escape much envied by the living.

But this was a different story. *This* body would be big trouble. Thanks to a fleeting moment of sentiment, Bolbol had promised to bury his father in the same grave as Bolbol's aunt—whom he had never even met. He had thought that his father would ask for some sort of precautionary guarantee of Nevine's rights to the family home, seeing as they had married only recently. The building had been reduced to a shell in an air raid, leaving intact only the bedroom where his father had passed his last days of love with Nevine before leaving the town of S with the help of opposition fighters . . .

Bolbol would never forget that scene. His father had been immaculate when the fighters brought him to Damascus from the besieged S; it was clear that they had taken good care of their comrade, this man who'd chosen to stay with them through more than three years of siege. They bade him an affectionate farewell, kissed him warmly, and saluted him. After enjoining Bolbol to be good to his father, they vanished down a well-guarded side road leading back to the orchards surrounding the village. Abdel Latif's eyes were gleaming as he tried and failed to raise his hand to wave to his comrades. He was exhausted and starving, having lost more than half his body weight; like everyone living under the siege, he hadn't eaten a full meal in months.

Now his body was laid out on a metal stretcher in a public hospital. A doctor told Bolbol, "People are dying in droves every single day. Be happy he managed to reach such an old age." Bolbol wasn't quite able to follow the doctor's instructions to be cheerful at his father's death, although he could grasp what was meant. He felt as though he were suffocating beneath the weight of his new predicament. The city streets were a wasteland after eight in the evening, and he had to move the body tomorrow morning, after it was released and before midday. A large consignment of soldiers' corpses would arrive at dawn from the outskirts of Damascus, where the fighting never stopped. There wouldn't be room for his father at the local morgue for long.

When Bolbol left the hospital, it was almost two o'clock in the morning. He decided that his father's last request ought to apply to the rest of the family, too, not just Bolbol himself: everyone ought to be equally responsible for carrying out Abdel Latif's last wish. He looked for a taxi to take him to his brother's house after successive attempts to phone him had failed. He considered texting Hussein the news, but it would have been beneath contempt to let him know that way. Things like that had to be said face-to-face, and the pain shared equally.

The soldiers guarding the hospital waved him toward the nearby Deraa Station—he would find a taxi there. Bolbol decided not to think too much about the gunfire he could hear. He put his hands in his pockets, quickened his pace, and swallowed his fear.

Even a short walk on a winter night like this was extremely hazardous: the patrols never stopped, and the streets were teeming with faceless gunmen. The power had been cut off in most quarters, and concrete blocks were piled high in front of the improvised "offices" set up by the national security branches, occupying most roads. Only residents could possibly have known which routes were permissible and which forbidden. From a distance, Bolbol saw a few men gathered in a circle around an upturned gas can in which some firewood had been set alight. He guessed that they were mostly taxi drivers trapped by the closure of various roads, waiting for dawn so they could go home. The last glimmer of his courage had almost flickered out by the time he found a taxi driver—listening serenely to Um Kulthoum on the car radio—willing to take him. Bolbol quickly reached an understanding with him and didn't argue with the fare that he was quoted.

They didn't talk at first, but after a few minutes Bolbol wanted to try and exorcise his fear. He told the driver that his father had died an hour ago in the hospital, of old age. The driver laughed and informed him that three of his brothers as well as all of their children had died a month before in an air strike. Both went quiet after this; the conversation was no longer on an even footing. Bolbol had been expecting a little sympathy from the driver. Nevertheless, the man behaved honorably and didn't drive away until he was sure that Bolbol was safe. Hussein opened the door, and when he saw Bolbol standing there at that time of the morning, he knew what had happened. He hugged his brother affectionately, led him inside, and made him some tea. He asked if Bolbol wanted to wash his face and promised to take care of everything that still needed to be done: finding a shroud, making the burial arrangements, fetching their sister, Fatima.

Bolbol felt himself become lighter and braver, his worries lifting away. He no longer cared that Hussein had completely ignored their father when Abdel Latif was in the hospital; the important thing was that Hussein wouldn't follow this up by abandoning him now. Bolbol was confident in his brother's ability to manage this sort of situation. Hussein had meandered around among several professions before taking a job as a minibus driver, and if nothing else this meant he'd gained considerable experience dealing with the state bureaucracy, and he had contacts all over the place. Without delay, Hussein dismantled the two seats immediately behind the driver's and rearranged them to form a shelf for the body to lie on. He said, "We'll lay the body here. That way there'll be enough room for everyone else to travel comfortably." He meant Bolbol and their sister, Fatima, but if their in-laws wanted to come along, too, well, they wouldn't be in the way. This idea was soon rejected, though: they couldn't imagine that anyone else would still harbor any sense of duty toward this man whose corpse would have to negotiate hundreds of miles to reach its final resting place.

By seven o'clock, Hussein had finished all the arrangements for the journey. He had brought their sister over from her house and blanked out the scrolling signs on his minibus, which he ordinarily used to work the Jaramana line. With the help of an electrician friend, he improvised an ambulance siren out of its horn. He also bought an air freshener, which he supposed would be needed on the long journey, and didn't forget to call another one of his friends who was able to supply four large blocks of ice. Despite the difficulty of his requests, his friends all had woken before dawn, offered him their condolences, and helped Hussein to arrange everything for the journey. The only thing still left to obtain before they could be on their way was the signature of the hospital director, who wouldn't be in before nine o'clock. They parked in front of the hospital gate to wait for him, but a morgue official asked them to remove their father's body immediately, as the freezers already needed to be emptied out to accommodate the fresh shipment of corpses that had just arrived, now simply heaped on the floor.

Bolbol didn't dare accompany Hussein when he went into the morgue. The corridors were full of the dark, sad faces of men and women waiting to receive the bodies of their loved ones. The orderly indicated that Hussein should search the southern side of the morgue, and Hussein almost threw up as he opened a fridge chock-full of bodies. He'd almost lost hope by the time he found his father's body; hundreds of corpses had been lost and forgotten in this chaos. It was clear that his father hadn't been dead for long. Hussein slipped three thousand liras to the official so that the orderly would be allowed to help him wash and shroud the body in the filthy bathroom reserved for the dead, which no one bothered to clean. The scene in the hospital was horrifying. Officers were pacing the corridors and shouting curses against the opposition fighters. Troops in full combat gear were wandering around aimlessly, smelling of battle. They had brought their friends, either wounded or killed, and dawdling there was their only way to escape or postpone returning to battle, where death would no doubt find them as well. Death always seemed near in this chaos.

Back at the van, Hussein arranged his father's body in such a way that he wouldn't have to see him and be distracted whenever he looked in the rearview mirror. He told Fatima to be quiet, even though she hadn't spoken a word, but she only sobbed harder. Hussein had always enjoyed ordering her around, ever since they were children, and Fatima obeyed him without argument; complying with her brother's demands gave her a sense of equilibrium and security. Hussein was furious at Bolbol when he noticed him leaning against a nearby wall and smoking as if he didn't have a care in the world. He slammed the door of the van and went back to the hospital gate to wait for the director, who had to sign the death certificate before the body could officially be released. It wasn't exactly the place to make small talk, but he couldn't help asking a woman, also waiting, if she knew when the director was expected. She shrugged and turned her face away. Hussein didn't bother trying to speak to anyone else, although he hated waiting in silence; he believed that a little chat would have alleviated their misery. He could feel the tension and anger hidden in the eyes of the petitioners who were packed in all around them.

At nine o'clock, the director arrived and signed the certificate. Immediately, Hussein told Bolbol to get in the bus and instructed Fatima to cover the body with the blankets that he had brought from his house. And also to shut up.

Hussein informed his siblings that removing the body had cost them ten thousand liras, adding that he was recording every expense in a small ledger. Without waiting for their reaction, he began strategizing about the quickest way out of Damascus. The streets would be clogged with traffic at this time of the morning, and the many checkpoints would be jammed; it might take hours to clear the city limits. His calculations proceeded based on his experience spending whole days in traffic as a minibus driver. The road through Abbasiyin Square would be best, although the security checkpoints had a particularly bad reputation in that area. Even *trying* to cross Sabaa Bahrat Square in downtown would be a disaster, he told himself.

So Hussein decided to chance Abbasiyin Square and tried to follow close behind a proper ambulance. He was stopped at the first checkpoint, which wouldn't allow him to travel along the main road, but he was still able to make some headway along an alternate route. The faux siren he'd installed in the minibus was no use whatsoever—no one made way for him. Amid the crowds and the chaos, Hussein recalled how funeral processions used to be respected back in peacetime—cars would pull over, passersby would stop and cast you genuinely sympathetic looks . . .

A row of additional ambulances suddenly descended on him, all heading out of the city. Inside each one were soldiers accompanying coffins; Hussein could see them through the small windows in their back doors. He tried to sneak in between two of the vehicles, but an angry yell and a cocked weapon from one of their furious occupants returned him to the line of civilian vehicles. When the last ambulance in the queue pulled up alongside the minibus, it slowed down, and a soldier leaned out of the window to spit copiously on him and berate him in the foulest possible language. Hussein looked at the spittle moistening his arm and was flooded with rage. Rage and then the desire to weep. Bolbol kept quiet and averted his eyes so as not to increase his brother's embarrassment. Fatima, for her part, no longer felt like crying; she was surprised at how few tears she had shed, all things considered. She decided to postpone expressing the remainder of her sadness and loss until the burial, which would no doubt be the most emotional part of the farewell to her father.

Since childhood, Hussein had been in the habit of memorizing entire pages of the cheap almanacs published by Islamic philanthropic organizations, containing famous sayings, aphorisms, verses from the Qur'an, and prophetic Hadith, and he used them in everyday speech to give his audience the impression of his being well read. He used to believe that he hadn't been created to live on the margins of life as a mere observer, but at that moment, looking at the deluge of vehicles inundating Abbasiyin Square, he felt terrifyingly powerless; he couldn't find an appropriate aphorism to break the strident silence dominating his brother and sister, yet he wanted very much to make them forget that he had just been spat on. He tried to remember something or other about life and death but couldn't come up with anything better than "Tend to the living—the dead are already gone." He didn't like it, however, because of how often the line was quoted by cowards justifying retreat. And in any case, today it might be a different matter—better to tend to the dead; after all, they now outnumbered the living. He went on to muse that they would all surely be dead in the not-too-distant future. This thought had given him exceptional courage over the previous four years. Not only had it served to increase his stoicism day by day, but he was far better able to withstand the many insults he received from checkpoint soldiers and Mukhabarat in the course of his work if he bore this thought in mind, since it allowed him to subscribe to the view that anyone who gave him a hard time would probably be dead today or tomorrow, or by next month at the latest. Not that this was a particularly pleasant notion, but it was an accurate one, and each citizen had to live under the shadow of this understanding. The inhabitants of the city regarded everyone they saw as not so much "alive" as "pre-dead." It gave them a little relief from their frustration and anger.

The bus crawled painfully toward the hundreds of vehicles flooding Abbasiyin Square. Three Suzuki pickup trucks with hoisted flags gleamed ahead of the siblings, heading in their direction; elderly men were standing in the open backs and trying to clear the road. One of them yelled through a bullhorn, loud and clear, "Martyrs, martyrs, martyrs!" He followed this up with "Make way for the martyrs, make way for the martyrs!" But no one cared. The Suzuki trucks approached Hussein's minibus and tried to escape the traffic. Hussein noted aloud that they were coming from Tishreen Military Hospital and added that there was no transport to take the poor to their graves. Bolbol couldn't take his eyes off the man with the bullhorn. He stared at him until he was lost from view.

There was no getting away from death, Bolbol told himself. It was a terrifying flood drowning everyone. He recalled the days when the regime still bothered to put effort into the funerals it staged for its fallen. On television, an ensemble would play some song written especially for the state's many martyrs, and on every coffin there would be a large bouquet bearing the name of the commander in chief of the army and the armed forces (who was also the president), another in the name of the minister of defense, and a third in the name of the deceased's comrades in arms in his squadron or department. A female anchor would announce the name, function, and rank of the martyr, and this would be followed with a shot of the family declaring how proud they were, how glorious it was, that their son had been martyred, faithfully laying down his life for the nation and the Leader. Always those two words—"nation" and "Leader." And yet, after several months, the band, the bouquets, and the flag disappeared; so did the female anchors crowing about the penniless boys martyred for their loyalty to the nation and the Leader; and so did all reverence for the word "martyr." Bolbol looked at the city as it dwindled around them. He remembered how passionate his coworkers had been when they used to tell their horror stories: searching for bodies that had been lost or buried improperly, through hospitals stuffed with corpses . . . Tracking down the remains of a loved one had become hard work—

even more so when a family, immediately upon being informed of the death of a son, was forced to go over to the battlefield and dig through a mass grave, or else among various devastated buildings and the iron skeletons of tanks and burned-out guns. But the bloom went off even these sorts of stories, eventually, and no one bothered to tell them anymore. The exceptional had become habitual, and tragedies were simply mundane—perhaps that was the worst part of this war. In any case, though, as Bolbol looked at his father's corpse, he felt a certain degree of distinction; at least *this* body was being cared for by its three children and not left to the mercy of the elements. He almost told Hussein and Fatima about their father's last moments—in fact, he was surprised that he hadn't already done so—but instead lay back, convinced that there would be plenty of time on the long drive to talk over the exploits of the departed, to recall a past that had never been particularly unhappy.

Hussein was still annoyed at himself. The thousands of sayings and aphorisms he'd spent twenty years memorizing had proved useless in the face of a bad traffic jam—but he refused to let his defective memory get the better of him. He repeated a few sayings on different topics, just to keep in practice: aphorisms on unfaithfulness and hope and the betrayal of friends. He considered this a useful exercise; these sayings might be required sometime soon, and they needed to be primed and ready. He called a few lines of Ahmad Shawqi to mind and recited them vehemently, enunciating majestically: "Crimson freedom has a door / Knocked by every blood-stained hand . . ." The following line only came back to him with difficulty: ". . . he will ever dwell among the pits." But no, he had mixed up Shawqi's poem with one by Shaby, "If One Day the People Wish to Live, Fate Must Respond." But this combination pleased him; if anything, it struck him as fortuitous that he'd accidentally blended two poems with very different meters and rhyme schemes. He had in fact read these lines dozens of times on the pages of his almanacs and liked them very much; he used them to shame cowards who preferred the regime to any unrest. He repeated both incomplete lines in a murmur as if in lament for his revolutionary father.

Bolbol paid no attention; he was content with the three previous months he and his father had spent talking everything over. Fatima understood the recitation as a belated reconciliation between Hussein and their father. She wanted to thank God out loud for this miraculous resolution, but Bolbol's heavy silence made her hesitate, and she decided to wait for a more suitable opportunity to voice her opinion on the long rift between father and son. True, their estrangement had gone through many different stages, and occasionally each man had even approached the other, trying to turn over a new leaf, but no matter what, their relationship never regained its original, cloudless perfection from the time when Hussein had been the spoiled favorite.

The soldiers at the last checkpoint within the limits of Damascus made do with a cursory glance over their papers and allowed them to pass. Many corpses were leaving the city today, and just as many were coming in. The sight of them was abhorrent to the mud-spattered soldiers; the bodies heralded their own imminent end, which they naturally wanted to forget. Hussein didn't look at his watch. He heaved a sigh of relief; he had been delivered from the traffic of Abbasiyin Square, and Damascus was falling away behind them. Now the goal would be to reach Anabiya before midnight. Fatima and Bolbol recovered their optimism and reviewed the necessities for their journey: bottles of mineral water, cigarettes, identity cards, and the little money they had left.

He died at the right time, Bolbol told himself. The body wouldn't rot as fast in this cold winter. They were fortunate he hadn't died in August, when flies swarm over and tear at the dead. Death is a solitary experience, of course, but nevertheless it lays heavy obligations on the living. There's a big difference between an old man who dies in his village, surrounded by family and close to the cemetery, and one who dies hundreds of kilometers away from them all. The living have a harder task ahead of them than the dead; no one wants to see their loved ones rot. They want them to look their best in death for that final memory that can never be erased. The last expression worn by a loved one necessarily comes to epitomize them. When the facial muscles of a suffering man slacken in the midst of his pain, his grief is what remains of him and he looks like nothing so much as a newborn child.

At the checkpoint outside the gate to Damascus, just before the highway, the soldier nodded inside the van and inquired what lay beneath the blanket. Bolbol said calmly, "My father's body." The soldier asked the question a second time, with a new edge in his voice, pointing to the heavy pile of blankets, and Bolbol reaffirmed his answer. The soldier motioned to Hussein to proceed into the GOODS TO DECLARE lane, where public-transport vehicles were lined up, and a different soldier, who was about twenty years old, was circling each one with a bomb detector. The soldier then left the checkpoint and went inside a one-room shed, previously a workshop and now used as an office as well as barracks for the checkpoint soldiers. After a few minutes, an officer marched toward the minibus, wrenched open the door, and ordered them to uncover the body. Bolbol lifted the blanket from his father's face. It was still fresh—his death still raw and tender. With studied callousness, the officer demanded the official documentation for the body, and

Fatima presented him with the death certificate signed by the director of the public hospital and the morgue official, together with their identity cards. He scrutinized the cards and then surprised them all by asking for the dead man's identity card as well. Bolbol almost started explaining to the man that all corpses share a single name—that they slip away from their histories and families in order to affirm their membership in one family alone, the family of the dead, and that no dead person can have any proof of identity beyond their death certificate—but Fatima slipped their father's identity card from her bag and offered it to the officer, who peered at the face of the body and then at the twenty-year-old picture on the card. In those days he had often laughed, their father; now, in death, his face was that of a stern, tough man. The officer took the identity cards and went back to his office. The three living occupants of the minibus exchanged glances and decided to wait in the bus without moving.

Hussein, in his place behind the wheel, was looking angrily at his watch and muttering inaudibly. One of the waiting truck drivers approached him and said plainly, "No goods can get through without the right *documents*." Hussein quickly got out of the minibus and went up to the makeshift office. He paid a bribe known as a goods-transit document, and their identity cards were returned. Feeling strangely victorious, he sped them all away from the checkpoint. Bolbol was thinking over the fact that his father was now a commodity like hookah coals, crates of tomatoes, sacks of onions. His ongoing silence discomfited Hussein, who announced that he had paid a thousand liras, and that they had to reach Anabiya before midnight.

For a moment Bolbol found himself wondering whether it might not be better to return to Damascus and arrange the burial in one of the graveyards there—although he knew this was absurd given how expensive graves were in Damascus. A good grave was so rare that people had begun advertising them in the classified ads, and they only had thirty-five thousand liras left among the three of them . . . Returning was out of the question; even if they had the money, how would they obtain official permission for a burial? Moreover, how could they convince the next shift of soldiers at the checkpoints they'd already passed that they had changed their minds? Or, indeed, that Abdel Latif had died in Damascus and not in a rebel town nearby?

After all, as a general rule, corpses don't much care about where they're buried. Just thinking about it frustrated Bolbol no end. It was a little past noon, he was tired, and he was fed up. Fatima lifted the blanket from her father's face, telling herself that a little fresh air, though cold, might do him good. She opened her window, even though the dead don't breathe and aren't likely to care whether the air is fresh or not. Bolbol told her to cover the body back up so the ice blocks packed tightly around it wouldn't melt, and Fatima complied without demur. Bolbol was now hoping they could all just ride in silence until they reached Anabiya. Their relatives would take care of the burial itself, and afterward he could escape from his family for the last time. He would go back to his nest and skulk in his room like a rat until his dream of moving to a faraway country was realized. There, in that distant land, he would inter himself in snow, and he would never complain about anything ever again. Right now, though, he couldn't keep from dwelling on the cramped and uncomfortable interior of the minibus, not to mention whatever surprises were bound to lie in store for them farther down the road, which he anticipated with dread. He couldn't think of anyone having successfully managed to transport a body all the way to Anabiya in three whole years.

Hussein felt uneasy at the silence, and since his memory didn't furnish him with a suitable pearl of wisdom, he snapped at Fatima to stop opening the window and then reminded his siblings spitefully that they wouldn't arrive at Anabiya before midnight, perhaps not even before dawn. Then he glanced at them in the rearview mirror, and the three of them exchanged looks of fear. All of their calculations had gone up in smoke; they'd already been delayed longer than they could have anticipated; there were few cars on the road, and the distant, blank wilderness—everything they could see, in fact—only made them more afraid.

At the beginning of the national highway, cars were turning onto a side road. Hussein asked a taxi driver if the highway was closed, and the man replied that there was a sniper up there, and he wasn't allowing anyone to pass. "He got *them* three hours ago," the driver added, pointing to four bodies lying on the road ahead: a man, a woman, a young man, and a girl. Bolbol considered the fact that they had chosen to die as they had lived: as a family. Hussein swerved the minibus onto the side road, following the other cars, and winding up in a series of narrow lanes. Somewhere nearby was being bombed, so close to them that they could see the bombs dropping out of the plane. Shrapnel was scattering around them. Hussein tried to block out everything but the road ahead. The last thing they needed was to find themselves pinned down in the middle of some burned-out olive grove.

A large number of cars were ahead of them. Doubtless one of the other drivers knew a safe route and was leading the charge. Bolbol wondered if they would wind up trapped where they were, but when he saw that all the other cars were now returning to the highway, hope was renewed. Hussein was already praising his own ingenuity in saving them from disaster; Bolbol was interested only in getting back to brooding about their dead father and wished Hussein would shut up. Bolbol noticed that the body was listing over; he tried to rearrange it to make it more stable. He considered tying it up somehow but wasn't prepared to have the debate this suggestion would open. Fatima reminded them of the sandwiches she'd brought for their long journey, and Hussein suggested that they pull over at the nearest rest stop when they began the approach to Homs. Bolbol hadn't eaten anything since the previous night. In his view, it was indecent to worry about food so soon after a parent's death.

Fatima was silent and put the sandwiches back in the plastic bag. Bolbol avoided looking at the right-hand side of the road. He was used to the sound of low-flying planes, the sounds of artillery and rocket launchers; for three years now there hadn't been a break in the noise. The bombardment of Qaboun and Jobar never stopped, and they could see traces of it on the buildings along the highway, but Bolbol wasn't interested—he remained indifferent to it all. Hussein drew their attention to the Qatifa checkpoint in the distance and said he would get right into the truck lane to save time. Bolbol made no objection and gave him some of his money. On the one hand, of course, Bolbol told himself, this was all a humiliating and ignominious experience, but then, on the other, it was difficult not to consider his father rather fortunate, given the thousands of corpses left out for birds of prey and other hungry scavengers . . . He tried not to dwell upon the four sniper victims who'd been left back on the highway, where no one dared to approach them, but his mind betrayed him, and he couldn't get the thought of them out of his head. All he wanted to do was lie down next to his father as he had done when he was a small boy, but the same fear that made him long for that comfort prevented him from sleeping so close to a dead man.

The long procession of trucks was exasperating; it would be hours before their turn came. Bolbol expected Hussein to try and expedite matters, but like him, Hussein was getting scared. He didn't dare to speak with the obviously irritable checkpoint guards. But Bolbol guessed that the agents manning the checkpoints were probably afraid, too; perhaps they would take pity on a dead man? He got out of the minibus and went over to the nearest officer and explained the situation with a concise and well-worded speech, but the officer didn't hear him; too many other people were talking to him as well, and Bolbol's voice was as weak and frightened as a wet baby bird in a moldy room. There was nothing for it: they were stuck in the line, with no way out. They were besieged by cars from all sides, and huge cement barriers prevented any vehicle from leaving its lane. On his way back to the minibus, Bolbol saw that Hussein was incensed at his behavior, as usual. He was telling Fatima that Bolbol was an idiot, a ditherer who had waited for them to reach the point of no return before lifting a finger to help, and then *still* failed to talk to the officer and convince him of their extraordinary circumstances. Fatima tried her best to alleviate the tension by telling both her brothers about her sister-in-law, who had been released from prison the previous week. The girl's face had turned yellow, she had lost half her body weight, and her head had been shaved to the bone. At night she raved deliriously. Fatima was sure she had been raped while she was inside. Hussein was ready to provide some pithy response, but Fatima went on, saying that the girl had scabies, too, so her family had been forced to isolate her in an old chicken coop on the roof, after all of which her fiancé dropped her and demanded compensation from her family.

The four bodies on the highway tarmac remained on Bolbol's mind, and now the story of Fatima's sister-in-law burrowed into him as well. It's often the case, in similar circumstances, on long journeys, that people will trade small talk and cheerful anecdotes to soften life's blows and distract from its cruelty: they'll talk about their children's achievements at school or the best season for making jam. But here in this minibus, such small talk as the siblings were able to muster did them absolutely no good; none of them could find any way to connect with the others. In ten years, the three of them hadn't been gathered in the same place for more than an hour or two during Eid, certainly not long enough for each to learn where life had brought the others. At first, when they'd left the hospital, they hadn't hidden their annoyance at being forced back together, but soon enough each sensed their common investment in avoiding any upsetting subjects. Here was a real opportunity to talk about whether they could possibly be a family again—but Hussein didn't care, Bolbol actively opposed it, and Fatima was too busy trying to play the role of the noble sister reuniting her family after the death of a parent. It was a role she had heard a lot about: it was something like her natural inheritance. The older brother inherits the role of the father, and the sister by necessity inherits the mother's role; but in this case it required a strength that Fatima, who'd grown old, didn't possess. She had become a mother, yes, but not like her own. She had given up her dreams of wealth, making do with a lot of complaining and occasionally hiding away a little money from her and her husband's salaries in a bank account no one knew about. She had become a miser on account of her humble income, collecting any castoffs from her childhood home and accepting charity from her in-laws. Her middling intelligence left her looking forever forlorn. All that remained to her now was the hope that either her son or her daughter would somehow compensate her for her lost dreams, so she might finally take revenge on the world for the loss of the pride she'd been famed for when she was a girl, convinced that she was striding purposefully toward a life of brilliance and happiness.

Fatima was nearly forty now, and the traces of her lost pride were still visible on her face. Everyone who loses their pride becomes a miser of a sort; their self-importance increases, their eyes die out, and their resentments accumulate. They incline to gossip and tell stories about all the heroic things that didn't happen in the life they never lived. Fatima, too, passed through all these stages and, in the end, surrendered. She focused on her son (who had entered a dentistry school) and her daughter. The latter was still only fourteen, but Fatima liked it when people said that they resembled each other, droning automatically, "What a pretty girl!" Fatima had prepared her children for a very different life and often repeated to them the story of her first marriage to a great businessman. In reality, he had been nothing more than a small-time fixer who liked running with the big shots. He facilitated their dealings with government agencies and carried out their dirty work, such as watching their wives whenever business took them abroad or accompanying their underage daughters on shopping trips to Beirut.

Fatima would sometimes recall the day they met. On that day, Fatima had been waiting for the bus that would take her to a teacher-training institute in Mezzeh. It was pouring rain, and the bus stop was crowded, and she accepted Mamdouh's invitation to give her a lift in all innocence. She thought he was a friend of her brother's and got into his car without more than an instant of hesitation. She was astonished when he told her that he was always seeing her at the bus stop and that he liked her. He added that he was a student of her father's at the high school. She accepted it, all of it, as quite normal: he liked her, and it wouldn't stop there. She secretly believed that most young men felt the same way about her and that this one just happened to be the only man with the courage to say so. Like all her classmates, she had composed many an imaginary tale about being pursued by lovers, and his presence in her life satisfied this vanity in front of her classmates. She intended them all to see it when her suitor drove her to the institute every morning, and she took her sweet time getting out of the car, speaking to him as if issuing orders while he nodded deferentially. Even though she had liked him from the first instant, she wouldn't surrender so easily; she dealt with him quite loftily and was coy about her feelings. Deep down, she held herself in high regard, and Mamdouh patiently professed himself delighted to obey her every whim. He was as much attracted to her illusions about him as to her, since she supposed him to be an exceptional person; she spoke about their future in an outlandish manner, full of unrealistic enthusiasm and optimism, and Mamdouh was delighted with it all. She liked his stylishness and his little gifts, which were limited to bottles of perfume, Italian shoes, and jeans, all ersatz but made to look like they came from grand shops in Damascus. She was absolutely entranced by his seductive words about love and the happy family they would be devoted to building.

It was a quiet sort of love story. Fatima convinced herself that even if Mamdouh wasn't rich *now*, a man with his connections, with such fine manners and so much wisdom about life, would doubtless get rich by and by, and so she married him despite her father's objections. Her father said it was impossible that such a proud girl should marry a man indistinguishable from any other, a man he described as "mercury," and moreover one who had no demonstrable moral values or virtues to prevent him from becoming a pimp. Fatima defended Mamdouh calmly, and her father eventually surrendered, although he foresaw her future misery, and the thought of it hurt him deeply.

Mamdouh tried to adapt to married life, but it turned out that his patience for his wife's grandiose delusions—about her beauty, her family's influence, her general estimation of herself—was limited. It was all exaggeration: she was just an ordinary, unremarkable girl. She persisted in believing that her looks and natural elegance were renowned, that everything she did could be described only as perfection, while in reality she fell far short of her ideal. From the very first month, Mamdouh knew the marriage was a mistake; he discovered that Fatima's misapprehensions—which he had assumed were just words, and words that would soon be forgotten at that—were for Fatima indisputable facts in which she had absolute faith. And despite her genuine attraction to Mamdouh, particularly in the early days of their marriage, when she was still working all her long-endured sexual frustration out of her system—frustration left over from those lonely years when other men had found her beauty too imposing to ever approach her—she was soon terribly bored. She put up with it and tried to give everyone the impression that they were happy together nonetheless. Her self-confidence and pride made her believe she was capable of remolding her husband. His supposed weakness and the supposed power (largely imaginary) she held over Mamdouh served to satisfy her ego, but she no longer felt so certain of controlling him as she had before their marriage. All her attempts to impose a different regimen on his life were unsuccessful. Their relationship began to lose all savor, and it didn't last the year. To Mamdouh, Fatima was just a short, failed experiment in matrimony. His ardor was slaked, and he could no longer stand to live with this remote and fatuous woman, whose family had allowed her to treat her fantasies as fact. Reflecting on his dilemma, he decided to escape before Fatima became a mother and his own folly also became a fact from which he could never be free. He told her he was going abroad to make his fortune and gave her the option of a divorce or waiting until he returned from Greece, adding that it was possible he might never come back.

After the divorce, her father said bitterly, "She married for the sake of some takeout from Broasted Express and the chance of sitting with some big shots in their fancy ballrooms." These big shots regarded Fatima as the wife of a servant, nothing more, but their good-natured acceptance of her presence among them led her to believe she could count herself as their friend, with the right to participate in all their private affairs. She would ask the wife of a Japanese company's local agent about the best slimming club in Damascus and wait gravely for a reply, or she would confess to the wife of a French oil company agent that she didn't want to have a child for a few more years so that she could keep her stomach from sagging for as long as possible. The following day, back in the school where she was now a teacher, she would yawn in the staff room and grumble nonchalantly about her husband's never-ending late nights with his friends and business associates. The aura of prestige always contains a little foolishness, and Fatima greatly enjoyed playing the fool, however unwittingly, especially when she saw the prospect of credulity in her colleagues' eyes.

After Mamdouh's departure, Fatima returned to her old room in the family home, reeling with dented pride, in utter disbelief that everything was over and that her total value had been reduced to six suitcases crammed with worn-out clothes and shoes, a collection of fake perfume bottles, and the balance of her dowry of two hundred thousand liras, which Mamdouh had paid after both parties signed the divorce contract.

That day, Bolbol had sat next to his father in his capacity as the elder brother, by no means enjoying this distinction. His father's concealed rage kept him silent for a long time; this insult to the dignity he had maintained all his life had cut him deeply, and Bolbol sympathized with this respectable man who had been forced, because of his idiotic daughter, to shake hands with a student he considered worthless. Their father settled the matter swiftly, opened the door, and asked Mamdouh to leave. That night was the first time Bolbol truly realized that his father would die one day. Abdel Latif had gone into his room, closed the door, and wouldn't speak to anyone for days. Afterward, as he did whenever he felt weak, he went to Anabiya, where he was content to walk through the meadows and respond to invitations from childhood friends to play cards and reminisce a little. After he returned from these visits, his confidence and sense of self were restored.

When it was their turn at the checkpoint, the agent on duty told Hussein that the Mukhabarat would have to check their identity cards while he examined the corpse. Bolbol sincerely wished that his father had indeed died on that day long ago, when it would have been so easy to carry out his request that he be buried with his sister. Kindhearted neighbors would have come by to condole with them as they had done when his mother died. On that occasion, a delegation of four men had accompanied the family to the graveyard, which was four hundred kilometers from the village, and one of them even hosted an additional 'aza for the departed on their return. The neighbors prepared a generous feast for the mourners, grateful that Ustadh Abdel Latif al-Salim had allowed them to share his grief.

Bolbol saw Hussein coming back, escorted by an agent waving his gun and gesturing to the rest of the family to get out of the van. Hussein stood next to Bolbol and whispered, "They're going to arrest the body." Bolbol assumed there must have been some mistake, but no, when the agent led them to a tiled, windowless room, opened the door, and pushed them roughly inside, he understood that things were serious. It was true: they had placed the corpse under arrest. Their father had been wanted by more than one branch of the Mukhabarat for more than two years now.

The cell was crowded with more than twenty people of different ages. One of them, a woman of about seventy, told Fatima without being asked that she was being held hostage in her son's stead, who had deserted from the army last year. Another, a young man of around twenty, missing a hand, told them that the Mukhabarat suspected him of having lost his hand fighting as an insurgent, and not in a car accident years before. He added that he and the two friends he was sitting with there in the improvised holding cell had been on their way to catch a boat from Turkey to Greece, intending to travel from there to Sweden. He'd never believed their journey would be as simple as that, particularly as their lives were bound to their identity cards, which showed their place of residence as Baba Amr, in the city of Homs. Like all young men from Baba Amr, one of the first places where revolution broke out and which was punished by merciless bombardment as a result, they had gotten accustomed to being stopped at every checkpoint. Meanwhile, other prisoners were snoring loudly or staring silently into the shadowy corners of the cell, their expressions making plain their sense of degradation. They had been here for some time, and bruises from beatings could be seen on their faces. One of them was wearing pants stained with clotted blood; his head was wrapped in his shirt. Bolbol tried to will himself to look at these people; no one knew what would happen to them once they were transferred to whichever branch of the Mukhabarat wanted them. He looked at Fatima, still listening to that old woman who wouldn't stop chattering about her son, saying that it didn't matter anymore if she died, and she was glad he'd deserted. Bolbol told himself that no doubt Fatima would now tell the old woman about her sister-in-law's rape and her fiancé's desertion; this last detail had stimulated Fatima's appetite for gossip.

From his position in the corner, tucked away as much as possible, Bolbol could see the faces in the shadows of the room: dark, afraid, and sad. The detainees murmured to one another in voices like the droning of an old bee, monotonous and incessant. It was impossible to say what would happen to any of them. No one could enter a place like this and know what was in store for them. So many people had disappeared in the previous four years, it was no longer even shocking; there were tens of thousands whose fates were unknown. Hussein asked Fatima to say that she was divorced from Mamdouh but not to mention her remarriage, believing that her first husband's name and regime connections might improve the siblings' standing with their jailers. Fatima nodded without asking why this mattered. She knew how much he liked giving commands, and she generally liked to obey him. Taking up their old roles made them feel less afraid, and they would go through these motions as often during their journey as they had—without ever understanding why—during their childhood.

The floor of the cell was cold, and the loud, nonstop conversation of the Mukhabarat agents came in through the one small window. Bolbol remained aloof from the detainees, careful not to say a word, careful not to get himself in trouble. He asked no questions and allowed no one to question him and avoided so much as feeling sympathy when he heard stories that ought to have aroused immeasurable rage and sadness. He could almost have fallen asleep were it not for the clanging of the huge iron door as it opened every now and again. His memory summoned up the tales he had heard of the horrendous tortures endured by detainees in just such situations. The facts related by those fortunate enough to be released from cells like these were discussed and circulated everywhere, too terrifying to be believed. In his heart he knew that he would never be able to endure torn-out fingernails or electrocution or suffocating indefinitely in a congested cell or being forced to walk over rotting corpses. Probably he would just die after his first session. He closed his eyes, oddly reassured by this. He, at least, would leave behind a corpse with no last will or request; he didn't even care if his body was reduced to ashes or left for the dogs to gnaw. When the time came, he would be capable of lying next to his father without fear. This thought gave him the courage he needed, without having to boast of any real or imaginary exploits.

The next agent to open the door asked for one of the relatives of the corpse in the minibus to please step forward. Hussein ignored him, still absorbed in a long conversation about car tires with the three young men who had been on their way to Sweden. His animated features communicated his deep satisfaction as a torrent of aphorisms flowed from his tongue with an eloquence wholly unsuited to this environment. Bolbol was forced to get up when the soldier beckoned him to follow.

He was brought to an officer who couldn't have been more

than thirty. All of the family's documents were in his hands: their identity cards and the death certificate signed in accordance with the proper regulations. The officer asked Bolbol for details of every single family member and friend of his father. He said he would transfer them to the main facility for questioning and detain the body, likewise in accordance with the proper regulations. Though the officer's cool tone left little hope, Bolbol pleaded with him to be allowed to continue with their journey, adding that he himself supported the current regime—he and his father had been estranged!—and going on to say that he had lived in the suburb of M, where a mix of religions was found, for more than twenty years. Bolbol heaped curses on his father for the benefit of the officer, who once again turned over the papers in his hands and looked at them contemptuously. The short silence that followed these pleas allowed Bolbol to hope that the officer wasn't serious about handing the family over to the Mukhabarat . . . but he didn't know how he could plead for mercy for his father's body.

The officer explained that according to their records, Bolbol's father was still alive and still wanted. It didn't matter if he had in the meantime turned into a cadaver. Then he added that his commanding officer would settle the matter in the end and asked Bolbol to go through to the other room to fill in and sign this and that form. Bolbol was dripping with sweat. They really were going to take the body. Yet another agent went into the holding cell and took the minibus keys from Hussein. He drove it to a nearby garage and locked it, notifying the guard that it wasn't to be taken off the premises without the express permission of the officer in charge.

This same agent came back and led Bolbol into the next room and said that it wasn't the first time this had happened. Another corpse had been arrested the previous month and sent under armed escort to Tishreen Military Hospital, where a committee had had to look into the matter and sign off on the body's status. The corpse wasn't surrendered to its family until all the appropriate procedures had been followed, which the agent then took it upon himself to explain at length. First, they entailed going to the civil-records office and updating the deceased's status, then going to the central registry and issuing a cable that would suspend the outstanding warrant. The body would be kept in custody until being transferred to the military hospital for examination, where the death of the wanted man would be confirmed and the legal procedures to permanently cancel the search warrant completed. The agent couldn't seem to make up his mind from one sentence to the next as to whether the state regarded a person as being merely a collection of documents or rather an entity of flesh, blood, and soul. Bolbol nodded desperately and asked the agent to go into more detail, but eventually he stopped talking and ordered his prisoner to go ahead and fill out the form.

Bolbol felt the pressure of the silent agent's observation as he wrote in the required details about his family members and the members of their extended families and then surrendered the form. Gathering his courage, he offered a bribe to the agent who had explained the procedures to him, referring to it demurely as a "goods-transit document." The agent gave him a sardonic glance, but they agreed on twenty thousand liras—if the body was released. The agent took Bolbol back to the holding cell and wished him luck, saying that he hoped the commanding officer would settle the matter swiftly, and adding that they would keep the family at the checkpoint till the arrival of the cable that would determine their fate.

Time passed slowly; the prisoners were all ensnared in their various conversations, which Bolbol resolved to ignore. He was thinking of the labyrinth they would be lost in if the Mukhabarat really decided to transfer the body to the military hospital. His fear increased every time he thought of the possibility that a person might be nothing more than a collection of papers. He heard the old woman describing the destruction of Homs to Fatima, adding that she had been arrested three times since the revolution—she pronounced the word openly and without fear—but that this was the first time she'd ever been held as a hostage. Bolbol wasn't surprised at the old woman's mettle; she reminded him of his father and his father's friends, in whose hearts fear had seemingly died forever. But he was surprised at Fatima's zeal in narrating the tale of her sister-in-law, which she naturally launched into as soon as she was given an opportunity. She asked the old woman if it was true that the secret police raped women being detained, and the woman laughed and murmured, "Men too," adding that a thousand years would pass before this outrage would be forgotten.

Whenever the door opened, an agent would throw a new prisoner inside. The cell was getting more and more intolerably crowded, but everyone knew that they wouldn't be there long; they couldn't be kept there all night, otherwise their jailers would already have separated the men from the women. Bolbol wondered whether there might not be a real prison in the nearby complex, something older and more permanent than this temporary setup, but he halted that train of thought immediately, telling himself that holding cells were one commodity still more than plentiful in his country. The door opened again: a mother and her two children came in. She wasn't kept waiting long. She sat by the old woman and Fatima and told them that she didn't know what she was being accused of; she had been on her way to Beirut, where her husband worked in construction, and they had ordered her to get off the bus she had boarded at Deir Azzour. A few minutes later, the woman said that she had six brothers in the Free Army, and now they had been forced to fight alongside a battalion of Islamic extremists in al-Mayadin, since their own funding had been cut off and their supplies had run out. She added that many Free Army troops had defected to the Islamist side because they supposedly had more money. The woman said all this in a loud voice; Bolbol kept a safe distance as he observed her.

Bolbol got up when he saw Hussein had at last run out of steam. He wanted to make the peril of their enforced idleness clear, to explain the labyrinth he had foreseen them all entering, had foreseen overwhelming them, but he changed his mind when he saw that his brother, even half asleep, was still blathering about tires. Bolbol went up to the cell door instead and caught the eye of the agent he'd spoken with earlier, miming that he wanted another word. The agent opened the cell door, and Bolbol reminded him of their agreement; the agent promised that everything would be all right if they raised the sum from twenty to thirty thousand. Bolbol said this was fine, but explained that they weren't from a well-off family and that this sum was all they had in the world. The agent returned Bolbol to the cell and asked him to stay close to the door.

Bolbol sat next to Hussein and explained everything to him. Hussein was taken aback; he'd secretly been hoping that the body's being impounded by the police might actually prove the best possible outcome—saving the family from who knew what dangers might still await them on their trip. Bolbol steeled himself to deliver the news that they could of course still be detained as hostages . . . Hussein scratched his head and found himself let down by his memory once again; no anecdote or saying seemed entirely germane to their situation. He pushed the question to one side and said that if the Mukhabarat had taken the corpse into custody, they would have to dispose of it themselves. They could burn it or sell the organs or throw it into a mass grave—what would the dead person care, after all? Bolbol was astonished. He felt his brother's burgeoning fear deeply, not to mention Hussein's ever-present wish to take revenge on their father one way or another. In Bolbol's opinion, though, contrary to Hussein's, losing the body to the security forces would plunge the family into a mire from which they'd never be able to extricate themselves—a trap in which details would get so tangled they would never figure out what had happened to them. Hussein agreed to leave Bolbol to sort everything out, and although Bolbol felt entirely impotent, he was less afraid at this moment than at any other time in his life.

An hour later, the same agent opened the door and pushed a new prisoner inside. Bolbol reminded him of their situation and their agreement, and the agent asked him to come outside. The money changed hands discreetly, after which the agent returned to the cell and pointed at Hussein and Fatima and told them to stand up and leave at once. He reminded them that they still needed to send the death certificate to the civil-records office and make sure their father was struck off the list of wanted criminals.

A few minutes later, they were waiting outside the officer's room. The agent who had pocketed their money opened the door for them and disappeared, leaving them to his superior, who proceeded to address them at length on the latest news of their case. He informed the family that his commanding officer had asked him to confirm the death of the criminal personally, and thereby close the file and allow his family to bury him. All three siblings stood in front of him politely and attentively as he spoke; they praised the kind heart of the commander, who had looked on their situation with a sympathetic eye and refrained from requiring that the body be sent to a medical committee to verify what was obviously true. After refusing to provide them with an official document verifying that the warrant for their father had been canceled, which would have prevented other checkpoints from holding and questioning them yet again, the officer concluded his short speech and said that their way would be clear after this checkpoint; their problems would lie with the checkpoints set up by the terrorists nearer to Aleppo. The officer said the word "terrorists" most emphatically, then indicated with a brief wave of his hand that they should leave before he changed his mind, or anyway before a telegram arrived demanding that the corpse be taken back into custody. In such a case, there would be no alternative but to obey orders. One gesture from the commander, he repeated, and their lives would once again be turned into a living hell.

It wasn't the first time they had been made to stand attentively in front of such exhortations, but it was certainly the first time they'd been so close to sliding into the labyrinth. Bolbol had by no means been confident of the outcome of all his negotiations, so he was overjoyed when the minibus was allowed to leave the checkpoint, and the whole complex soon lay some distance behind them. He felt he'd been very close to the ultimate moment—the moment he had avoided for four years. He had felt this same giddiness before, whenever he escaped arrest for a crime he hadn't committed. On those occasions, his identity card with its incriminating birthplace had been the principal problem; now, the body of his father, the wanted man, had almost drowned them all.

Evening brought back all their fear and confusion, however.

Hussein was offended now that Bolbol had struck the deal alone. He considered it irresponsible for an amateur like him to have handled a case as grave as theirs—it ought to have called for his own expert negotiation and people-reading skills. He managed not to complain about it and made do with stating that they had to think of where they would spend the night, adding a casual comment that thirty thousand liras was pretty steep just to ensure safe conduct for a shipment of smuggled goods. Bolbol was afraid that Hussein would conclude by saying that their father wasn't worth this sum when he was alive, so how could he be worth it dead? Really the price should have dropped by at least three quarters, as with selling used shoes.

Hussein didn't say it—but neither could he keep quiet. In fact, he soon suggested that they toss the body out on the roadside, asking his brother and sister how confident they were that they would pass other checkpoints without trouble. They would be right back where they started if the next checkpoint agents discovered that their father was a wanted man. He added that the dogs were eating plenty of bodies nowadays, so what difference did it make? Why didn't they just leave it or bury it anywhere and go back to Damascus?

Bolbol could tell that Hussein wasn't joking this time; he wanted an answer, wanted his brother and sister to make a decision. Bolbol wanted to ignore him, but suddenly a great strength welled up inside him, and he declared he wouldn't abandon his father's body before his last wish was carried out. Fatima agreed and asked Hussein to speed up, even though it would be impossible for them to arrive at Anabiya that night in any case. The highway came to an end a few kilometers before Homs, and they would have to use the side roads, which were dangerous at night; no rational being would even consider traveling them in the company of a dead man.

Whenever Bolbol saw trucks crossing checkpoints with ease, he wished his father's body would turn into a sack of cumin; it was hard to see any downside to such a transformation—in fact, reaching a state of mutual understanding with a sack of cumin would be easier and far less dangerous. He deeply regretted promising his father to do as he'd asked. Forget about changing Abdel Latif into a sack of cumin—Bolbol would have been content to see himself transformed into a man with a little less sympathy.

The night before, he had sat on the bed next to his father while Abdel Latif told him in a feeble voice that his death was very near. Bolbol tried to divert his father's attention from these forebodings and thought briefly that his father was just having a nightmare, thanks to the death all around and the bombings that hadn't been silent for three years—that Abdel Latif was entering one of his states of delirium, which had become more and more frequent in the past month. Of course, you didn't have to be sick to have the same problems. Everyone suffered from insomnia and interrupted sleep these days, from panic attacks and nervous breakdowns; everyone spent entire nights discussing sleep aids, such as chamomile flowers brewed with rosemary, milk mixed with crushed garlic, or Faustan-brand sleeping pills; Bolbol, too, liked to talk over the recipes he'd tried, or to discuss with his colleagues how best to cover their windows with plastic wrap so that the glass wouldn't become shrapnel when it shattered. Recipes and helpful hints were also frequent topics of discussion for the people stuck at checkpoints for hours in the scorching afternoons and under the pouring rain. Taking naps was good; it helped the dreary evenings pass a little more quickly. Small things like that could cheer people up . . . or, alternatively, could destroy their lives and drive them out into the unknown, as in the case of this corpse, which had begun to turn rotten. When they left the hospital, they hadn't wondered what would happen to them. All three were too busy calculating how long it had been since they had last spoken to one another. Their throats were clogged with words that would rust and waste away if they weren't finally let out. Fatima at least wanted to regain some tenderness in her relationships with her brothers, but Bolbol had no desire to concede a thing to his siblings. Certainly there had been times when he wanted to return to that old familial harmony, but usually he felt that there was simply too much distance between them now. Getting away from them was the only positive thing he'd accomplished in the last ten years, he thought sometimes. And if they were honest, his sister and brother felt the same way, painful though it would be for anyone to admit—all believed that they had already done more than their duty for the family. Now it was time to consider their own lives.

Yes, the previous night, their father had felt keenly that he was dying. He had done everything he wanted to do in this life and had said everything he needed to say during his stay with Bolbol. But despite the illness, Bolbol hadn't believed his father would really die. It wasn't credible that anyone could still die of natural causes in this day and age. Even his neighbor Um Elias had been murdered, though she was in her eighties. A young relative and his friends conspired to break into her house and force open her strongbox, which everyone said contained millions of liras and several kilograms of gold. She put up a fight and recognized them, so they killed her. The police were even forced to follow it up and do a little actual police work so the killing wouldn't be recorded as a sectarian crime. That would have sent the Christian inhabitants of the quarter into a panic.

Not that the neighbors were too upset about old Um Elias, who had made a living selling miserly amounts of watered-down alcohol to them, but nevertheless they came as a body and spat at the young man in question, barely twenty years old, as he was forced into a police car. The police took him to the apartment in Rukneddine where he'd hidden the stolen goods in a well next to the graveyard. His two accomplices lived in the same building, and they didn't try to flee but surrendered and confessed in full. The following morning the three criminals were quietly brought before an examining magistrate. He was frustrated, as the crime of murder no longer called for such caution and care, and the criminals' easy confession increased his irritation. They would all find a way to avoid prison anyhow, the easiest route being to accept a position among the murderers of the regime militias, though there was always the chance that the resistance might storm the prison, knock down the walls, and destroy their files regardless.

In recent months, when people died, no one bothered asking after the hows and the whys. They already knew the answers all too well: bombings, torture during detention, kidnappings, a sniper's bullet, a battle. As for dying of grief, for example, or being let down by your body, deaths like that were rare—and no one lamented a death that didn't have any outrage attached to it.

Before Bolbol and his siblings left Damascus, he had called his office and requested a leave of absence. He received the indifferent condolences of his colleagues over the phone and asked that no one take the trouble of condoling with him in person, or indeed trouble themselves with helping him arrange the burial. He was still feeling the same deeply rooted fury as when the young doctor on duty told him his father's heart had stopped. If his father had died three months earlier, when he was still in the village of S, then everything would have been easy. The cemeteries there were large and plentiful, and any one of the people still living in the town could have buried him with all the consideration due to the great and illustrious *ustadh*, their comrade in revolution from its first day to his last. They would have considered him a martyr. Bolbol's only responsibility would have been to hear about it—and then pass along word to Hussein and Fatima and spread the news by calling their few relatives still in Anabiya, some of whom would certainly have supported Bolbol to carry out his duty of looking mournful and organizing a small 'aza for a few close friends. But that body lying on its hospital bed, and the glances of the on-call doctor—they only made Bolbol feel trapped. Death had become hard work. Just as hard as living, in Bolbol's view.

The doctor had instructed the orderlies to cover Abdel Latif's face and carry him to the morgue, and then asked Bolbol to sign for the body and get it off the premises before the following afternoon. If not, they would be forced to deal with it themselves. Priority in the overcrowded hospital morgue was given to the bodies of soldiers.

When he used to think about it, Bolbol hadn't reckoned on his father's death being such a disaster for him. He had half hoped that if Abdel Latif needed to die nearby, it would be somewhere closed off by a siege or while Bolbol was traveling far away. In such a case, he would have been absolved from the duty of arranging everything, and responsibility for his father's last wish would have had to be shouldered by Hussein, who wouldn't have hesitated to ignore it.

One night, three days before Abdel Latif died, Bolbol took his father to the hospital after his pains grew worse. It was lucky they stumbled across a taxi by the all-night *fuul* restaurant. Finding a driver willing to cross the city from east to west, not to mention finding a vacant bed in the public hospital, was such a stroke of luck that God should have received their utmost thanks—and Bolbol really did do his best to feel grateful. He gave the taxi driver the fare he had requested plus a tip for helping his father onto a stretcher; he insisted on staying with Bolbol until he was assured that Abdel Latif wouldn't get abandoned by the hospital staff in some corridor. Then again, the driver, too, probably preferred to be in the hospital than on the dangerous streets at night. Bolbol didn't ask him why he didn't go home; he was afraid of the answer. On an earlier occasion, trying to make small talk in a taxi, he had been unwise enough to ask the driver when his shift was over and he could go home, but the driver had sneered and described his house in Zamalka in detail, including the fact that it had been bombed and his wife lay dead beneath the rubble. In the end he had asked Bolbol, "So what home do you mean, sir?"

For months, Bolbol had avoided talking to anyone he didn't know or even leaving the house. Going outside was hard work. He was content to travel back and forth from work and read state newspapers ostentatiously on the bus. On his days off, he watched black-and-white Egyptian films on cable and grieved for this golden bygone era. He didn't know why he put himself through this, but at least this was a pastime that no one could possibly find suspicious; everyone was mourning for the beautiful days that they'd lost. Longer holidays such as Eid he spent making different types of pickles. He liked the new strategies he'd developed in order to keep himself sane, even though they were all strictly short-term arrangements. He didn't dare acknowledge that his life was a collection of trivial acts that would sooner or later have to come to an end.

One day, his isolation was punctured. One of his father's neighbors' sons—an engineering student turned combatant in the Free Syrian Army—called Bolbol and informed him that his father's health made it very difficult for him to remain in the besieged village. Bolbol couldn't bring himself to say anything in reply— not out of shock from hearing about his father's deterioration, but from fear of being arrested for speaking to a person who lived in S. The caller didn't have a lot of time and said that they had been fortunate enough to manage to smuggle the *ustadh* out to the abandoned gas station at the edge of the village. He asked Bolbol to arrive at six o'clock that evening to take him away.

The call had come at three in the afternoon. Bolbol couldn't chance saying a word to this person calling from an unknown number. What if the line was tapped? He was absolutely certain that the regime monitored every word coming out of the village. He had to think of a way out of this terrible mistake. Suddenly one of his rare bursts of self-assurance led him to decide to resolve the matter. He thought he would call Hussein. His brother should help in a situation like this. He dialed Hussein's number and was overcome with frustration when he heard that phone service had been temporarily interrupted. There was still time, though. Hussein would probably get back to him when he saw the missed call. Bolbol sat in a neighborhood restaurant in Saruja and asked for beans and rice. He contemplated what he was about to do to himself: his father was going to come and live with him in his small house. Well, maybe his father wouldn't be able to endure being in a district loyal to the regime.

Bolbol had worked hard to gain the trust of his neighborhood.

The details on his identity card marked him out for suspicion; for four years now, similar details had spelled catastrophe for many others. Thousands of people disappeared without a trace, simply for being born in areas controlled by the opposition, just as many regime supporters had disappeared in those same areas. Kidnappings, ransoms, and random arrests were widespread and tit-for-tat responses meant they only escalated in frequency. People's movements were tightly controlled. Any error could be very costly.

Bolbol minimized his time in public. To get to work he took the special bus for public employees, and to get home in the evening he took the same route back—like so many others whose identity cards and official documents happened to list the names of various now burned-out towns under "Birthplace." He abandoned his few remaining old habits, such as visiting a coffeehouse every Friday, or loafing around Bab Tuma. He cut short any burgeoning friendships with his colleagues; all they ever did together was repeat the same conversations about rising prices anyway . . . and by the time they started furtively discussing indications that they had gleaned which pointed to recent regime losses, using code words familiar to opposition sympathizers, Bolbol had already taken to ignoring them. He didn't want to venture so much as an ambiguous comment—he simply acted as if he hadn't heard anything at all and then returned to the subject of his pickling projects, grumbling about the rising price of eggplant.

Three months before the long drive to Anabiya, there was a knock on Bolbol's door at dawn. Three young men came in, boys from the neighborhood, all armed, accompanied by a local official who treated Bolbol with something like contempt. They ignored all his questions and overturned everything in the house. Not even the big portrait of the president in the middle of the living room won him any favor. Bolbol was offended, but kept quiet. He'd already scoured his home of everything that might have caused him harm in this situation: purging each and every suspicious belonging and even canceling all the television channels that regime supporters considered "biased," such as Al Jazeera and Al Arabiya, and filling his "Favorites" list with pro-regime channels: first came Al Manar and Al Mayadeen (the satellite channels run by Hezbollah), followed by Alalam from Iran, the Syrian News Channel, and then various other innocuous choices, like National Geographic, some food channels, and so forth. He'd gone over every inch of the place dozens of times to confirm to himself that the house was "clean." He only wished he could change his ID number and his place of birth. Anyway, the soldiers searched the house carefully and left without apology, letting Bolbol drown in the chaos of his scattered possessions. They cursed him and his hometown, as usual, but Bolbol did his best to ignore it; he told himself they were just goading him into reacting so they had an excuse to kill him. Of course, if they shot him, his blood would be spilled for nothing. Defending himself against some mild abuse would hardly make him a martyr. When they were well and truly gone, he congratulated himself on successfully passing this thousandth security check. After this he gradually gained the qualified approval of his poverty-stricken neighbors, who likewise used to curse his birthplace loudly whenever he walked down the street. He had chosen to live in this poor neighborhood after his divorce from Hiyam; she had made it a condition that he leave all their furniture with her to pay off the balance of her dowry and in exchange for her raising their only son—another Abdel Latif. The boy had been named after his grandfather, as though to prove that Bolbol still had strong links to his family, in the absence of any other evidence.

Really, all of Bolbol's behavior was an imitation of his father's—an attempt to live longer in his shadow. That respected gentleman, weighted with idealism, lived in the past, a remnant of some dreamlike former age. His vocabulary and habits dated back to a different world and would not conform to standards of the present day. Bolbol's father boasted of belonging to an era of "the greatest values and elegance," as he called the sixties, adding that it had been quite lovely to boot. Bolbol often caught himself using the same flowery old words as his father. And he still remembered his father's hysterical reaction when Hussein dismissed his precious 1960s as just a mirage—announcing that everything people said about those days was a lie that should finally be put to rest, and that those years were in fact the era of all the Muslim world's defeats. His father had been furious for the rest of the day. That was probably the first time any member of the family had dared to contradict him or sully his sacrosanct memories.

As Abdel Latif had aged, he only became more attached to those memories of his youth, down to the tiniest details: a certain way of shining his shoes, a particularly elegant necktie, a way of speaking concisely and listening respectfully, making witty comments and telling anecdotes whenever his old friends were gathered. It was important to him to be charming, to hold a constructive and enjoyable salon. He considered his duties sacred, and the town of S never saw a funeral in which he wasn't a participant. He remembered all his friends' birthdays and other special occasions and shared the few supplies he was able to see brought in from Anabiya. According to his students, he was a strange man, though likewise a respected inhabitant of their town for more than forty years, who had arrived to teach in the school and soon became one of them. They originally called him the Anabiyan, in reference to his hometown, but everyone forgot this nickname with the passage of time, and he became, simply, Ustadh Abdel Latif.

Bolbol couldn't get through to Hussein. He felt cold to his bones. There was no choice but to go alone to pick up his father. The sheer density of the checkpoints between him and the rendez-vous point meant the length of the journey was out of his control, but he still managed to arrive at the appointed time. When he saw his father leaning on the wall of the abandoned gas station, Bolbol felt empty inside. His father was somewhat dazed and had lost a lot of weight; his face was haggard, his breath was foul, and it was clear that he hadn't eaten for some days. Even so, he was clean-shaven, wore a tie, and his clothes were spotless.

Abdel Latif smiled when he saw Bolbol coming toward him. Bolbol squeezed his father's hand. A group of armed young men appeared from nowhere, some of whom Bolbol recognized, and they all raised their hands in farewell to their comrade as they passed. Abdel Latif refused to lie down in the back seat of the taxi. Bolbol asked his father not to talk to the driver; he might be an in-former, and Bolbol knew the sorts of things his father was likely to say—open praise for the people of his rebel town and curses for the regime. Bolbol didn't say a word, praying that everything would work out. He asked Abdel Latif what medicines he needed, but his father just shook his head and proceeded to glower at every check-point soldier with overt resentment.

When they got home, Bolbol laid him down on the bed and went out to find a doctor. He reflected that the doctors of this neighborhood might also be informers who would consider Abdel Latif a terrorist if they knew where he'd been these last few years—stubbornly clinging on inside that besieged village. But there were rumors about a back-street doctor named Nizar, who had been thrown in jail at the beginning of the revolution, and who'd had some public clashes with the rest of the neighborhood when he refused to give up his home in it. After tracking him down, Bolbol more or less explained the situation, and the doctor—who turned out to be a kind and conscientious young man—accompanied Bolbol to his house as soon as he was finished with one more consultation. On the way, Bolbol told him that they were originally from the town of S, a veiled reference to where their sympathies lay. The doctor caught it at once, and the name of the town was all it took to rouse the young doctor's fervent respect.

The doctor was assiduous in his care. Abdel Latif always used to say that the children of the revolution were everywhere, which was why they would, in the end, prevail. The doctor was surprised to find a portrait of the president hanging in the living room but made no comment about it on that first visit. The next day, Bolbol explained his position in the neighborhood, implying that he himself was a clandestine revolutionary. The doctor didn't care for this obvious dissimulation, considering Bolbol's tack to be little better than collaboration with the regime, but he well understood Bolbol's anxiety and felt reassured as to his basic good nature when Bolbol gave him a couple of jars of pickled cucumbers and peppers. The doctor brought over various drugs free of charge and became a firm friend of Abdel Latif. He visited every day, and the two would whisper together. Their eyes would gleam when Bolbol's father told his doctor friend stories of life inside the siege; they laughed and spoke vehemently and with great hope of victory.

But on the third day of his father's treatment, Bolbol returned from work to find that the president's portrait had been removed from its usual place on the wall. Abdel Latif gave him no opportunity to ask about it, and Bolbol didn't dare object. He put the picture in his bedroom, but there it kept him up at night. This was odd; it was just a picture, after all, but spending night after night in the same room with it caused Bolbol's worst and most terrifying preoccupations to resume. He covered up the portrait and propped it in a corner of the living room, behind the metal cupboard where he kept his plates. He didn't dare to throw it out or tear it up; he would need it as long as he lived in this neighborhood. Between Bolbol's unwillingness to challenge his father directly, and Abdel Latif's studied avoidance of the topic, they both eventually forgot about it entirely.

Bolbol insisted on closing all the windows in the house for fear that the laughter of his father and the doctor would leak out and catch the attention of someone passing along the alley, who might then stick around to hear their conversations or the revolutionary songs they sang together between bouts of exchanging news from the battlefronts and commentary on political developments. The two of them were agreed that it was a revolution against the entire world, not just against the regime. Abdel Latif still loved big words, and he used plenty of them when describing the things that had happened during the brutal siege, when those who had remained behind had been forced to cook the leaves off the trees and to eat grass. They made bread from chaff, and shared what little they had left.

Their conversations about their inevitable victory conveyed nothing to Bolbol. His only thought was of his father's illness—particularly, how he might rescue himself from the predicament it had caused. Bolbol offered to help his father bathe but was refused; Abdel Latif didn't like seeing himself as a weak old man. Blood analyses showed that his illness was worsening and that hope of recovery was slight. Behind the siege lines, there had been whole months when he hadn't taken his medicine, whole days together that he hadn't eaten. He kept telling Bolbol about the siege, as if asking him not to forget, but Bolbol wanted very much to forget everything that had happened over the past four years. He felt like someone else—a stranger. His father deserved a true son of the revolution, someone brave like Dr. Nizar. The doctor wasn't afraid of being associated with the revolution and had refused to flee the country even after he was arrested and tortured for three months. Bolbol couldn't bear to hear him telling the details to Abdel Latif, who in turn regaled Nizar with tales of the torture undergone by the many other detainees he had known. These prisoners had returned hating the regime more than ever; when they spoke of what they'd endured, it was as though they were implying that revenge was the very least they could do in response. Bolbol's father described in exhaustive terms how, in prison, many had transformed from peaceful revolutionaries to advocates of the utmost violence against the regime and its troops. He added, "Prison can kill you. The person who leaves is not necessarily you, even though they have your appearance." Few retained their self-control and their reason; few remained loyal to their initial ideals. The terrible pressure of each successive story told in Bolbol's house made him wish he were deaf—but he despised himself when he tried to avoid listening. It was only in the final weeks that he really began to worry that his father would die. The day they went to the hospital was the first time that Bolbol really thought about the chaos that could surround a body after death, given the state of things. It didn't even occur to him that his father had been serious about that last wish he had repeatedly extracted Bolbol's solemn promise to carry out.

Bolbol, Hussein, and Fatima successfully made it past the third checkpoint after the town of Deir Atiya, but the bleak road ahead didn't exactly inspire them with confidence. Night was falling, and they had only gotten a quarter of the way: they were nowhere near Anabiya. The same mysterious number from which Bolbol had received his instructions as to where to collect his father on the outskirts of S had called his phone a number of times since that awful day—and now Bolbol was regretting that he'd never picked it up again. He was sure his father's friends wouldn't have let the *ustadh* be buried so far away from them. Perhaps they were even more resourceful than he'd ever guessed, these children of the revolution—they had managed to infiltrate everywhere, communicating by way of a system of secret codes. Maybe those men could have collected the body from anywhere at all and brought it anywhere with no problem. Maybe *they* should have been tasked with arranging the burial. Bolbol was suddenly confident that Abdel Latif's friends could easily have spirited his father's body away from the hospital and buried him in the new cemetery he had himself laid out during the siege in S. Then the dead man would have breathed freely, so to speak.

What did his father's body mean? It was a harsh but justified question that night. All three of them were wondering it, but none had a clear answer. Silence had settled over the minibus. Hussein stayed silent to stifle his anger; Fatima was trying not to breathe, so they would forget she was there. The sounds of missiles and anti-tank bombs were getting closer; Hussein said dispassionately, "They're bombing Homs," before retreating back into his silence. They were all hoping for a miracle to come and save them from this desolation, the fear they couldn't put into words, which burrowed into them all the same. These lulls offered a rare opportunity to talk but always came at inappropriate times, when no one was capable of speaking.

Fatima opened her window again. A cold breeze crept in. She suggested uncovering the body, but neither of her brothers replied, and she wasn't about to reach out herself and draw back the blankets. Instead she tried to mop up some of the water streaming over the floor of the van from the melting ice blocks packed around the corpse. She was frightened, thinking about the terrifying smell oozing from the body's pores, and her fingers were trembling by the time Hussein said they had no choice but to spend the night in the town of Z—but they didn't know which side road to take, and the main highway between Homs and Aleppo had been closed for more than two years.

Hussein turned the minibus in what he thought was the right direction and sped on through the gloom. The road was full of holes, and Bolbol and Fatima held on grimly as the vehicle lurched and almost toppled over. Unable to hold on to anything, the body shuddered. Hussein's rage was evident by now; he tried to call some friends to fix up a place to stay, raised his voice more than once, and eventually halted at the roadside, cursing the unreliable cell signal. Bolbol told him coolly not to worry about where they would stay; they would go to Lamia's house. Fatima's eyes glistened, and she looked at Bolbol sympathetically. Hussein said nothing, but a few minutes later he asked what sort of welcome they were likely to get from Lamia, in her husband's house, after all these years. Bolbol was positive that it would work out, and in fact he only needed to tell Lamia in a steady voice that they would be in Z in a quarter of an hour, and that they needed her help, in order to be proved right. She was as kind and generous as ever, Bolbol thought as he hung up; she had begged them to be careful and promised to wait for them at the entrance to the town with her husband. The checkpoint there had a bad reputation as far as dealing with strangers; they had started filtering out and disappearing travelers who had been forced to pass through the town, or ransoming off the children from rich families.

Bolbol felt oddly powerful; Lamia's voice had energized him. Hussein, meanwhile, felt defeated; he hadn't expected he would need Lamia today of all days. Bolbol had resumed his friendship with her some years earlier. He had met her husband and made a concerted effort to behave like a friend to them both, not an old lover purposely stirring up a husband's jealousy, as Zuhayr, Lamia's husband, had believed at first.

In that first meeting, several years after their graduation, he had invited Lamia and Zuhayr to dinner along with two other couples to celebrate meeting again after so long. Hiyam, Bolbol's wife, and Zuhayr were outsiders in that clique, listening as the ex-classmates laughed and recounted stories of their friends at college. In telling these stories, they realized that, if they were really honest with themselves, not a single one of them had made much of a mark during their student days; they hadn't made trouble, they hadn't protested the administration, hadn't distributed pamphlets for far-right or far-left parties, hadn't tried hashish or lived on the edge in any way. They'd all been rather pathetically well behaved. To conceal this, they conjured up some additional stories about their own small acts of valor—and all conspired to hide the fact that they were merely plagiarizing untold stories from their classmates' biographies.

Bolbol wasn't a source of concern to Lamia's husband, which was all he really cared to know about him at this moment. The men never became close, but neither were they enemies. Bolbol would never have believed that Zuhayr, a powerful man and a former political prisoner, could ever fear a man like himself, who was afraid of his own shadow. Bolbol wished he could close his eyes and relive all his memories with Lamia and, this time, change things. The poems he had written her, the letters with which he had pursued her over summer holidays . . . He'd poured his heart and soul into those poems; he liked to believe that, at the very least, she'd found them too amusing to throw away. If she had stayed with him, he would be a different person entirely, he was sure. Lamia would be sad to hear of Abdel Latif's death; she'd liked him very much. In fact, they had remained close over the years; Lamia would visit or call every now and again, sometimes bringing books by and accepting gifts in return. Equally, she had remained friends with Bolbol's mother, who'd maintained her tradition of cooking *molokhiya* for Lamia—the girl's favorite dish—and she would always insist on giving Lamia a selection of the pickles she was famous for, known locally as Um Nabil's Miracle. Lamia had always found time to visit Bolbol's family, and although these visits grew rarer after graduation, they were a sufficient expression of mutual respect and affection.

Now, crammed into his seat and reviewing all these memories, Bolbol realized that his own pickling skills must have come from his mother. Everything he did was a copy. It wasn't too pleasant to discover that he was just an imitation of his family, repeating throughout his life the very acts he used to despise.

Bolbol said to himself that Lamia was an angel, that she would defend his father's body with all her strength. The soldiers at the checkpoint into Z were irritated at being unable to "interrogate" these strangers as much as they would have liked—the family would have been rich pickings for any checkpoint. Unfortunately for the soldiers, Lamia had informed Zuhayr of the problem posed by the family's identity cards, and he had instantly comprehended the delicacy of the situation. He'd beaten them to the checkpoint, bringing along his uncle, who was connected to influential men in the regime, in order to mediate their swift passage through. Bolbol quickly explained their problems, giving a digest of their adventures to date: the congestion at the checkpoints and their difficulty in leaving Damascus in the first place, adding that they had been traveling now for ten hours. The staff at the checkpoint, a mixture of Mukhabarat agents and volunteers from the town, was unsympathetic but didn't spend too long scrutinizing their papers. They made do with examining the death certificate and then allowed the travelers to pass without even a mutter, though, under other circumstances, and at the very least, the family deserved a good round of cursing out, seeing as they embodied all the necessary qualifications for such—in the view of any checkpoint manned by the Mukhabarat or any of the sectarian groups funded, unofficially, by the regime.

Driving along in the dark, the siblings hadn't noticed the changes that had overtaken the body. Lamia was upset when she saw the current state of it. Everyone was taken aback by her racking sobs, and her tears caused them to weaken as well. Hussein wept, and Fatima saw her opportunity and plunged into a protracted fit of bawling. Zuhayr acted quickly and drove them to the small public hospital. Thanks to his uncle's intercession, the hospital director allowed the body to spend the night in the morgue. The terrible burden was lifted. No one looked at Abdel Latif, afraid of finding his body so disfigured that they would agree to dump it in any hole in the ground—even throw it to the stray dogs.

Lamia was slender as a rail, and her long, thick hair was the color of carob. Her face was innocent, and her smile deeply reassuring. She knew no evil and had been born to give without any expectation of return. Now, after all these years, Bolbol supposed that she regarded him as little more than a sick man in need of her care. When they were younger, however, and parted by distance, she'd read his letters and believed that someone else must have written those texts so full of double entendres and poetic flights of fancy. These letters were the venue in which he could say how much he worshipped her. He wrote that it wasn't right for the throne of a goddess like her to be touched by an ephemeral human—better for eagles to spirit it away while it lay vacant. He still remembered some of his letters by heart, since he'd read and revised and hesitated over them so many times before sending. And then there were the letters he *hadn't* sent, which Lamia didn't even know about—the ones that openly expressed his fervent desire and hunger for her body.

Once, Lamia admitted to him how impatiently she'd waited for his letters throughout the scorching summer holidays in Z, how she was overjoyed when the postman knocked on her family's door and waved a letter at her with a smile. Bolbol had broken into a sweat when she said this and couldn't admit that he loved her to tears. Now he believed Lamia was the only ideal that could salvage his life and perhaps even turn him into a less fragile person.

But he had been too afraid of seeing her hurt to admit all this: the scene of what he assumed would be their inevitable separation haunted his thoughts. He didn't know why, but he was positive it would end badly, that she would say, *I love you, but I can't marry a Muslim.* He hadn't listened to the advice of their mutual friends when they encouraged him to confess his love. They had said that love was more important than marriage; everything else would come later—but on the evening of their arrival at her home, led by her husband, Bolbol felt that he had acted correctly. She wasn't a hard-line Christian, but in the end she would never have wanted to anger her kindhearted, simple country family, who wouldn't have been able to pay for a wedding anyhow. Bolbol quickly warmed up to this reasoning and declared himself well satisfied by his paralysis over the years.

Zuhayr was behaving with his usual gallantry. When Lamia opened the door to her house, Bolbol was struck by how exhausted she looked; he regretted having increased her troubles. More than thirty children were inside, eating dinner. Men and women were coming and going through the four open rooms on the spacious ground floor. That Lamia was hosting displaced people needed no explanation. No one could be surprised by the appearance of strangers; everyone was used to new arrivals crossing their path at any time of day or night. Zuhayr saved the siblings their explanations and simply introduced them as old friends from S on their way to bury their father's body in Anabiya, praising the father as a great revolutionary in the process. Dropping these names was enough of an explanation.

Bolbol was deeply moved by Lamia's sympathetic glances as she held back her tears and accompanied Fatima to the women's room. All three of the siblings looked appalling, but no one noticed or found it unusual; they had all gone through similar ordeals. When she came back, Lamia squeezed Bolbol's hand, pleased that he was carrying out his father's last wish; she described his father as a great man, a martyr, and a revolutionary. She gave Bolbol no time to explain everything they had gone through on the road and went on to say that she was cooking for six families and thirty children, assisting them and making them as comfortable as she could. Zuhayr was kind to the siblings and thanked them for asking if they could help. Really, both husband and wife were like people from another age, Bolbol thought as he watched Zuhayr and Lamia gladly and indefatigably attend to the needs of each of their guests. They were nothing like his neighbors, who had driven out three families, displaced from Yarmouk Camp, on the pretext that they were extremists, probably terrorists, merely because the women wore the hijab. The sight of the expelled made one's heart bleed; but, then, the sight of the impoverished local women was simply sickening. They encouraged their children to pelt the homeless families with stones, yelling curses at these traitors who'd turned their backs on a regime that had housed them, raised them, and educated them in its schools.

Hussein put an abrupt end to the discussion. He asked Lamia for two blankets and a pillow, and after dinner he slipped out to the bus, spread out on its floor, and fell into a deep sleep. Zuhayr suggested to Bolbol, who was grappling with his usual shyness, that he might like to bathe, but added cheerfully that he would have to heat the water in the cistern using firewood, not gas; the electricity only came on for two or three hours a day. Bolbol thanked him and asked for somewhere to lie down. He was so exhausted he could no longer grasp what the men here were saying, passing the time by discussing the latest news or trying to phone someone who had stayed in the besieged city of Homs. The story of their father's body got no sympathy from them; they had seen too many bodies already. As ever, death was so close to them that they had stopped giving it any particular consideration.

Zuhayr generously offered to let Bolbol sleep on his and Lamia's own bed in the corner of the kitchen, but Bolbol chose instead to use a twice-folded blanket for a mattress, then another to cover himself up. He couldn't get over the fact that Zuhayr and Lamia were sleeping here now after giving everything they had to refugees from Homs—total strangers. Lamia repeated Abdel Latif's favorite saying in a low voice: "The children of the revolution are everywhere." Bolbol shut the kitchen door and tried to sleep. He was cold and slow to feel any warmth seep into his body. He tried to push away evil thoughts: Lamia slept here, right there on that bed in the corner of the large kitchen, leaving her bedroom to the children. Here, her breath circulated every night . . . The mattress, only a few centimeters away, smelled strongly of Lamia. Bolbol was bewildered by his growing state of arousal. There was, of course, one way for him to relax—he didn't even feel especially ashamed at the prospect of betraying a man and a woman who had shown him every generosity. After all, the horrific tension was almost killing him, he had no way of sleeping, his senses were inflamed. Even crying would be better than doing nothing; he wished he could manage it. Crying would relax him, wash him clean. And no one would ask a man transporting his father's corpse across the country why he was crying. Bolbol buried his head in his blanket and heard a knocking sound in his head. He began to feel that he would surely die here; in fact, he craved it; Lamia would then bury him with her own beautiful hands—such a terrible tragedy for her! It got to be eleven o'clock at night, and intermingling voices were still coming from the large room where everyone else was gathered as if for a party. He even heard distant laughter. Yes, there was only one way of relaxing. So Bolbol closed his eyes and tried to recall a particular image of Lamia. When they were students, she had brought over some extra course materials for him, and his mother had persuaded her not to head home for Deir Rahibat but to stay the night with them. Bolbol had spied on her at dawn as she was sleeping in Fatima's room. She was like an angel in that bed, her legs revealed by a short cotton nightshirt. Her breasts were firm, and there was the ghost of a smile on her face . . . But now the shame came flooding in. Bolbol scrambled to his feet. He left the kitchen, lit a cigarette, and began to feel calmer. He quieted his conscience; he would sleep, he wanted to sleep, he needed to sleep so he could take his father's body to Anabiya. From there he would cross the border to Turkey and never come back to this country again. What an excellent new idea. He went back to the kitchen and lay down. The voices in the next room receded, and he fell asleep.

Only a couple of hours later, he was shaken awake into a state of instant terror. Hussein was standing by his head, shouting that the nurses were throwing their father's body out into the street. Lamia was waiting for them in the minibus, worried and angry. They had called her to come and take the body away because, once again, the bodies of soldiers killed in a nearby battle were being brought to the hospital.

Zuhayr had gone ahead; as they arrived, they could hear him fighting with one of the nurses who had now taken up cursing their father. Bolbol went into the morgue to sign for the body so Hussein and Zuhayr could carry it back to the bus. It was a terrifying scene. There were more than forty corpses there in military dress; some had lost their lower extremities, others half their heads. A furious officer was speaking to someone out of sight, requesting more ambulances from the hospital in Homs. Bolbol felt sick. He managed to reach the office amid the chaos, but the nurse there didn't understand what he wanted. Bolbol asked for the doctor on duty. The nurses were opening the morgue fridge and piling bodies on top of one another like lemon crates; their tiny fridge hadn't been designed to deal with so many bodies. Bolbol dug through the mound of papers on the office desk and found the release forms.

Clutching these, he looked through the large register, signed his own name next to his father's, and left like he was fleeing hell, almost deranged by fear. If someone thought to ask him for his identity card in all this chaos, he could wind up dead.

On the ground floor of the hospital, a large number of people from the surrounding towns and villages were looking for the bodies of their sons who had died that night. The furious nurse was still cursing Abdel Latif, calling him a terrorist, threatening Zuhayr and Lamia and insulting their whole family. Everyone piled into the minibus, which was thankfully ready to leave. Lamia looked sadly at Abdel Latif's face. It had begun to swell; its skin was turning blue and a shade of green that looked almost moldy. Back at the house they drank coffee while Lamia rewrapped Abdel Latif's shroud, removing the smelly blankets that were still soaked from the slabs of ice and replacing them with clean ones. She also placed sweet basil around the corpse's head, perfumed him all over, and gave Fatima the large bottle of cologne to sprinkle on him from time to time. Then the five of them sat in silence, sipping their coffee, surrounding the dead man, and waiting for dawn.

A BOUQUET FLOATING
DOWN A RIVER

At dawn, the minibus hurried away from Z.

The air was cold, and the cologne wafting through the car put the siblings in a serene state of mind. The feeling that they had the whole day ahead of them made them feel confident of arriving at Anabiya before nightfall. The road was narrow, and the big passenger buses passing alongside them made them less desolate and afraid; they weren't alone out here. The bus passengers looked pitiful, and they seemed to have been traveling a long time. Their clothes were tattered and poor, and desperation had settled on their faces as they stared at the road ahead. Most of the buses were old, their glass windows shattered, and on the backs of each were bundled the possessions of these people fleeing the country for somewhere safer. It was a mass exodus, hundreds of thousands of people heading from the north and the east toward the unknown.

Bolbol closed his eyes and relaxed. The cool breeze had revived him and woke again his longing for the old days with Lamia. He'd felt proud when she had looked at him with affection for carrying out his father's last wish. He had declared to Lamia that he would see to it that Abdel Latif was buried with Aunt Layla (whose story Lamia knew a little about) no matter how dangerous the journey became—saying that he would carry out his father's last wish even if it cost him his life. In front of Lamia, he affected to be careless about his life, as he imagined a brave man might. She wasn't surprised; he had a history of doing idiotic things no one would have believed him capable of.

When Zuhayr had disappeared into prison, who knew where, Bolbol had gone to meet an influential officer, a relative of one of his friends, and asked outright about his whereabouts. Even now Bolbol couldn't forget the quizzical look on the man's face as he sought to clarify the nature of the relationship between Bolbol and Zuhayr. That simple question, asked for the sake of a person he didn't really know, could have consigned Bolbol to an endless nightmare. And Lamia still remembered the night her mother died; she had been astonished to see Bolbol arriving before dawn, wanting to help with the burial. He had traveled all night despite the challenge of finding transport at that time. He had done many things for her over the years, and after the looks of gratitude she had given him he began to feel that he was carrying out his father's instructions solely on her account.

Lamia was one of the few people—perhaps the only one—who gave Bolbol the courage to act recklessly. She never knew it, but his greatest follies had been committed on account of just a few words she'd once spoken in defense of his character, calling him "bold" and "impetuous" when his other friends preferred "indecisive" and "cowardly." Her belief in the courage he in fact lacked had helped him commit more than a few sins in his time (sadly, they went unremembered by all), but despite everything, he had never been brave enough to declare his love for her. Even now his knees started to shake as he imagined what she would say to him: *The right moment for this passed a long time ago.*

Discovering love is like seeing a bouquet floating down a river. You have to catch it at the right time, or the river will sweep it away: it won't wait for long. You have only a few intense, mad moments to give voice to your profound desires. In fact, there had been plenty of bouquets floating tranquilly by, rocking gently close at hand, easily within Bolbol's reach . . . Lamia had waited for him to say something, especially after the long summer holidays were over, but Bolbol stayed silent as usual or merely suggested a walk in Bab Tuma. Eventually she realized that the years she had spent waiting for him to pick up those bouquets floating down the river were over, but despite knowing that they had missed their chance, she didn't conceal her happiness at receiving his letters nor her longing for the next. And so, the thread of their usual conversations would resume where it had been broken by their separation while the river swept the bouquet away.

Whenever she went home for the holidays, she was astonished at the letters that were already waiting for her in her hometown. Bolbol wrote that the very sound of her footsteps was his joy. He even described her handbag in terms borrowed extensively from an ode of the great poet Riyadh al-Saleh al-Hussein. He told her that he had read the poem in question the previous day, on account of her, and on account of her he had also gone to the empty college canteen and sat on their seat in the garden. She replied to every one of his holiday letters, told him how much she missed him, and she didn't bother to hide her happiness at everything he wrote. Sometimes she put a few small wildflowers in her replies, letters that he read dozens of times and kept in a secret place in his closet, afraid they would fall into someone else's hands. For him, these weren't letters but an enormous and personal secret. They were like precious icons hidden in the deepest vaults of a monastery, forbidden and untouched for hundreds of years. As time passed, the secret cast a hidden magic over things; what Bolbol wanted was for Lamia's letters to become enshrined just as he imagined them, a real collection of icons he might suddenly reveal to his future children, after many years, so they would be forced to see their father in an entirely new light.

Yes, he'd missed his chance to pick up that bouquet hundreds of times. Deep down, he still believed that she was a goddess who deserved to be worshipped, not approached. One touch from her was enough for him; he couldn't imagine her as a wife chopping onions, her clothes reeking of cooking smells. But now everything had been lost, regardless, and he was content with what remained of their relationship. Here and now she looked like an angel to Bolbol, an angel reaching out her hand to save the drowning; humanity's only hope lay in her delicate fingers, which could grant life with one affectionate touch.

Bolbol had convinced himself that merely retaining her friendship was a miracle for which he should thank God. He would wait for her to visit Damascus and then take her to the restaurants she loved. Sometimes, and quite intentionally, he took her to places of special importance to their past relationship, where he was tempted to reach out and take her hand. She was polite and friendly to him in those moments, but the silence which soon settled over them made it clear that the past was the past. Then they would return to their favorite topic of conversation when things became awkward: Bolbol would speak and she would listen as he complained about his wife, who thought that buying a new sofa would be preferable to climbing up to the roof of the world and taking in the view. He told her about his wife's repugnant smell, her hardness and utter lack of concern about him. He complained about their sex life; she called the deed "homework" and laughed endlessly at this little witticism. He described her yellow teeth and her never-ending list of demands: fix the boiler, stock up enough fuel for winter, invite her sister and her husband for dinner. Bolbol would then go on to describe what happened whenever the four of them met: his brother-in-law talked constantly about house prices and would end the evening by advising Bolbol in his hoarse voice to convince his father to sell the large family house or to knock it down and build an apartment block so Abdel Latif could sell off the individual apartments. Bolbol didn't know how to extricate himself from this situation, he said, but he never allowed his impatience with his wife or her family to show. He remained the same kind man as ever, who allowed his foolish brother-in-law to appear smart and continually advise him how to arrange his life. Still, Bolbol always concluded this litany by restating his regret at having married a woman who didn't know the poetry of Riyadh al-Saleh al-Hussein—whose conversation consisted entirely of repeating the silly jokes she had been told by colleagues during her trivial day.

As he looked at his shrouded father, Bolbol told himself that he had no regrets at not trying to convince him to sell the house with the flowers Lamia had loved. She used to exchange seedlings with Abdel Latif and spent hours helping him arrange the flower beds. It gave them both indescribable joy, a joy shared by Bolbol's mother, who adored her plants to the point of madness. Bolbol had often observed his mother and father in the garden, lingering over the harvest of their three olive trees. They behaved like the seasonal workers, eating breakfast under the tree and discussing how much of the harvest to give their friends. Bolbol told Lamia that the flowers were a love token between his parents; he meant that they were a secret token of his own love for her, one of many. He didn't dare tell her that he lingered to breathe in the fragrance of every flower she herself had pruned or caressed.

Lamia didn't take too many of the things Bolbol said seriously, but even so, she was an eager listener. He was a different man when he spoke to her; his eyes were bright, his face alive—though he was careful not to be overheard. She knew that he was polite to his brother-in-law, that he didn't argue with his wife but gave in to all her demands. He didn't really care if his wife loved the poetry of Riyadh al-Saleh al-Hussein or not.

Back when Zuhayr was still in prison, Lamia would visit Damascus and insist on spending a lot of time with Bolbol, listening to his complaints. It wasn't that she was getting revenge on him by wallowing in his unhappiness; on the contrary, she sympathized deeply with her old friend. Hearing him, she thought of and enjoyed Bolbol's image of her as an angel. As for herself, she didn't complain: she was strong and didn't want Zuhayr to compromise in exchange for his freedom. She summarized the difficulties caused for her by the Mukhabarat in a few sentences—how they were harassing her at work and in her social circle, which was not really so different from the world of Bolbol's wife. Lamia didn't tell Bolbol that she, too, repeated the same jokes told by all low-ranking public employees, that her house clothes stank of onions, and that she often helped her friends with their simple household errands; equally, she didn't tell him it had been some time now since she last read the poetry of Riyadh al-Saleh al-Hussein, and she never took his diwan down from her bookshelf anymore.

But back when they had graduated and Lamia returned to her hometown and married Zuhayr, her visits grew more and more infrequent, and she lost all interest in those flower beds, just as Bolbol's father lost interest in them after his wife's death. One after another, the flowers withered and died, but Bolbol still tried to enjoy the scent of the rosebushes that Lamia had once tended.

Bolbol used to see his father looking miserably at the garden that had changed so utterly, staring with grief in his heart. For him, it had become a place that spoke only of loss, a leftover from a happier and vanished age. After his wife's death, Abdel Latif changed considerably; he no longer cared much about little details, and the things in his life all lost their shine. He refused Fatima's offer to clear the closet of her mother's clothes and many belongings, and he became suspicious that she might do it in his absence. His misgivings increased dramatically whenever Fatima visited him; he would lock the door to her mother's room and put the key in his pocket. He wouldn't even allow anyone to clean it unless he was present, a clear sign that he wanted his memories left undisturbed, or so it seemed to everyone. He spent a lot of time reading history and sitting silently in front of the television. He wished he would die, but death wouldn't grant his wish, no matter how much he pleaded. He spent five years in this way, longing for death as if he and his wife had made a secret pact to depart this life together, although when at last she had deserted him, he had simply let her go.

After his wife's death, Abdel Latif rarely referred to the dear love he had just buried. He didn't mention her much or reminisce about the details of his life with her, as if he had lost the vocabulary to speak of his happier past. No one doubted seventy-year-old Abdel Latif's love for his wife. Everything was proof of it: the rarity of their fights, the way they clung to each other—the image of the happy family (so much like all other happy families) that they projected wherever they went. But Bolbol often thought that the true meaning of love was what he had never experienced and what was now lost to him. He was reminded of all this when he first brought his ailing father back to his house. Bolbol examined him closely; he would almost have sworn that this man wasn't his father. Starvation had left its scars on his aged body, and his eyes had an odd gleam to them. Abdel Latif wasted no time in telling Bolbol that he had distributed his mother's clothes to the few neighbors who had stayed behind during the siege. And, by the way, the garden had returned to its former splendor, though now all it grew was basil and wormwood, not counting the three olive trees, which he hoped would hold out for a few more years at least. He added, "Nevine and the martyrs love wormwood." Without giving Bolbol time to ask, his father told him neutrally that he had married her, Nevine, and that she was the one who had pushed him to escape the besieged town. She had told him resolutely, "Leave this sacred ground." His father was silent for a long time before carefully addressing Bolbol's questions over the next few days. Bolbol was very frightened and didn't fully grasp what his father had said that night.

The next day Bolbol had wondered about the connections between Nevine, the martyrs, and the wormwood. He told the doctor who'd accompanied him that his father was a little delirious, but the doctor discovered that his patient, although on his deathbed, was fully alert and not delirious in the least.

Of course, Bolbol understood why his father had distributed his mother's clothing; after all, what would a man on the brink of death do with the clothes of a woman who had died several years earlier? The people under siege shared everything—food, clothes, whatever they had that would keep them alive. But his father surprised him when he added the following night that every door should be thrown open to love, that love could sweep away the past all at once, which had helped to cleanse his being and strip away the withered branches that would never put out leaves again. It was agonizing, of course, to slice off your awful past and throw it away, but it was necessary if you were to catch the bouquet of roses floating down the river and carry it safely to the other side . . .

Bolbol had thought his father might be raving, because he was speaking in clear but disjointed phrases, like people do when suffering from partial memory loss or maybe while sifting through a surfeit of memories, the whole tumultuous chaos of the last four years. Bolbol listened with a lump in his throat; he considered his mother's clothes to be his father's business, and of his own accord he relinquished his own stake in whatever other household goods could be divided up between Fatima and Hussein. Meanwhile, his memories of Lamia never left him; what remained of them would have to sustain him. He felt empty and couldn't sleep that night, thinking of the unsent letters to Lamia he had kept. Over the following days, he began to empathize with his father for the first time—his suffering had been kept hidden for years.

Forty-five years earlier, Nevine had been a lovely woman. She entered the teacher's lounge one day and without any ado introduced herself as the substitute art teacher. Abdel Latif stared with a passion that embarrassed her. He had been searching for love at first sight and believed he had found it at last. A few days later, Nevine opened up about her background: she was a university student at the Faculty of Fine Arts in Damascus; she was teaching art to cover her course fees. Her father was a math teacher and her mother a primary-school teacher in al-Mayadin. Her family lived in the village of Muhassan near Deir Azzour, known as Little Moscow. Nevine had chosen to live in a small house in the meadows around S. She was nice to her students. Abdel Latif would wait until she was entering or leaving the school to waylay her, inventing some excuse for conversation. He told her about the geography and history of the Euphrates, and Nevine responded politely, merely confirming that his information was correct, in much the same way she replied to the blandishments of all her male colleagues—something about her accent, from the Euphrates region, made them all try to flirt with her. But she wouldn't allow anyone into her private life, which was much quieter than was suspected by her small-town neighbors and the bachelor teachers. Quite simply, she was a middle-class girl from an educated family, conservative in most things, despite her clothes, which spoke of a liberality and particularity that, nonetheless, no one found especially provocative. When she wandered around S, which at that time was a small town of no more than ten thousand people, she seemed the archetypal *fellaha* from some distant village, rather than a painter fighting against tradition.

Abdel Latif didn't dare to be frank about his feelings, much less his ambition to marry her. He lay awake at night, feeling as though he were drowning in a gray and indescribable space, somewhere between love and desire. There in S, everyone was a villager, each about the same as the others, but Nevine was the exception—her every quality struck him as entrancing: her beautiful voice when she sang old Iraqi songs, and her great kindness, made her seem like a leaf in an autumn gale.

The first three months after they met had been the most difficult for Abdel Latif. He was always trying to hint to Nevine how he felt about her: to signal all his pleasure and fear. True, he had trouble believing that this girl who taught three days a week and spent the rest of her time in art school was really as innocent as she looked, but he didn't care. He believed that she liked him back, but was too anxious to find out for sure, and so went on loving her silently and sleeplessly.

He went to Anabiya as usual to spend the fortnight's holiday with his family, who no longer objected to his choice to live so far away from them—indeed, for years now his family had done its best to make him feel welcome and tiptoed around any subject that might annoy or enrage him. The subject of his sister Layla was closed—the family no longer mentioned her at all. Her story might be too painful to be forgotten, but everyone was willing to try. They conspired to efface it by concocting fairy tales to cover the truth, relying on the sound principle that if you really want to erase or distort a story, you should turn it into several different stories with different endings and plenty of incidental details. They said, for example, that Layla had committed suicide because she suffered from incurable leprosy or that she was hideous and had been concealing a congenital defect since birth, and the legend that she had been a beautiful girl was a lie. The most horrible story is always the one that people believe, in the end, but nevertheless, the truth never dies, even if its voice is so faint no one can hear it. The true story was perfectly clear to those with ears to hear it: Layla was beautiful and strong-willed, and she refused to accept the humble, cringing life others had chosen for her. Instead, she had made a choice of her own—to die.

Abdel Latif returned from his holiday firmly convinced that Nevine wasn't some brief infatuation. Her smile had never left him for a single instant. He felt like a man who not only hadn't caught the bouquet floating down the river but had dived into the river's depths and drowned. He resolved to make a clean breast of all this to her after his return to S and was therefore somewhat taken aback to find that his dear friend Najib Abdullah had married Nevine while he was away.

Without preamble, Najib had gone to Muhassan with his whole family in tow and asked Nevine's family for her hand. Everything was settled without difficulty. They were married, and Nevine moved into her husband's house in the middle of his family's large estate. Everything was as it should be, apart from Abdel Latif's suffering, which accumulated in devastating silence. Nevine was the only one who ever caught the least sign of that suffering, especially during the big party the couple threw to celebrate their marriage. Abdel Latif couldn't hide his longing for her, nor his overwhelming regret at being too late to have caught the bouquet. She ignored him then, and it was years before she sought him out to lessen the torments of this man who had loved her for so long.

Everything was concluded without fuss. Despite her unhappiness in her marriage, she never admitted to having made a mistake she, too, would silently regret. She'd known that Abdel Latif wasn't the man for her; she liked him well enough, but not enough to marry and live with him. For several months after her wedding Abdel Latif did nothing, and remained alone, striving to get over his wound. He avoided Nevine and made excuses whenever his friend Najib Abdullah invited him around—Najib, who never even noticed that he'd stolen the girl his friend hoped to marry. But then there was a lot Najib didn't know: he was also unable to see that he was living with a woman who dreamed strange dreams and possessed a sensitivity so exquisite as to be excessive. To Najib, everything was normal; his mother had pointed this woman out, so he broached the topic of marriage with her, and Nevine didn't refuse. Everything was soon over and done with, and life went on smoothly and happily. It wasn't long before monotony imposed the rhythm of forgetfulness on everyone but Abdel Latif. Her perfume, even at a distance, still stirred him, her walk dazzled him, and at times her penetrating eyes threatened to destroy his defenses and expose his weakness. Nevine forgot all about her own art; she became a normal mother and teacher, accepting the duties of her lot without complaint. Within a few years she was like all the other women of S; she never used her beautiful voice, forgot her Iraqi songs, and even lost her sweet accent, which now only slipped out on rare occasions.

Bolbol found it all hard to believe. He just couldn't think of his father as a lonely, unrequited lover. At last he understood the secret of Abdel Latif's love for Iraqi songs! For whenever Nevine abandoned something from her past, Abdel Latif reflexively picked it up and kept it, polishing it anew and storing it in some remote corner of his life. He kept many of Nevine's old paintings, dusting them off and rescuing them from decay where they had been left in the school storeroom. And yet, despite everything, this same supposedly sensitive man berated Bolbol bitterly when the latter slunk back to the family seat after his divorce, the bereaved man showing a cruelty in the midst of his grief that Bolbol found unbearable.

This return to the family home was supposed to lighten the

suffering of both the widowed father and the divorced son. Lamia, when she visited them, couldn't bear to see Abdel Latif so bereft as he marked five years after his wife's death. He wouldn't indulge her suggestion of taking him back to her village for a long visit, even though she declared with enthusiasm that it was more than fitting given the closeness of their friendship, adding that a long visit would delight Zuhayr and their two children, too, and that perhaps Abdel Latif could help her revive her parsley. He just looked at her and smiled, then went off to prepare dinner. He told her, "When your beloved goes away, they take the keys of happiness with them and throw them into that deep pit known as the grave." His wife hadn't left him any happiness, he said, but had taken everything with her: sleep, the secrets of cooking, their morning coffees together and evening walks through the town. Now he was abandoned, alone, waiting to die—she had taken everything with her. Not that he told Lamia about his depression—and he'd never told anyone that it had been forty years since he had last tasted happiness, on that holiday to Anabiya when he was dreaming about Nevine. No, for him, everything was finished. His memories of his wife were a simile, so to speak—an interregnum, no more, resembling love—before he could be with his true beloved. So much time had passed, and Nevine was still surprised by Abdel Latif's occasional furtive glances; most oddly, in recent years these glances had begun to break through her reserve, leaving her bewildered. From her depths, pleasant feelings surfaced that she couldn't describe.

Surrendering to one's memories is the best way of escaping the wounds they preserve; constant repetition robs them of their brilliance and sanctity. So as the minibus was leaving the checkpoint at Z, that's just what Bolbol did, swamped with pain as he was, feeling as though he were sinking into the earth . . . The morning was serene, and a peculiar silence had settled after a night of intense bombardment, but they knew it wouldn't last the closer they got to the zones where the fighting had been at its most intense for two and a half years. The opposition forces had captured the principal roads, weakening the regime forces and threatening their supplies of fuel and wheat . . . Bolbol tuned out and once more revisited his father's last nights in his house. Abdel Latif had been exhausted and overcome with pain; he knew he wouldn't survive, and again a vehement desire to die seized him and never left him.

His father spoke in a faltering voice about death and love, about the revolution and the martyrs, about the great future waiting for the children who had been born in these past four years and those who were yet unborn. An image of his wife returned to him, but he didn't linger on it for long. He prayed for mercy on her soul in a few conventional phrases, just as people did before the war when a stranger's funeral passed by. He elaborated on his relationship with his beloved Nevine. Bolbol understood this desire to narrate everything all over again, to reveal a side of himself that no one had known. Abdel Latif wanted to leave his final story in Bolbol's hands—not only his final wish. Abdel Latif was increasingly cheerful as the day drew nearer when he would lie in Layla's grave. He still missed her, in spite of everything, and was delighted whenever he heard the fantastic stories that star-crossed lovers wove around her, although they personally preferred to live loveless rather than die for their grand romantic dreams. These failed lovers, this host of ordinary men and women who had surrendered to the ways of this cruel earth, considered Layla their patron saint. They left roses on her neglected grave in secret, composed songs to her, and described her savage beauty with endless fascination.

Abdel Latif may have stopped mentioning the mother of his children, but nevertheless Bolbol recalled that his father had been assiduous in visiting her grave on holidays, as custom demanded. Still, the decades they had lived together were enough. Nevine compensated him for all his losses and had restored life to his soul and his body. The dead are more comfortable when they're buried beside their loved ones; they speak to one another in a secret code impenetrable to the living. If it wasn't for his sister Layla, and Nevine's wish that Abdel Latif be far away from her when he died and was buried, he wouldn't have asked to be interred in Anabiya. Nevine had refused to allow him to be buried in the same grave as her. How could he have found rest among the graves of her son and her husband, Najib Abdullah, his old friend? Several times he asked her to reconsider and allow him to stay close to her, as he wanted to die in her arms, but she wouldn't discuss the matter. She wasn't interested in surviving any more loved ones. She had no intention of being a custodian for any more graves.

Nevine had begun to believe that she would be around for many more years to come. This abundance of time dazed her. Nothing would satisfy her save going back to the land of her childhood. She wanted to cast off everything that might hamper her from flying freely away down that lengthy road lined with meadows . . . She liked to think that there she would go back to singing the sad songs of her childhood that befitted her two martyred sons; there she would be rid of her burdens, and everything superfluous would be shed. Men were plentiful everywhere; there was no use getting attached to one. Abdel Latif couldn't change her mind, even as she moved in with him. The most wretched of creatures are those who are worshipped; what Nevine wanted was something far better: to be someone who worshipped and adored, not just another beloved worshipped by someone who adored her. She realized why she had always been miserable: she had never been a lover herself.

And so, Abdel Latif kept insisting that Bolbol be his audience during his last days. Bolbol alone knew about his father's secret love; he imagined Hussein's shocked expression when he discovered that the family home in S was to be split four ways instead of three—the only inheritance remaining to them.

One morning, Abdel Latif woke up early, eyes bright and face flushed. The previous night he had spoken to Nevine over a satellite phone belonging to a squadron commander he knew well. He'd beamed when he saw that there was an unknown number on the line, and he closed the door of his room behind him, emerging cheerfully a few minutes later to say that he would go to sleep early that night, after which he went right back into his room. This shyness struck Bolbol as rather peculiar, under the circumstances. In the morning, he found his father drinking coffee in the kitchen, and Bolbol's cup was already waiting for him. His father surprised him by saying that if he'd lived much longer, he would have been nothing but the caretaker of the martyrs' graveyard, which he had constructed himself. He cared for the plants and the flowers and the trees and listened to the raucous laughter of the departed martyrs every night. He spoke to them about their blood, which hadn't been spilled in vain; he told them how the tyrant would soon depart, and children would go to school in clean clothes again, with heads held high and eyes filled with faith in their future. He spoke to Bolbol about martyrdom and revolution, confident in victory, and he didn't want to hear any criticism. When Bolbol made his opinion clear, saying that the revolution was over and had become a civil war, and how the regime's superior army would win in the end, his father made do with shaking his head and smoking voraciously without comment, ignoring what his son was telling him. Bolbol was irritated at being ignored and wanted to add that the international community—Russia, America, and all the West—was agreed that the regime should stay and that it would outlast this orphaned revolution, but Abdel Latif was done with the conversation, seeing how it would only corrupt his dreams. He didn't want to be cruel to his son, but made it clear that he was here to talk and Bolbol here to listen, nothing more; in a few days he would be far away, and then Bolbol could go back to his opinions and his capitulation, could go on living in a neighborhood supporting the regime. He could dance to the sectarian songs broadcast by the speakers fixed above the houses where Hezbollah agents, who no longer hid their faces, gathered openly with National Defense troops—militias that the regime had recruited and armed, made up of volunteers, mostly regime supporters and Iraqi Shi'ites. Most members of these militias were unemployed or had criminal records, and no restraint was placed on their capacity to insult, arrest, and murder at will. They inspired terror even in fellow loyalists.

When Bolbol passed them, he greeted them as cheerily as he could manage; he tried to smile and never let his voice falter in calling out to them. His father, on the other hand, once spat on the ground in a clear show of defiance and said to Bolbol, "These traitors and invaders should all drop dead." Bolbol tried to hurry their pace. He begged his father to stop his puerile behavior. Militias like these could kill anyone without having to answer for it. He told his father a dozen stories about what they had done to people, especially families who were sympathetic to the revolution. For instance, they burned down a family's house when they discovered the son had been arrested at a checkpoint for smuggling medicine into the areas of Homs still under siege. On another occasion they kidnapped a girl from a neighboring district who died after being raped continuously for four days, and her family was forced to officially declare that she had died in a road accident if they wanted to get her body back. The neighbors stayed silent; deep down, many approved of the punishment her family had received. No one came to mourn with the girl's family after her body was thrown into their living room, wounds still fresh. The family couldn't bear to stay and left for Argentina to join distant relatives of the girl's father. As for the father himself, he refused to leave the country before getting revenge on his daughter's murderers, whom he knew by name. He returned to his hometown near Homs and shut himself away there, waiting for the moment when he could point a gun in the faces of the murderers. He hung a list of their names on his wall.

Bolbol did his best to avoid hearing such stories, but some still managed to reach him. Somehow his ordinary, enormous baseline level of fear had managed to worsen since his father came to stay. He believed that the walls containing his usual fear—like a musty, battle-scarred citadel—had finally been knocked down, and he was falling into open space. He couldn't keep it up forever; living in this neighborhood made him pay for his life twice over. He was deeply lonely, and at the same time didn't want to belong to any community. He was far from neutral in his mind: for example, he couldn't stop himself from feeling cheered whenever he saw a funeral procession for the regime's casualties pass by. He couldn't meet their eyes in the posters hung on city walls declaring them to be martyrs. But fear prevented him from even gossiping with his coworkers when they gloated over the growing worries of the regime's supporters, who were also beginning be afraid. Fear had become the only true opposition; it was now each individual versus their own fear, and no one trusted the regime any longer. The ongoing impasse was too terrible to be endured, and everyone had begun to speak of their fear openly. Anyone who had been confident of victory a year before began to feel powerless and weak, increasingly vulnerable, even in mortal peril. Since he was incapable of close observation of anyone else, Bolbol kept an eye on himself, only to discover that he was the most craven of all.

In the final months of 2013, the city had begun to feel a new pressure that no one could explain. In rare moments of clarity, Bolbol would say to himself that it was due to the idea of revenge, pure and simple, taking alarming root in the regime; it no longer wanted to win so much as to punish. He mused sardonically on this dreadful idea: he would wake up one day and see his street empty, everyone having run for their lives. The district chief had already fled, having spared no effort in surveilling every inhabitant of the neighborhood during his tenure. He wrote reports on all the suspicious characters there, including his own relatives, as had the young men who weren't content with supporting the regime but carried weapons and insulted their childhood friends and generally made everyone's life hell. Suspicions alone were enough to lead to corpses lining the streets. Suspicions alone were enough to cause someone to disappear without a trace.

Bolbol didn't ask many questions, frightened of getting tangled in the same net of hatred and turning into yet another person bent on revenge. He would find a means of getting rid of his fear, he told himself, but it was difficult to get rid of the thought of revenge. It wasn't even enough for your enemy to be dead for the fire of vengeance to be extinguished; you had to be the one to murder him yourself if your bloodlust was ever to be satisfied. It was terrifying to see such sentiments no longer hidden but plainly written on silent faces expressing nothing but wrath.

His father regretted leaving the land of the martyrs, as he proudly called his village. He wanted to sit quietly that night, but he was afraid of dying with Bolbol's defeatist talk being the last words he heard from his weak, used-up son. He got up, went to the kitchen, and began to peel some potatoes; despite being clearly exhausted he was resolved to fry some the way Nevine made them. He cheered himself up by returning once again to her story, caring little that Bolbol found it painful to think of her as his father's second wife and sweetheart, not Auntie Nevine, the wife of his father's old friend. Afterward, Bolbol had the ridiculous idea of avenging his mother somehow . . . and then he fantasized about doing the same thing with Lamia if Zuhayr died: this time he would kneel at her feet and beg to be allowed to remain at her side. He used to think that love meant a happy old age with your beloved—as if the years before that were worth nothing, merely something to be gotten through in order for the lover to reach the moment when his torment would stop, a new life would begin, and the daydreams he had enjoyed hundreds of times in his warm bed would be reconstructed in reality. Happy were those who spent their old age with their lover. Old age was a deliberate reliving of childhood, and the time that separated these stages was just a distraction, however long it lasted, even if this meant years had to be willfully squandered before you could begin to understand their superfluity. This is what happened to his father when he met Nevine again. As for her, she didn't need much time to think over his proposal. Mainly she was surprised by his folly. She'd thought that things between them had died, or else grown so obsolete that they could no longer mean anything to anyone. A few indirect comments weren't a declaration of love under any circumstances—just as some shy and occasional glances were hardly a confession of desire.

She was astonished that Abdel Latif could still describe the first time she entered the school. He remembered the color of her socks, the style of her shoes, her white blouse and black skirt. He was eloquent in describing her perfume, the shape of her neck, her laughter, and the color of her eyes. He only left off describing each detail in order to return to it a moment later, this time more vehemently. Nevine was bewildered. She didn't mask her longing for the days when S was still a small village crossed by one long, straight road, when it was surrounded by groves of olives, peaches, and apricots and grapevines. Its houses were spacious and welcoming then, the doors were always left open, and you could count the number of strangers on one hand. It was only a few kilometers from Damascus, but the road to the city used to be lined with meadows, of which only a few remained now.

She liked to have someone from those times around to reminisce with. In truth, she'd barely paid any attention to those attractions back when they'd really existed, but now she liked to give them central, undisputed pride of place in her memories. She'd had another life in art school that no one from S knew about, but in the end, it hadn't been enough for her. That life consisted of a single failed love story, adolescent in its simplicity. She had been in love with the same young man as all the girls in her university class. She was the first to withdraw from the race, unable to bear being so totally ignored. Withdrawal suited her conservative personality and her lack of self-confidence, frightened as she was of the passions and caprices of the city. She guarded this story closely, considering it a dangerous secret, a failed sexual adventure, a one-time-only experience. Her reticence went unappreciated by her colleagues at the art college, where disorder and stupidity were an integral part of student life.

She thought of the long night when she met Abdel Latif again. They were both caring for a young man who had been hit by a sniper bullet, which had ripped through his shoulder. His prognosis was good, and there was no real cause for concern. The battle had stopped for some days, but the truce wouldn't last. Everyone could see the hordes of regime forces at the entrances to the town; tanks and defense artillery had been stationed there, checkpoints made of sandbags had sprung up, and snipers had proliferated on every tall building that overlooked the town. That night there was a full moon, and everything was quiet. Abdel Latif had spent days rearranging every detail in the field hospital. He made a list of all the medications in the stores as well as the names of the patients who had been discharged, along with the casualties whose burials he organized meticulously in the new graveyard he'd built, with numbered graves. When preparing this new cemetery for the victims of the siege, he made sure to gather flowers for them all—something that caused Nevine to reflect that this man must have changed considerably since she'd last seen him. He seemed different from the other men his age: younger, more vigorous. Nothing frightened him anymore. He would rush into the heat of battle alongside the young men and drag the wounded to safety, heedless of dying himself. A strange energy welled up from inside him, and despite his long workdays he made do with only a few hours of sleep a night and never forgot a single detail required by the field hospital or the graveyard.

She felt him panting like a teenager, and it wasn't long before he reached for her hand and squeezed it with disconcerting force. She thought it was just an expression of the solidarity called for in such circumstances, but even so she felt a not-entirely-innocent sensation flowing through her veins. He would never find a better opportunity than this to declare the love he felt compelled to reveal. He talked for more than an hour, and Nevine listened without comment—not that he gave her any chance to respond, to correct his interpretation of the facts he related with such confidence; he just stood up when he was finished and walked out. He left the hospital for what remained of his house: a single bedroom and the remnants of the kitchen, whose eastern wall had been destroyed, leaving it open to the garden. He was used to living in these ruins and refused to leave the house; he told his friends, who asked him to move somewhere safer—somewhere with a cellar that might protect him from the aerial bombardment—that whatever remained of his own home was good enough for him. He wouldn't leave his bed; to do so would make him feel like a stranger to himself. Homesickness always began with leaving one's bed, he said, and abandoning the little items you use every day that have become a part of you. Leaving these objects behind is extremely difficult and is always a herald of misfortune.

He wasn't the only man who refused to leave his shell of a home, but even so his determination to stay put seemed incomprehensible. His remaining friends and acquaintances explained it as reluctance to leave his memories of his wife, but the truth was that Abdel Latif didn't want to leave the place where, for years, he had daydreamed about Nevine. The night of his confession, he slept deeper than he had for years, while Nevine sat alone on her bench in the garden of the field hospital, unable to move. She thought of what Abdel Latif had said and tried to piece together his precise words, the various expressions he had used. She couldn't remember anything in concrete terms, but she had to admit that the thought of shaking up her life was attractive. She was delighted to discover there were men who had been in love with her for years without speaking a word to her about it; she'd always hated being the country girl afraid of the city who hadn't felt able to turn down the first suitable offer of marriage. And after accepting, she hadn't been able to back out; Najib Abdullah never gave her a logical enough reason for retreating from her foolish decision, agreeing to be joined to a man she didn't love. She hadn't noticed that life had already presented her with a bouquet floating quickly down the nearby river; she hadn't seen it until it was too late, when it didn't mean anything anymore. What was the point of clinging to memories as life went by? They were only good for digging up more pain, she thought.

Abdel Latif didn't pursue her, exactly, but neither could she forget what he'd said. He was always present nearby, like a moth fluttering around her. He had decided to burn; no more slow living for Abdel Latif—that was what he thought as he saw her furtive looks at him changing every day. He felt surrounded by a wall of time protecting him from frustration and sluggishness. He was confident she wouldn't let him drown in the whirlpool again. He didn't know where he found the courage to act so recklessly in the early years of the revolution, doing so many things he used to find horrifying. He opened his wife's wardrobe, and the smell of moldy clothes wafted in his face. Even now he refused to look inside. He asked a girl who took care of donated goods to cart everything away, and he cleared the house of his wife's clothes at last. Later he decided that this wasn't enough; he asked a group of young men to take the whole wardrobe out of the house and dispose of it; some nails in the wall would be enough to hang his few clothes on. *If you want to expel someone from your memory, you need to remove their scent from your presence entirely.*

He asked himself: What do the martyrs need? Nothing, was

his reply, and he went on: Even if they were alive, nothing. He liked the idea of renunciation and asceticism in these times, the same way he liked seeing himself as a living martyr seeking death at every moment, a man who had truly destroyed the walls of fear by reviving a cherished notion: that of the brave man who couldn't have cared less about that cruelest of all humanity's fears—death. He kept a vial of poison in his pocket, small but enough for a quick death, and planned to swallow it if he were ever arrested. He wouldn't give them the pleasure of torturing him. He thought of all the courageous people he had read about in the histories of various other revolutions who had climbed the scaffold without faltering, spitting on their murderers and striding forward into oblivion with total composure and resolution.

Meanwhile, Nevine thought for a long time about all she had left: nothing but graves. Once again, she was an outsider longing for her childhood home. Her sons' friends tried to alleviate her loneliness, but how to carry on living was the greater problem. Basically, there was no one left; at night the town was completely desolate. A few thousand people still clung on, but they couldn't go outside after curfew. Few houses had completely escaped destruction, and the town had become communal property; what remained wouldn't sustain anyone for more than a few weeks. Supplies were exhausted; animals were dead; water pipes and electric wires were completely destroyed. Everyone was thinking up other ways of surviving, with never a moment free from considering the question of how to keep clinging on to life. They had to dig up old wells, remember the old ways of storing the beans that grew wild around the edges of the nearby meadows. Reaching the distant fields full of produce had become impossible; regime troops had closed off all the entrances and exits to the town, and four large military campaigns had allowed them to occupy observation posts and embed large groups of snipers around the place who kept watch over every possible—and impossible—way of reaching the fields.

Everyone wanted to smash their mirrors. It was hard enough looking at other people's faces without feeling miserable, let alone one's own. They had heard about starvation from books and fairy tales, but now they were experiencing it for themselves, along with selfishness and a new lust for survival. People fought fiercely over a handful of herbs and a few wild mushrooms. Everything had changed in the small town, and what had been normality a few months earlier now became unimaginable. Abdel Latif walked the empty streets among the destroyed houses, looking for some scrap of food that might have been forgotten, a few handfuls of bulgur wheat or rice, a little corn or olive oil, the remains of some ground lentils, but he never found anything, as others had been there before him. He spent hours combing through the rubble, walking through nearby scrubland looking for anything edible: rabbit, dog, cat—anything would do, and everything had become acceptable. People slaughtered dogs and invented new recipes for them; they drove cats out of every corner. Many people died of starvation. He didn't want to go home empty-handed; the sweetheart waiting for him there was withering away with each passing day. Their late-woken feelings helped them both to find their innocence once again; they knew all the phases of the moon and kept watch for each.

Because Nevine hadn't kept him waiting long. She said that she didn't want to spend the rest of her life alone. Abdel Latif understood her well enough.

That day was in the winter of 2013, two weeks before Christmas. Abdel Latif had been to the church earlier in the afternoon—

it had been substantially destroyed in the last bombardment. Father Walim had been one of the last Christians to leave before the siege finally closed around the town, and he had charged Abdel Latif with looking after what remained of the church, reassuring him that the archbishop had already moved all the manuscripts and icons to an unknown location in Lebanon. Abdel Latif understood him well enough, too: he had to care for the soul of the place—that was his task. So every now and then he would go there and wander around the rubble. Only a small part of the large hall was still standing, and in the middle of it a door led to a narrow room holding priests' robes and some small bottles of oil. Abdel Latif was astonished that these had been left untouched; the looters hadn't spared anything else—not even the huge bell this church and all the other churches in the area used to boast of. Syrian ironmongers had made it especially for a church in Antakya, but they were so proud of their craftsmanship they didn't want to see it hanging so far away, and so they hid it instead. A few years later they gifted it to the church in S, where they could enjoy its peals every Sunday.

Abdel Latif went inside and spent some time reading a book he found in the rubble; the book was torn, but there was still a possibility its binding could be repaired. When he left the church in the evening, Nevine was sitting on a large boulder outside, waiting for him. He was surprised to see her there. He sat beside her, and she repeated that she didn't want to spend the rest of her life alone. The two of them went quiet and didn't move. Then Abdel Latif took hold of her hand and kissed her timidly. He pulled her into an embrace, and they sank into a long kiss; Abdel Latif immediately considered it the only real kiss in his life. Still, they both acted quite properly. They stood up and went to the house of their friend

Sheikh Abdel Sattar and asked him to marry them. Nevine invited the few remaining friends of her sons to witness the signing of the marriage contract.

Happily, a few people were still around to celebrate the wedding with them—the front lines were relatively quiet that night, so there was no need for every man to be at his post. The wedding was perfectly ordinary, and not in the least bit strange, as Nevine had feared—it was simply an occasion for joy. Fighters fired into the air to celebrate the newlyweds, and no one who remained in the town—sharing their hunger, thirst, and cold, caring for the graves of the martyrs—refused Ustadh Abdel Latif's invitation. He felt a powerful sense of renewed connection to everything, and there were new, different feelings now, too, driving away the image of himself he'd been nursing all these years—an elderly man killing time as he waited to die. He took up once more all his old and powerful ideals about revolution and living an honorable life. Deep down he felt himself to be fortunate; he would witness the end of a regime that had brought him nothing but shame since his youth. His former party comrades had betrayed every principle and pounced upon every advantage, had imprisoned their old friends for years at a time, and hadn't hesitated to sell out their cause to stay in power.

Life settled down after the siege closed around the town. Abdel Latif no longer had anything to do but pass the time. He planted flowers on graves and in the walkways of his graveyard, which he hadn't expected to grow so huge. He organized everything, numbering the graves and recording every detail in a large register: the names of the victims, how they had died, their last words, their family names and ID numbers, and a full description, including height, eye color, skin tone, and any distinguishing marks. Perhaps no one would stay in town for much longer, he used to think, but the day would come when they would all return, and when they did, they should know where their loved ones were buried. He didn't know why people would want to know this, as such, but considered running the graveyard a sacred duty just the same; the living looked after themselves well enough.

Despite starvation, everyone still clung to hope and spoke optimistically about the days to come. They realized that despair meant drowning in the abyss, so kept faith with the confidence that was the only possession they had left. The regime, with all its might behind it, inflicted unimaginable losses in every battle, but the people of S couldn't retreat; they had burned all their bridges.

Nevine was surprised she was still capable of doing so much. She would talk animatedly about her previous life, and Abdel Latif would listen sympathetically. He lit candles for her every night, and they would reorder the place afresh. Outside they would move lightly among the ruins, exchanging kisses in the abandoned, shattered houses. They took shelter from a rain shower under a roof, embracing each other as though they might be separated at any moment. They had no time to search for the right term to define their new life together even though they both liked big words. They relished all the small details they had been missing in their lives. They went hungry with each other and with everyone else, and they gathered grasses and concocted soups out of narcissus bulbs and nameless herbs. They hoarded salt carefully, made bread from whatever remnants of lentils, chickpeas, or beans were available, or really out of anything that could make up for the flour that was usually missing. The usable roads linking S to a nearby town that wasn't under siege were secret and few, and they brought in only a small quantity of medicine and flour. Abdel Latif and Nevine didn't approve of the monopoly that the fighting men had on the majority of the smuggled goods, but they didn't have time to find fault or to fight over a handful of flour. They worked vigorously to plant Abdel Latif's garden with vegetables they could dry and store, such as beans, eggplants, tomatoes, and a few ears of corn; under siege, one didn't have the luxury of choice.

Nevine couldn't shake off her fear of winding up alone. Abdel Latif no longer gave her the time or space to talk freely about her past life; they had discussed the past enough to forget it. He was always keeping her occupied with daily plans, and she soon fell in with him and entered enthusiastically into their new life. She joined him in making butterfly nets and ran behind them like a small child, indifferent to the bombs and missiles exploding incessantly nearby. She was convinced that the best way of beating the war was to stop talking about it. She had stopped being afraid of dying a long time before and was even more reckless than Abdel Latif, who would rush off to the front lines swinging a first-aid kit at the least provocation. Nevine would walk calmly through the empty streets, looking at the bombs raining down over the town, and the only thought she gave them was this: They won't kill anyone, unless it's from fear. There was no one left for the bombs to blow up, after all. They'd already murdered everyone there was to murder; now they were destroying only already destroyed houses. The fighters could protect themselves well enough by digging long trenches and erecting secret fortifications, shoring up their already strong defense lines. In the end, though, war is war, and it wouldn't be over easily or quickly. It carried its stench with it wherever it reached, wafting over everyone, leaving nothing as it had been. It altered souls, thoughts, dreams; it tested everyone's capacity for endurance.

Nevine's resolution not to spend her remaining years alone

wasn't trivial. She knew she would die, but not soon. It took many tries before she could tear off the vines of loneliness, which began by constricting her breathing and ended by giving her the crushing sensation that nothing else lay in store for her. She woke alone every morning, unconcerned with the preoccupations shared by the rest of mankind. Nevine no longer thought of being a grandmother; that dream was over, and now she was suspended in space. She wouldn't reconsider her break with her husband's family; her absurd battle with them for influence had wasted enough time already. She'd spent years embroiled in gratuitous conflicts whose triviality she felt only now. Everything she had built was destroyed—the family, the house—the only thing she could do now was wait to die, but death remained such a distant prospect, in her mind. Victory in the revolution meant nothing to her anymore, other than the chance of seeing her son's murderers dragged through the streets. She was gripped by fantasies of revenge for losses for which there was no possible restitution. After losing their compassion, a person becomes little more than another corpse abandoned by the roadside, one that should really be buried. She knew that she was already just such a body, but she still needed to die before she could find peace under the earth. And for her, dying was the hardest work of all.

A year after her marriage to Abdel Latif, Nevine's feelings had changed. She no longer felt she was waiting to die, and she no longer wanted to stay in S, but then she couldn't let herself move away from her son's grave. She didn't like living so close to the dead, but whenever she thought about leaving, she felt paralyzed—her legs went numb. Sometimes she felt a great yearning for the gossip and fleeting quarrels with her former sisters-in-law, who once tried to intervene in her life, but all that was finished. They had always been haughty women, convinced they belonged to such a powerful family; now, they were migrants in refugee camps, expecting sympathy. They had lost everything: their houses, their children, and their lives of plenty.

As he listened to his father go on and on about Nevine, his town, and his revolution, Bolbol could only assume that he was making it all up. It wasn't possible for a man in his seventies and a woman over sixty, the mother of two martyrs, no less, to chase through meadows after butterflies and write each other love letters as if they were separated by a great distance; equally, it was impossible to sit in the sights of a never-ending military bombardment and yet spend hours talking about the moon. But, then again, he could hardly call his father a liar.

In those moments, Abdel Latif had wanted to tell Bolbol that he was no longer a lonely old man in need of care; he hadn't been toppled; he had regained his former vitality, and all at once. He reflected on his life without anger, he entertained no illusions, nor did he let himself get carried away. In this, father and son were much alike: Bolbol understood the truth of his own life, too, in those days—that he had changed considerably, and that the solitude whose merits he discussed with Abdel Latif wasn't so terrible. He still remembered how his name had changed from Nabil to Bolbol; Lamia began to call him Bolbol as a pet name, and in the early days of his solitary life he had liked hearing others use the same name that Lamia used. His original name was almost completely forgotten at this point. Whenever Bolbol saw it on official documents, he felt it belonged to someone else. "Bolbol" sounded lighter and more human to him, whereas "Nabil" suggested some well-adjusted man still dreaming of a grand future. Recently, Bolbol had lost even the impulse to dream and make plans; carrying out his father's last wish was an exercise of what little remained of his will. After all, you have to do *something* if you aren't just going to lie down and die—if you don't want to sink down to the center of the earth.

The corpse swaying to and fro in the minibus was the only truth he had left. He still thought of it as a real person, a collection of tangible, worldly sensations: it could do things; it wasn't just a gelatinous lump. It had a family, and that family still had a long way to go, and on the journey maybe they might even talk like real siblings again.

They traveled fifty kilometers in four hours. Agents at three checkpoints were relatively patient with the family when they saw the bloated body. The third checkpoint allowed them to pass using the lane reserved for military use only, and hope was revived that they might reach Anabiya before evening. Along the road, the signs of battles were clearly visible: damaged tanks, burned-out cars, dried bloodstains. The houses by the road were destroyed and abandoned, and other houses in the distance seemed to have been scorched. Very few people and animals moved through the streets of the small semi-abandoned villages; the only visible morning activities were death and exodus. A double-cab pickup passed them on the road, filled with soldiers armed to the teeth. They flagged down the minibus and the other cars and ordered them to stop and clear the road for a line of tanks. The people in the stopped cars avoided looking at the long convoy. Hussein approached a car driven by a man in his sixties, traveling with his wife and a daughter, who looked around thirteen. A Pullman coach stopped behind them, taking passengers to Aleppo, some of whom got out to smoke. Hussein joined them to chat, waving his hand at Bolbol and Fatima and nodding along with whatever the passengers were saying. It was the very picture of people brought together by tragedy, far from home, trying to dismiss their fear by making small talk.

The tank convoy was still passing when planes swooped over-head. The drivers and their passengers watched the planes bomb some place invisible from this vantage point, and the sound those bombs made gave the strong impression that death was even more imminent than usual. The line of vehicles and their marooned pas-sengers reflected that it was useless to try to resist death. Everyone surrendered to what was to come; no one thought of running away. Where would they go? Hussein came back to the minibus as every-one tried to stick together or else find somewhere to hide; very few were still wandering around bored and smoking. The minutes of horror eventually passed, the airplanes left, and silence descended on the vast wilderness. The final military vehicle accompanying the line of tanks signaled that it was all right for the civilians to continue, so long as none of them overtook the convoy.

It was now almost one o'clock; reaching Anabiya before sun-set again seemed a lost cause. Most of the idling cars pulled out all at once; of course, every one of the travelers wanted to reach their destinations before nightfall. After five kilometers, however, they all had to stop again; the cars that had tried to overtake the rest reappeared, and their drivers signaled to everyone that they couldn't go forward. Volleys of bullets could be heard nearby, behind a hill only a few kilometers away.

Bolbol considered their predicament. Once again, where would they go? There was nowhere but here, out in the open. They stopped the minibus by one of the big passenger coaches, and some other cars stopped close to them. They all stood there for an hour or two. Then the sound of gunfire stopped, and news passed among the vehicles that a battalion of guerrillas had attacked the line of tanks and had now retreated to their original positions. The tanks had been diverted onto the military road leading to the villages south of Aleppo. Six tanks from the convoy were burned out; one of them contained the remnants of a dead man that his comrades had left as food for wild animals.

It was the only corpse visible. Smoke was still rising from the rest of the destroyed tanks. Bolbol thought of this body and dreaded Hussein seeing it, in case it led him to play that same old broken record he'd been spinning since they left home: that bodies weren't important in war, loved ones could make do with a torn shirt or a severed leg wrapped in a shroud inside a closed coffin ... Many families had buried their loved ones without once laying eyes on the horrifying sight of their dismembered corpses.

Bolbol knew that if his father weren't a cadaver, he would be going on and on about all the features of the area. He would be telling his children the names of the local villages, would be listing the flora and fauna, the produce the region was famed for, even its precise elevation above sea level. It had been his favorite hobby, to explain the geography of each district he passed through, but a corpse couldn't do any of that.

Evening began to fall. Reaching Anabiya before midnight was out of the question. Bolbol convinced himself that everything would be easy once they reached Aleppo; only forty kilometers separated Aleppo and Anabiya, and they would travel that distance easily, especially as they were from the area and belonged to a well-known family. His father, who had fled his family more than forty-five years earlier, would nonetheless be saved by its name. Bolbol shared his optimism with Hussein and Fatima, but was discomfited by their silence. Hussein was wondering despairingly, *But when will we reach Aleppo?* Fatima's frightened face made it plain to the others that their predicament, stuck on a half-impassable road crossing abandoned villages and boundless wilderness, wouldn't be an easy one to escape. Hussein was now convinced that patience was the only thing that might save them, and he no longer suggested burying the body by the side of the road or in one of the graveyards belonging to these small villages. (He had pointed out that they could always come back after a time to retrieve it—no one would steal a stranger's body—but, then, bodies won't wait: they soon rot and melt into the earth.)

The siblings tried to limit conversation and made monosyllabic replies to any questions. All three were thinking how they would need to work together as a family in order to get their father's body to its last resting place; all were thinking about how they would return to their loneliness and isolation after the burial, how they would have to avoid looking into one another's eyes for fear of discovering the extent of the gulf separating them. The blissful days of their childhood, when they would exchange secrets, when they could still believe that their life was happy and full of ease, were well and truly over. What had happened couldn't be explained, but they were no longer anything like their childhood selves. Hussein more than either of the others was a stranger to his original character; Fatima and Bolbol, like their father before them, couldn't believe he had changed so much. He was no longer a smart, ambitious, strong young man but had become an entirely different person. Anyone who didn't know him would think he was going out of his way to get himself killed.

Hussein had been closest to the siblings' parents and was the most spoiled. He won all the prizes at school and captained the soccer team to unimaginable victories all around and outside Damascus before returning borne aloft on his classmates' shoulders. He would lead his friends on crazy adventures in the alleys of Bab Tuma, where they would skulk and make dates with girls, spending hours in those cafés that allowed teenagers to press against and fondle one another in darkened corners. He invented lies for the benefit of their credulous families and took these girls on long trips to the meadows of Ghouta to woo them with his guitar to the songs of Muhammad Jamal and Sabah before spiriting his beloveds away behind some nearby trees where they would exchange long kisses and he would touch their breasts. He encouraged all his friends to be reckless and take chances. He kept their secrets and passed a terrible judgment on anyone who broke their word. All the girls trusted him and asked him to help them solve their romantic problems—this or that teenage drama, such as someone threatening to shame his girlfriend by sending some rather personal pictures to her family after a fight. Hussein would intervene forcefully, put a stop to the threat, speak to the boyfriend as though he were the girl's brother, and that was usually the end of the matter. The muscles he was beginning to build up from sports helped him to make credible threats, and he emerged victorious from the many fights he waded into.

Everything changed for Hussein when he reached high school: by that time he was no longer an idealistic boy, but had grown strong and athletic. A woman in her thirties fell in love with him, and within a few months she had transformed him into her bodyguard, escorting her on mysterious errands. He stayed with her for days at a time in the apartment she rented that overlooked the Mezzeh highway and he would return exhausted from being kept up all night. He wouldn't brook any discussion with his father; when he was bombarded with questions, he packed a suitcase and left for weeks, and no one in his family knew where he'd gone.

Hussein left school before finishing his high-school degree and settled happily into his new life. The night of their big fight, he was insolent to the father who was only trying to help him. After calmly telling him that they had to speak as equals, Hussein explained, in blunt language, that he had no desire to repeat his father's small-town life of teaching and respectability. He said he hated the world of weaklings; he wanted to live among the powerful. He would creep into their lives and become one of them; he would share their wealth, sleep with beautiful women, travel to different countries, and live in a mansion in the richest part of town.

His father proceeded cautiously in this discussion. He explained the concept of strength of mind, but was mired in customs and traditions that couldn't convince his son. As for Hussein, he spoke harsh truths that couldn't be denied. He pointed out Abdel Latif was the most highly regarded geography teacher in the school, and even so his meager salary alone couldn't keep the family afloat for two whole weeks. His wife was forced to earn a paltry sum shelling peas and beans and peeling garlic for the grocery stores in the rich parts of town. Hussein added coolly that he didn't want his wife to peel garlic and chop vegetables for rich women in exchange for a few pennies.

Hussein went on. He told his father quietly that Abdel Latif might know all about Brazil and the topography of the Alps, but he didn't know what went on in his neighbors' houses. He didn't know that in this utopia, families sold their daughters to rich Arab tourists who demanded some enjoyment while passing through (of course, legitimized by a temporary marriage contract), and he didn't know that women who worked in the civil service would go out with men in exchange for a pair of shoes, and they didn't have to be expensive ones. His father choked at this and no longer knew how to defend his way of life. He stood accused, along with all the sons of his generation, of the fear and cowardice that had brought his country to the point where it was willing to sell its daughters.

This sort of talk was unheard of in Abdel Latif's house. In the silence following Hussein's tirade, he wondered if his father might not die of shock that very moment. Abdel Latif couldn't believe that this was his son, not yet nineteen—a young man caring nothing for the values his father prized above everything else: honor and integrity and morality. Before Hussein got sluggishly to his feet and left the house, he declared these values worth no more than his mother's plastic slippers and suggested his father accompany him for a few days to see the real marvels of the city. But Abdel Latif had long since refused to ride in Hussein's car, a Golf 1976 that his lover had bought to make it easier for him to accompany her and her friends on their private errands. His clients weren't stingy when it came to encouraging Hussein to fulfill their special requests—an extra pinch of hashish or a few grams of cocaine—with alacrity; besides, all Hussein really ever wanted was enough cash for dinner in a restaurant in Bloudan with a girl who was wearing only a skimpy negligee under her coat.

Abdel Latif managed one last sentence. He told Hussein that he couldn't be both a pimp and his son. Hussein took exception to the word "pimp." He took out his identity card and scratched out his father's name: "I'll write 'shit' in its place," he said as he stormed out, leaving nothing but confusion in his wake.

None of Hussein's family saw him for two years after that. Abdel Latif forbade anyone from mentioning his name. He judged what had happened to be reason enough to consider his son dead. Sometime later, a woman who didn't give her name called to inform them that their son was an inmate at Adra Prison, something to do with drugs.

Hussein, who had been his father's pride and joy, had become his shame, and Bolbol was no good as a replacement: his weakness and anxiety had never exactly endeared him to Abdel Latif. This didn't especially bother Bolbol. No one ever bets on the weak. Strength of mind, that quality of which his father used to speak so highly, was Bolbol's only departure from the weakness that otherwise seemed to define his character, but the fact was that Abdel Latif had only really valued Hussein's physical strength and refused to lay a wager on Bolbol's mind. Bolbol was happy to be overlooked; he didn't want to be a racehorse, and he didn't have the energy to realize the dreams of a family that struck him as not only defeated, but one whose defeat only grew larger with each passing day—larger in every heart and in every corner of their home.

Hussein's cruel words shocked them with facts they had been doing their best to avoid. They had been living in this small town for many years, but they were still outsiders. Despite their perpetual belief that they weren't poor, in truth they were not at all well off, as most families working in the public sector weren't. Everything around them, everything their father had built, Hussein turned to rubble in seconds. Their father hadn't had the courage to live in Damascus, for fear of getting lost; he liked gatherings where everyone was somehow linked by familial or party ties. He couldn't bear the thought of being a stranger in a large city, but in the end he'd still become the stranger he had never wanted to be. At first, whenever Abdel Latif was mentioned by a native of S, they reiterated his connection to Anabiya: it wasn't easy to escape that identity, but even this would pass in time. Returning to Anabiya was no longer feasible. It seemed very far away; as if all his friends had died or had forgotten their childhood, or indeed anything that linked them with Abdel Latif as members of the same generation.

After Hussein left the house, their father was silent for three days. He didn't leave his room and ate only a few morsels. His wife was indifferent to the behavior of both. Bolbol soon thought it might be a good idea for him to get away for a while himself; Abdel Latif wouldn't be able to get past what had happened as long as he knew Bolbol, his other son, who had witnessed everything, was around. Bolbol asked permission to travel to Anabiya, as he did every year, to spend a few days with his kindhearted aunt Amina—a good way to keep himself from being underfoot. He told his mother, "I'll be back in a week, and everything will be fine again."

His grandfather's house in Anabiya was long gone. There was only a collection of relatives left there, most of whom had forgotten some time ago that Bolbol's family ever existed, particularly after Abdel Latif refused to participate in their various and venerable family feuds, which he considered a backward practice for the latter half of the twentieth century. Only Aunt Amina had continued to care. On Bolbol's visits she would tell him their family history, and he would try to piece together the story of his father's flight from his village and his family. The story his aunt always told had parts missing, and she stopped at the first mention of the three knights, as they were known in the village: Abdel Latif and his cousins, Jamil and Abdel Karim. They were the first young men in the village to get their high-school diplomas, tramping the muddy winter lanes half barefoot to reach the school in Afrin, which in the early sixties was still a small, clean town. It required the strength of a mule to make that journey every morning and to return every night. Beneath the pouring rain, the three would cross the fields on foot, sometimes sleeping at a friend's house or in a mosque when floods closed the road. They couldn't afford to rent a small room in town, and their determination to finish school forced their families to save small amounts to cover their fees.

Abdel Latif would boast of how they lived: the whole winter they would cook lentil soup and bulgur wheat and walk barefoot to school; they would distribute Baath Party leaflets and get thrown in jail; they would face the whip and still hold out. Knowledge was a battle and politics a sacrifice, as well as a contest, he would conclude to his audience, who had heard the tale hundreds of times. No one in Anabiya remembered those battles now, but they certainly didn't forget Bolbol's uncle, Lieutenant Colonel Jamil, who, if he'd had better luck, might have wound up president of the republic. As it was he had been betrayed by certain friends who'd slandered him and his associates. As the price for their defamatory comments, those men had accepted an amount of influence that still wasn't exhausted forty years later. Everything was upside down, now: the whole family was branded as traitors, and the slanderers were considered heroes.

The corpse of Abdel Latif, now laid out on a minibus seat, gave no indication of the man's past strength of conviction—that Palestine would one day be fully liberated, for example, and that he would one day pray with his friends in al-Aqsa Mosque. Forty years earlier Abdel Latif had picked up his tin suitcase and left his village for good, after he had failed to support his sister Layla in her refusal to marry a man she didn't love. Not even when she said, "I'll set myself on fire before I marry a man who stinks of rotten onions." And, sure enough, on the day of the wedding she had been forced into, she stood on the roof of her family's tall house in her white dress, poured out a jug of kerosene, and set herself alight, carrying out the threat no one had taken seriously. She whirled around like a Sufi to best let the flames take her body, which had become a charred corpse before anyone could reach her. Abdel Latif had watched her from a distance, weeping for her silently, as his three children were doing now for him: despite how bad life had become, death could still seem terribly cruel.

Yes, as the minibus traveled on, the three siblings preferred to focus on memories and stories rather than think about being stuck on this journey. Bolbol said to himself, If I'd seen even half of this coming, I would have buried him anywhere there was space . . . Taking his father's body to his friends in S would have been easier by far. They had fallen into Abdel Latif's trap. As well as their burden his body was now their only means of escape—because it did still stir up some sympathy, sometimes, and it was the only justification they could point to for their being together on the road at such a time.

They were delighted when the next checkpoint showed them a little compassion. Bolbol reflected that in war, little things like that were enough to give you hope: a considerate soldier at a checkpoint, a checkpoint without traffic, a bomb falling a hundred meters away from you on a car that had cut you off and taken your turn in line . . . *Chance has just given us a new life! If that car hadn't shown up, the bomb would have fallen on us!* This is how people think when even their highest hopes have been brought so low to the ground. The happiness of being able to end your journey at last completely overwhelms your sadness for the victims when you see their charred remains as you pass their car. You need to set aside your compassion so you don't wind up facing yourself and acknowledging the bitter truth: in the face of a meaningless death, hanging on to the self becomes a task as sacred as it is selfish. Over the past twelve hundred days, Bolbol had often reflected on the numerous coincidences that had saved his life. He even began to act as though fate had taken a special interest in him; when somebody panicked and pushed past him onto a bus, he told himself that being forced to take a later bus was no doubt for the best. The first bus was probably going to be hit by a bomb or maybe get caught up in a sudden firefight. Death passes by, and you can't grasp it. In war, death is blind. It never stops to look at its victims.

For the first time, it occurred to Bolbol that the road, with all its rituals and its twists and turns, resembled the people who traveled on it: In the early morning, the dew-laden trees in the distance and the moist earth on either side of the minibus had filled him with optimism. By the afternoon, however, he was exhausted. The changeable weather was damper than usual; storms would blow up and then subside. The three passengers were focused entirely on arriving; they couldn't bear enduring the body's company for another night. It had begun to rot in earnest now, and the cologne, which Fatima desperately sprinkled over it every few minutes, no longer helped.

Hussein seemed calm now. It helped Bolbol and Fatima to relax. They once again postponed the exchange of accusations they had each been nurturing. Bolbol stood the most accused, of course, for having embroiled everyone in this hellish journey they were no longer sure would ever end. The bravery they had boasted of had turned into a nightmare; the moment of their decision now seemed one of insane recklessness, but, even so, a secret satisfaction was creeping into Bolbol. He was no longer the person he had been for four years. He wished he could go back to the beginning, as he was now, so he could spit in his petty neighbors' faces for perpetually spying on him and never trusting him.

He began to understand the secret of his father's regained

strength late in life: his psychic wounds all healing at once, his attitude changing, his no longer acting like a rotten fish waiting to be thrown into the nearest gutter. His eyes got back their twinkle; his body seemed to regain its youthful elegance; he started shaving again; he wore his new favorite clothes. Like a young man he exchanged his threadbare suits for jeans, T-shirts, and sneakers to help him outrun sniper fire. He didn't sit and wait for the protests to pass his house but went to the mosque two hours before the afternoon prayer. He had never prayed in his life—everyone knew he was there to wait for the protests. He spoke with the young people and ignored their pleas to wait for them in front of his house where the protest passed every Friday. He thought up slogans and discussed new ideas. He reread the histories of revolutions and underlined many sentences. He offered copious explanations of the greatest revolutions in history, and his abundant enthusiasm made him into an icon. He resumed his role in the town as the respected teacher who was still fondly remembered by his students, and he lived the bitterness and the glory of the revolution alongside them. When Bolbol met up with his father for the penultimate time, he saw that Abdel Latif was no longer an old man filled with bitterness and loss, just waiting to die; he was an active man whose telephone rang at all hours, who had high hopes of living to see the regime fall and breathing in the freedom for which he had waited for so long.

In early May 2011, Bolbol found Lamia knocking at his door unexpectedly. Her eyes blazed, and she said, "There's no time to lose, we're going to S." Without waiting for a reply, she went on to say she was joining the protests that day. Bolbol couldn't get out of it, and they arrived at ten o'clock in the morning. She hugged Abdel Latif and embarked on a strange conversation with him about their moribund town, which expected sparks to fly today.

Bolbol instantly resumed his other personality, the reckless, impulsive one that Lamia believed in, and went out with them. He was afraid, but when they blended with the huge crowd he could pretend he had broken with his former life, at least for the time being; peculiar feelings struck him and he shouted defiantly. His voice was weak at first, almost mute in contrast to his father's and Lamia's, who raised their hands in the air, their voices as strong as the other twenty thousand people shouting at once. Their voices rocked the town, whose entrances were being guarded by young men observing the road. They signaled to the other protesters when they spotted vehicles carrying soldiers approaching the town. After half an hour Bolbol merged with the others and truly began to shout. He felt a vehement delight; the moment he buried his fear was like his first orgasm. He tried to regain that feeling several times; although he couldn't return to it, he could never forget it. It was an incomplete, unrepeatable pleasure, and it remained suspended in his life like the pendulum of a clock. More than twenty cars bristling with Mukhabarat and machine guns charged the protest and opened fire at close range. Bolbol saw bodies fall in a horrifying scene. Lamia, prostrate on the ground, was helped up by a young man who took her arm and escaped with her into a narrow alley. They were close to his father's house, but Abdel Latif wouldn't budge; he wanted to accept his own portion of death. Dead bodies were strewn everywhere. The Mukhabarat retreated after less than an hour— but that was more than enough time for a massacre. When Bolbol reached his father's house, Lamia was waiting for him. She asked about his father, and he told her he had left Abdel Latif standing there, waiting for a merciful bullet. Again, the sound of gunfire broke out, and they heard young people running and cursing the regime and the Mukhabarat. Lamia opened the door when she saw that the neighbors had all done the same—letting the protesters seek shelter in their houses.

It was a great day. His father relived it a thousand times. As for Bolbol, that one visit was enough for him. Lamia stopped knocking on his door in the morning to take him with her to his father's house.

She told him she felt an affinity with the martyrs who had fallen that day. She'd spent that night in Abdel Latif's house, and they'd both helped to treat the wounded over at Nevine's larger house, which had been turned into a field hospital. The town didn't sleep; the families of the fallen kept vigil by the bodies of their sons and daughters. The army and the Mukhabarat patrols made relentless house raids and arrested scores of young people. Bolbol stayed alone in his father's house. Abdel Latif and Lamia didn't return before dawn. Bolbol heard them talking about the wounded by name. He tossed and turned, but didn't get up. Lamia slept in Fatima's room. Before she and Abdel Latif went to sleep, Bolbol heard his father ask her to wake him in the morning so they could go to the funerals.

Come morning, Bolbol didn't dare flee, afraid that Lamia would think he was a coward. He tried to think of something that would cheer her up, and so prepared a large breakfast, but she and his father ate only a few mouthfuls and drank a few sips of coffee before they left to go back to the field hospital. Loudspeakers at the mosque were inviting people to attend the funerals after the afternoon prayer; public defiance was at its height. Bolbol wondered if fear might finally have changed sides; Lamia told him that she had seen soldiers looking terrified the moment they opened fire on unarmed people. But no, Bolbol told himself, this was artistic license, nothing more. How could someone holding a weapon be frightened by unarmed people waving nothing but their bare hands? Yet her innocent eyes seemed to tell him that lies and exaggeration were simply foreign to Lamia; on the contrary, she was always humble in her estimation of herself, deferring to others and overvaluing their roles in her life. Often, she had made Bolbol feel he was very important to her, asking him to do small favors and thanking him profusely afterward. She was the type who considered the presence of others to be a reward in itself. Bolbol was relieved when Lamia and his father didn't ask him to accompany them to the field hospital. He went back to bed. He was still there when the funeral procession approached the house; curiosity prevented him from going back to sleep. He climbed to the roof and saw a flood of people below. Women were performing *zagharid*, ululating triumphantly, and roses and rice were being thrown from balconies. His father climbed the steps to the church with Father Walim; they grasped the rope of the huge bell and tolled it with all their strength while twenty thousand people raised their fists in the air in reply. It was an awe-inspiring scene, and Bolbol didn't notice the tears slipping down his own cheeks.

Lamia was in the middle of the crowd, weeping and shouting; even where he stood on the roof, he could tell that her voice was screamed almost raw. The funeral procession passed, and a few minutes later Bolbol heard the sound of gunfire. Six young men and a woman were killed close to where Lamia stood; she spent the night delirious, her mind refusing to grasp what had happened. Bolbol's fear returned and increased; he felt as though he personally were under siege. His father paced the living room furiously and spoke on the phone to his friend Nadir, a math teacher, telling him he would meet him at the graveyard. He hung up and left in a hurry. Bolbol followed him with a recklessness he hadn't thought himself capable of, but then he, too, was furious.

Lamia wouldn't listen when his father said that women shouldn't attend the burial. She followed them, and all three hurried to the graveyard. The streets of S were deserted, and the smell of death wafted through the houses and alleys. The electricity had been cut off, and they were all enveloped in darkness. As they went through the narrow alleys, men were preparing to pray over the bodies. Lamia headed toward a group of women, relatives of the dead. Bolbol sat on a tombstone and watched from a distance. His childhood friends kissed him hastily in greeting and continued to where the men were completing the burial rites. The faces of the martyrs gleamed in the light of the full moon.

Lamia was still filled with rage as they left S. She cursed the regime with a wide variety of obscenities while Bolbol kept quiet, unsure how to make her feel better. She left him suddenly in the neighborhood of Baramkeh. She kissed him affectionately and hailed a taxi to take her to the bus depot, and then Bolbol was suddenly alone in the middle of the traffic, a small rabbit in a sea of people. The faces of the crowds around him were impassive, and he panted for deliverance.

Now Bolbol was staring outside the minibus, switching from one side of the road to the other. If this nightmare ever ended, and they ever reached Anabiya, he would wash his hands of the past entirely. He no longer had a father or a mother, and all links to his siblings would be severed for good. He would insist that his own son bury him in the nearest possible graveyard. He didn't want anyone to read the Fatiha over his grave; what good did that do the dead? Everything the living did for the dead just highlighted the solitude of the dead and satisfied the vanity of the living; all that chatter in remembrance of a dead person's good qualities was nothing more than jockeying for social position. Few would have objected if the three siblings had tossed their father's body into a ditch, but perhaps they, too, were taking risks only in order to win admiring glances from their friends and neighbors. Those looks hadn't meant much to them before, but now they could see themselves being consumed by the supposed nobility of their task. If they succumbed to such vanity, they could easily wind up joining the ranks of the self-righteous, those people who consider themselves worthy of passing judgment on everyone who can't live up to their own high moral standards—a group united only by its isolation.

By now they were pessimistic about ever reaching Anabiya at all. Bolbol had switched roles with Hussein, who had taken on the role of the sensible older brother, praising his father and trying to keep Bolbol and Fatima calm. At the ninth checkpoint, the guards were actually kind to them. They told them to hurry if they wanted to reach Anabiya before midnight and pointed out where the next checkpoint would be. They said it belonged to the security services and advised the siblings to answer any questions briefly and without any obstruction; the agents manning that station were miserable, as they hadn't been on leave in months. The siblings prepared themselves, and Bolbol left it to Hussein to decide whether to take the lane for goods or for passengers. Hussein stopped a few meters before the start of the bottleneck at the checkpoint and hurried to the officer in charge. He explained their situation and asked to be allowed to pass in view of their special circumstances, mentioning that the body had begun to rot. The officer came with him to the minibus and glanced at the corpse. He ordered them to go into the goods lane and kept hold of their documents. Hussein said, "When we get to the Free Army territory, everything will be easier. Our identity cards will help us to cross checkpoints quickly." Fatima closed her eyes and murmured a prayer; it occurred to Bolbol, as he looked at her, that this journey had turned her into an old woman. Despair had crept into her heart. He said to Hussein that they still had a little money left, which might speed up their passage through the checkpoint and help them get their identity cards back. Hussein pointed coolly outside. They were trapped inside a lane closed off by huge cement blocks and couldn't leave until all the cars in front of them had passed through; money wouldn't do a thing.

Cars on the other side of the barrier were asking Hussein about the road ahead, and he replied wryly, "There's always someone who knows the road, and everyone follows him." A man who opened his car window was taken aback when Hussein yelled to him without warning that they were carrying a corpse, which was why they were in the goods lane. The man tried to avoid looking at them and continued his conversation with his corpulent wife, who watched them out of the corner of her eye. In a wave of black glee, Hussein asked the driver of another small car for an aspirin because the stink of the corpse had given him a headache. The man just fiddled with his steering wheel without replying to Hussein, who said to his siblings, "We have to have some fun. In a few hours we'll all be dead of cold, or of the smell." He turned up the volume of his tape player a little and began to drum out the rhythm of the songs. Fatima glared at him, but Hussein didn't care. Bolbol prayed to all the gods that their task would end successfully, with everyone still sane. No one could predict Hussein's reactions now, and Bolbol couldn't complete the journey by himself. He needed Hussein to be in his right mind; he was more than familiar with this other face of his, which sneered at everything. Life had wounded him deeply; he had lost all his dreams, and his present was nothing but a nihilistic wait for nothing in particular. He would always be a private driver for a group of Russian dancers working in a club in

Damascus, waiting outside their cheap hotel to convey them to the cabaret, coming back at four in the morning to bring them home again. His life had become one long errand. By day he worked as a minibus driver just to get out of his house.

It wasn't for this that Hussein had broken with Abdel Latif. He'd dreamed of leading an empire, not of becoming a petty driver for a bunch of women who sometimes ordered him to pull over and negotiate with potential clients on their behalf. In those moments he felt like a disgusting insect or, as his father put it, a cheap pimp. He worked for free for a small, obscure gang that sold things on behalf of a large, well-known gang. They were connected to the Mukhabarat and worked openly to sell Russian escorts, hashish, cocaine, and heroin. But he was on the lowest level in this gang, with no hope of ascending to become a full member. Everything was finished, in his opinion. He was no good for anything anymore.

Hussein, persisting in his drumming, switched to the radio and began to sing along loudly to the Saria Sawas song playing. The solemnity and dignity of the presence of death was dispelled. Fatima looked at Bolbol, hoping perhaps that he would reestablish order. For his part, Bolbol was amused by what he saw and wished he could join in the singing; such futility could only be defeated by song and laughter. Often, he had seen people sitting silent and despondent at an ʿaza, avoiding one another's gazes so they wouldn't burst out laughing and ruin the mourning.

They would be waiting a long time if things carried on this slowly. The agents at the checkpoint were scrutinizing everything: identity cards, bags, cups. They examined the cars carefully, shooting out unexpected questions about the passengers' occupations and intended destinations, questions that were normal in themselves but disconcerting when asked by an armed group of men more like a mob than an official squadron. They stood at the checkpoints with their fingers on their triggers. Their clothes and headscarves denoted sectarian affiliations; Hezbollah badges mixed with the green badges of the Iraqi Shi'ite groups who were working with the death squads established by the regime. There were no curbs on their behavior; they were entitled to pass judgment on any person for any infringement, execute them, and throw them in a mass grave, or else just leave them where they fell for their family to pick up and take away.

After an hour and a half of waiting, the minibus pulled up to the checkpoint proper. The three siblings didn't speak until spoken to. The bearded agent who poked his head into the van was astonished at the body. Hussein explained everything in a defeated tone, seeking a little more sympathy on account of the rapidly disintegrating corpse. Abdel Latif's tissues had slackened, and his pores had fissured; his lower half had turned blue, his stomach had inflated, and the stench was overpowering. The agent asked them to pull over on the right and get out of the vehicle. Half an hour later they were a pitiful sight; Fatima was trembling with cold, and Hussein wore an unusually imploring look. No one spoke to them or asked any questions. This limbo of waiting could be so perilous; sometimes, soldiers would drag young men off the buses and spirit them away into nearby buildings before allowing the vehicles to pass through.

Of course, this checkpoint, like so many others, seemed less like a proper checkpoint than a small barracks surrounded by tanks. A short improvised tower was positioned on the barracks roof with snipers stationed inside, observing everyone, perpetually ready to kill. There was thunder in the air, and suddenly it was no longer distant thunder but right on top of them. The storm was approaching, but time was crawling by as usual. Bolbol found himself imagining his family stuck in place for a whole day, or a whole week. It was becoming impossible to believe that their father's body merited such risk and sacrifice, that it should be treated so respectfully, when death reaped hundreds every day throughout the length and breadth of the country. Who could possibly make such an argument now?

Bolbol exchanged a glance with Hussein that they both understood. Bolbol approached another agent guarding the checkpoint who was smoking calmly and tried to explain their situation to him. They needed to reach Anabiya before midnight in order to be rid of the pestilential corpse. The agent referred him back to the officer inside the building, adding that they couldn't pass without his permission. The corpse had become an object of revulsion without an identity; it wasn't merchandise and it wasn't a person. After death a person becomes a third sort of thing, neither animal nor mineral. Records are closed on their account; they are struck out of the family ledgers with a red line; their belongings are thrown into garbage bags or picked over by scavengers from near and far. No one asks old bedsheets about the warmth of the bodies they once protected in the heat of passion. After the file is closed on a dead person, all these little details are shed piece by piece by the memories of the living. Everything is consigned to oblivion and nothingness.

Bolbol went to the officer in charge with an attitude of supplication. In a trembling voice, he explained that time was of the essence; he spoke about the dignity of the dead, not mentioning that they were stuck with this corpse if they couldn't reach Anabiya. He made himself look wretched, begging without complaining. He hated how naturally the pose came to him; a brave man would say something different, would affirm his right to move about freely and take his father's body to its graveyard in good time . . .

The officer looked at Bolbol coldly, used to the blandishments of those who had fallen inside his trap. As far as he was concerned, all these people hated him and wouldn't have any mercy if their situations were reversed. The roles of executioner and victim were eternally being exchanged, were they not?

Bolbol thought of the pouring rain and raging storm outside. Night would fall soon, and they wouldn't be able to finish their journey in this weather. The officer said that transporting bodies in this fashion was forbidden, but because he believed that they were acting without malice, he was waiting for confirmation of the death certificate. Bolbol offered to try and get the pronouncing doctor on his cell phone, but the man in charge cut him off sharply: "Life and death are only a matter of official documents." He pointed at the fax machine on his desk. Bolbol asked permission, again, to call someone at the hospital who might be able to expedite matters, and the officer nodded his acquiescence. Bolbol dialed the doctor's number and explained the problem to him. The doctor promised to look for the fax from the checkpoint and to get back to them as quickly as possible.

Bolbol had almost no money left; he blamed himself for having wasted it, for not having properly calculated the cost of their long journey: he should have divided the sum between the total number of anticipated checkpoints. They had nothing they could sell here—Bolbol's phone was ancient and wouldn't fetch more than a thousand liras, while Hussein would never relinquish his phone for any price—and the two thousand liras left in the siblings' collective possession wouldn't get them anything. The doctor called back and told Bolbol that the hospital's fax machine had been out of order for three months. Only then did Bolbol remember Fatima's ring and wondered how much it might fetch. He went back out into the driving rain and explained the situation to Hussein and Fatima, who were huddled in the minibus for shelter, but still soaked right through. Fatima had slipped her feet under the blanket that served as their father's shroud. Hussein explained that he couldn't turn on the heat; they needed to save gas.

They all looked at one another, acknowledging that they were lost in the wilderness, until an agent rapped on the bus's window and gestured at Bolbol to get back out. The agent returned the documents to him and said that a fax had arrived from the hospital; the officer was allowing them to proceed. They couldn't believe they were being allowed to go on their way. The minibus set off, and Hussein put as much distance as he could between themselves and the checkpoint. He regained his good spirits, and Fatima muttered strange litanies and asked him to look through his cassette tapes for a prayer for traveling. Hussein didn't reply; he was busy speaking to one of his friends on the phone, telling him the name of the village they'd passed through a few minutes earlier. His friend told him there were still ten kilometers until they reached the final regime checkpoint. After that, they would enter the territory of the Free Syrian Army. Hussein focused on the road. The rain stopped, but the wind picked up speed; it tilted the minibus, and the corpse began to topple. Bolbol grabbed it before it could fall over and considered laying it flat on the floor. He dismissed the idea, however; to move it would be to risk revealing even more of its decay. They did their best to ignore the stink, though they were on the brink of passing out: the cologne mixed with the corpse's odor weighed the air with a putrid, lethal stench, and the biting cold outside prevented them from opening any windows.

Each sibling was too ashamed now to admit that they regretted ever setting out on this journey. Why hadn't they looked for a more convenient graveyard, or maybe called one of those charities that volunteered to finance burials for strangers to the city?

Their silence also made it clear just how little they could stand spending so much time with one another. An entire day was intolerable; there was nothing left in them of the affectionate siblings of old. The ties of blood simply weren't enough to sustain the falsehood of family harmony given all the things that now divided them—a lie that in any case had disintegrated long before. When Hussein told their father what they were all thinking, back then, he paid the price of his recklessness; Bolbol meanwhile kept trying to live the lie of respect and the sacred family bond. There were many times he would have liked to tell his father that he was cruel to his children and kind only to his students and strangers. The image Abdel Latif presented to the world was paramount; he cared too much about what people said about him and believed only the best of what they said. He didn't respect his children's weaknesses because he didn't remember his own, nor his old inability to escape with Layla from his own family's influence. He had waited for her to turn to ash before he let out a stifled cry and left Anabiya for good—Anabiya, where now he wanted to be buried. Bolbol wanted to ask him: *Why, after you left it all behind—those cruel faces that knew no mercy—why would you want to be buried on their cursed land?*

It wasn't the first time he had pictured himself standing in front of his father, speechifying to him, telling him to his face that he was a weak, emasculated man with barely a quarter of a dream to brag of, which wasn't nearly enough to achieve anything effective. His tirade would conclude: *You're like me, but you wrap your delu-*

sions in big words about the liberation of Palestine, which your generation left to rot. Or maybe something about the respectable family Abdel Latif had always wanted, filled with successful, educated, socialist children working in respectable professions: *Like all poor people you want your children to become doctors or engineers, but your uniqueness is a fantasy and the cost of it has buried us.*

When Bolbol decided to study philosophy, he felt he was disappointing his father. All his life Abdel Latif had venerated the great philosophers who had changed humanity, but for his own children he wanted professions that would safeguard them against going without. But Bolbol felt incapable of doing anything differently. He wanted to understand the world, and tried to be one of the best students, but everything went against him: his teachers despised thought and sold grades and exam answers to the highest bidders; everything that ran most counter to the essence of philosophy existed in abundance in the philosophy department. They despised debate, politics, reflection, and research; the faculty guided students to storefronts where hucksters sold extracts from lectures and where the professors took a commission from every sale. As for the lecturers who tried to reimpose the kind of philosophy that actually provoked reflection, they were either dismissed or finally shut themselves up at home in despair. Student informers wrote reports accusing them of sedition, inciting atheism, and cursing the party as well as Arab nationalism. Thought was a veritable crime, and it necessitated interrogation.

Bolbol soon lost his enthusiasm. He bought lecture notes and followed the teachings of professors who vaunted the ideas and wisdom of the Leader. He didn't dare admit his cowardice to Lamia. When he was with her, he was possessed by his old image of himself, of which nothing now remained but the remnants of his old, dead ambition. He became one of the herd that only wants a degree to get a job. Soon he was employed at the Institute of Food Storage and Refrigeration, where he recorded the quantities of tomatoes and onions prepared for warehousing and then, at the end of the season, would record how many tons had gone bad. It was trivial work that required no philosophy. Bolbol stopped caring about new ideas, and day by day he became a model employee—scared of everything. What frightened him most were those perilous situations in which he found himself agreeing with Lamia when she spoke of necessary change; she would declare loudly that the populace had reached the last stages of servility and that revolution was the only way of uprooting society's backwardness, as well as the dictatorship, and bringing to account the murderers who had plundered the country from east to west. Abdel Latif agreed with her enthusiastically, and Bolbol chorused his agreement, too, but deep down his heart was cold like a rotten quince. How it pained him now, the hypocrisy he had shown on so many positions just to satisfy Lamia and retain the privilege of her friendship. If it pleased her, it was enough for him. Even today, the look she had given him that morning as she bid him goodbye was all he'd needed to hoist his father's body onto his back and carry it through checkpoints, storms, and the arid wilderness.

They were alone on the road again. All other cars disappeared, night fell, and the scene went back to being terrifying. Bolbol felt bleak, Fatima's face plainly showed her apprehension, and Hussein was worried they were lost. They listened to the storm, and none of them cared about the state of their father's corpse or whether it fell off the seat. Blueness now suffused the chest almost up to the neck, but they didn't look at it anymore, so as to avoid seeing the bloating. Hussein had even stopped making proclamations about what time they would arrive. They had traveled more than a hundred kilometers and began to convince themselves they were over halfway there. At this point, they told themselves, mired in the unknown, going on was surely preferable to heading back.

The searchlights of the next checkpoint appeared in the distance. They slowed down. When they reached it, the soldiers on guard looked at the family in astonishment. These soldiers' outfits were different, nothing like the uniforms at the other checkpoints. These soldiers were also poorer looking than they should have been, as if they had been cut off in this part of the world—they were certainly soldiers, as opposed to Mukhabarat or private militia, but they had been stationed here on the front lines in the full expectation they would die. A soldier of no more than twenty opened the car door and examined the body, aghast. He looked at everyone's identity cards, smiled, and said he was from a village near Anabiya; he knew the family name. They exhaled in relief and smiled back at him. He took pity on the dead man and, leaning his head into the car, he told the siblings that at the next checkpoint, which belonged to the Free Army, they should find his cousin Hamada. He might help them secure accommodation till morning; they certainly couldn't keep traveling tonight. Then he raised his hand in farewell and allowed them to pass.

It was fewer than five kilometers to the Free Army's checkpoint. They asked for Hamada and added the name of his village; Hamada came out, looking surprised, and scrutinized the siblings. They introduced themselves and explained their task to him. He asked them if they knew what it meant to be traveling this road at this time of night. He genuinely wanted to be useful to them and offered to help them find somewhere to stay overnight in a nearby village, at least until dawn, when they could proceed with their journey. The siblings were adamant that they had to reach Anabiya before then; the state of the corpse would brook no delay: they had to bury it as quickly as possible if it wasn't to disintegrate entirely. Hamada saw from their faces that they were hungry, so he suggested that they join him for dinner. Hussein asked if Hamada would provide them with a written directive to the following checkpoints certifying that he knew them and requesting facilitation of their passage. Hamada laughed and informed them that his influence extended about five meters from the point where they were parked. Every squadron at every checkpoint had its own system, and such a letter would be disastrous if it fell into the hands of hostiles. At that moment, the siblings realized they were truly in unfamiliar territory.

Hussein agreed to drink some tea and wait a little. After all, it would be no use arriving in the middle of the night; they couldn't very well wake their uncles and cousins and ask them to bury a dead man at midnight. Fatima asked Hamada for some spirits so she could rub down the distended corpse. They drank hot tea, and Hamada supplied them with a small bottle of spirits and some cans of food. He guessed correctly that they were embarrassed to ask anything of people whose appearance so clearly demonstrated their poverty.

Hamada's face was delicate and gaunt. He told them he had defected from the army a year and a half previously and joined this battalion, which had no funding. He said that his cousin at the previous checkpoint hadn't wanted to defect, preferring to stay with the regime—and now, even if he wanted to defect, it would be difficult for him to do so, as snipers lay in wait on every road. Hamada finished by saying that his cousin hadn't visited his family in three years. He said that the two checkpoints were waging a pitched battle for supremacy that was entirely imaginary; they wanted to keep the peace here, but they had been forgotten by everyone else. He would have talked till morning, repeating that the war was a futile bit of madness with no end in sight; it had been a long time since he had seen anyone from his region who would understand how lonely he was. He asked them to look up his father, a good friend of their uncle, when they passed by his village, so they could tell him that Hamada was doing all right. Hamada added that he spoke to his father on the telephone, but a personally delivered message still meant something in that region.

When Hamada bid them goodbye, he warned them to watch out for extremist squadrons, insisting that Fatima cover her hair thoroughly. Hussein embraced him like a brother and wished him victory. The family only realized their mistake after they left the checkpoint, all three siblings thinking the same thing, but afraid to speak the words out loud: Why hadn't they asked Hamada's help in burying the body in the graveyard of *his* village? After the war was over, they could go back to collect the remains. But the ease of their last couple of crossings had given them confidence they had passed the worst. At last, they had reached the liberated areas, and their identity cards were no longer a problem; no one would look at them with contempt and suspicion for being born in S and having roots in Anabiya. Bolbol remembered his father's rousing words: "The children of the revolution are everywhere." They discussed Hamada and his cousin with amazement and sympathy in order to expel any negative feelings that might slip back into their souls thanks to the continuing stormy weather. They weren't alone on the road anymore, or not so completely; at one point they were overtaken by a few modern SUVs scurrying along with fighters inside. One of these pulled alongside, and its occupants waved to Hussein to turn

off his lights; they didn't respond to his plea in return to be allowed to travel behind them, and after a hundred meters the vehicle
turned onto a muddy side road. Without lights, then, the minibus
seemed like a big coffin shared by Bolbol, Hussein, Fatima, and
the body. The calmest of the four was the corpse, of course, which
knew no fear or worry; blue tinged, it swelled with perfect equanimity and didn't care that it might explode at any moment. When
it vanished, at last, it would do so willingly, unconcerned with wars,
soldiers, or checkpoints.

Bolbol thought about his mother. She hadn't expected his
father's body to be buried beside her. She hadn't even left enough
space beside her grave for it.

She had often endured his unjustified rage. The image of them
tending flowers in the garden in total harmony was a lie his mother
had been forced to live for all forty years of their married life. When
she was angry, she would mourn her lot in curt phrases. It took
years of Bolbol's hearing these tiny complaints before he came to
understand the tragedy of her life: she was a maid to a man who
had left his land and his family to invent an imaginary history for
himself. She missed Anabiya and its meadows. She didn't care about
anything her husband did; she didn't want to become a sophisticated woman. She adored the strong consonants of her country accent and kept silent whenever her husband started to tell his
family history to visitors. Believing that he was being creative, not
that he was simply a liar, she no longer bothered to correct him as
to names and relationships. The only really interesting character
Abdel Latif had known was his sister Layla, who had set herself on
fire—but he never once mentioned her. She had been a close friend
of Bolbol's mother, who described her as a wonderful girl and
recalled her kind heart and beautiful voice when she sang for her

friends as they prepared okra, squash, and tomatoes on mild summer evenings. Layla had memorized every song, it seemed, and her zest for life made her popular among all the girls her age; they would gather at her father's house, and she would teach them beauty regimens. She experienced an early heartbreak when she fell in love with her cousin, Lieutenant Colonel Jamil, who left her and married an idiotic fair-skinned girl from a powerful family rich in land. Bolbol's aunt told her friends her beloved had essentially sold her, had given her up in exchange for an enormous dowry and powerful connections, but on the day he was executed, she tore her clothes and lamented as a wife would grieve her husband. She couldn't endure the weight of her few memories of Jamil. She stepped up to the coffin, pushed aside the soldiers who surrounded it, wouldn't let anyone near the traitor, and beat on the coffin lid, wanting to wake him as she used to do whenever she could steal a few moments to go to his room. She would shake him awake and stroke his face with her delicate hand, staring at him in a way he found irresistible. Her laughing eyes, her fresh scent, and her strange elegance among the *fellahin* made her seem like someone from a different era and place. She wasn't shabby and second-rate, like the other women of the area.

Her open mourning for Lieutenant Colonel Jamil was a real scandal for the family. She had gone further than a girl of any respectable family was permitted to go. The men gawked at her, her father couldn't hide his fury, and the women of the family took her home, locked her in her room, and returned to the funeral as if nothing had happened. Everyone waited for a verdict from her father and three brothers. All that happened, however, was that her father was silent for a month, then everything went back to normal. After all, Lieutenant Colonel Jamil *deserved* to have girls rending their garments in frenzied mourning on his account (or so the family, which had tasted power for the first time through his advantageous marriage, decided to believe). Six months after this incident, Layla's father informed her that an appointment had been made to recite the Fatiha over Hamdan, after which she would have to marry him in a month's time; she was to accompany the women of the family to Aleppo for the preparations in the meantime. Layla couldn't accept this; she went to her father's room and told him outright she would never marry Hamdan. Then she asked to speak with her brother Abdel Latif and told him that he had to intervene, adding that she wouldn't be turned into a cow in the house of a man she didn't love, and she wouldn't live as her mother had lived. She didn't know what form she wanted her life to take, but she was certain about what life she *didn't* want. She knew her wishes were exceptional but was confident that her brother Abdel Latif wouldn't throw her to the wolves of their family. They spoke for a long time, but he was afraid of being seen protecting and supporting her, which would have been a pointless battle in any case, especially after the scandal of her behavior at Lieutenant Colonel Jamil's funeral. What Layla wanted was to distance herself from this land of ruin and finish her education; she was the only girl in the village who had even gotten through middle school—with the encouragement of her brother, who was now lying dead in a cold minibus on a distant road. Yes, she'd wanted a different life, the one she thought that she deserved. No one believed the threats she made; no one believed that she would really make them regret their decision. She told Bolbol's mother she would become a blazing torch, burning her family and lighting the way for other women.

She used to love long words, just like Abdel Latif. She composed unusual sentences and could spend hours reciting poetry and criticizing the refinement of its composition. She was an inexhaustible mass of sensations. No one could believe their eyes when they saw her on her wedding night. She contented herself with being among her friends, including Bolbol's mother, in the weeks leading up to the wedding; she wouldn't allow any women from the groom's family, or even her own, to help her. She celebrated her body: removed her body hair like the girls in the city did, and Bolbol's mother rubbed her with creams. Then she put on her white dress, went up to the roof, and pulled up the stepladder behind her. She had prepared everything the day before: the bottle of kerosene and the matches. She looked down at the revelers in the courtyard, where the party was at its height, before she began to laugh, and set herself alight. Her body was extinguished amid the stupefaction of the men and the weeping of the women, who couldn't believe they had lost their dear friend forever.

But nothing changed after Layla's suicide. Girls were still made to abandon their education after primary school, their families decided whom they would marry, and any girl who left the herd was slaughtered—but Bolbol's grandfather was no longer the same man. He shut himself away and died ten years later, full of regret that he hadn't taken her threats seriously. He had loved Layla and thought of her as the true heir of his own mother, who used to recite poetry to her husband. Many people still quoted her poetry and sang those sweet songs of hers. As well as composing love songs, she'd sung about many local events, recording them for posterity: the anonymous Storyteller of Anabiya. But no one had corrected the official history, in which her poetry and songs were usually attributed to Bolbol's great-uncle. There was nothing in the history of the region about how that skinny little woman had passed all her anxiety on to her granddaughter decades later, and as for Layla herself, no one said anything about her, save that she had set herself on fire to hide her disgrace.

Now almost everyone was dead. Only a single uncle and a few cousins were left; most had fled for the camps in Turkey or were in prison or had joined the Free Army and its battalions, fighting one another as well as the regime. No one was waiting for the three siblings in Anabiya except for a few men who were already exhausted from burying so many dead over the last four years. But those few men would be enough to witness the accomplishment of Abdel Latif's last request, although they had forgotten him long ago. His occasional family visits to Anabiya hadn't been enough to reestablish the connections he'd broken after Layla's death.

On those visits, Abdel Latif would exaggeratedly praise his new town and its inhabitants, trying to sound as though he'd found a new place to belong. He took no pleasure in fighting, in angry shouting matches. In reality, of course, Damascus did nothing to help him find a new identity for himself, and he ended up living in a small town on its margins, afraid of everything, like everyone who'd fled the countryside. Whenever he ran up against any bureaucracy, he would be asked about his relationship to the traitor Lieutenant Colonel Jamil; he would be struck dumb and reflect how, like him, they must be rather afraid if after all these years they still hadn't forgotten Jamil. In this country, people like to say "The page doesn't turn after death"; the dead pass on their actions and attributes to their children and through them to their grandchildren. Everything you do is closely observed, and your official records may as well be locked behind an iron wall: impossible for any civilian to read or alter.

And in one of the calmer moments of that stormy night in the minibus, it occurred to Bolbol that, as for all citizens, his father's full record would still be in the hands of the Mukhabarat. Bolbol was assailed by a peculiar curiosity. He wished he could obtain those pages and read over them: what they said about Abdel Latif, how it had been more than forty years since he first arrived in S, that small town near Damascus, and then what they had written on the final pages. Thinking about these things distracted him from telling his brother and sister about Nevine, which he'd been meaning to do. It also prevented him from replying to Hussein, who had again worked himself into a rage over their stupidity for not getting rid of the body long before now.

Fatima spoke up to inform her brothers that the corpse was splitting apart. Bolbol immediately tried to change the subject, as if what she had said was of no concern. He wasn't in the least bit interested in dwelling on the state of the body. He'd always known that keeping it intact and in the same state as when they left the hospital two days earlier was simply impossible. And when Fatima took it upon herself—out of her sense of duty, Bolbol supposed— to lift the blanket off of the corpse and reveal the nightmare under- neath, which the brothers could only have guessed at, Bolbol wished she would just drop dead as well. The dead turn to shit. And even if Abdel Latif's corpse had *literally* turned to shit, they still wouldn't be able to just wipe him away. Their memories were like acid inside them, boring eternally down into their depths and cover- ing their hearts with pockmarks—just as the sight of Layla burn- ing like a corncob ate at Abdel Latif's heart until the day he died.

Fatima wouldn't leave well enough alone. She kept drawing her brothers' attention to the ragged body, from which a string of pus had started to trickle from a tear. Hussein stopped the minibus, turned to Fatima, and shouted angrily, "Let it! Let it turn to shit!" He cursed his father and his family and glared furiously at Bolbol, who wouldn't meet his eye. Bolbol was afraid he wouldn't be able to bear what Hussein would say next. For some time now, he'd been glowering at Bolbol in the rearview mirror; they hadn't expected to pass another night on the move. Silent tears were, as usual, dripping down Fatima's cheeks, and a peculiar compulsion made Bolbol now decide that he wouldn't go on allowing Hussein to behave however he liked toward them. Bolbol would carry out his father's wish even if he had to carry him to Anabiya himself. He felt greatly comforted by this decision, but he kept silent and wouldn't respond to Hussein's provocation.

Images of their childhood had besieged them ever since leaving Damascus, of course, but now they were positively suffocating Bolbol. They weren't all bad, but with the passage of time, those innocent moments had been made strange. Neither he nor Hussein could save the other; they were two sides of the same coin: Hussein was the face of bravery and buffoonery, and Bolbol of cowardice and capitulation. Both had lost the battle with life. Now all three siblings were like strangers to this corpse that, however much it had lost, still retained the advantage of being able to lie there without caring.

The drumming of the pouring rain was hammering their nerves. Twenty kilometers later the optimism they had felt at leaving the previous checkpoint finally ran out. They were back in the unknown. A group of cars overtook them, speeding erratically along the road. The armed men within had harsh faces and long beards. Their dark complexions made them look like foreigners; only one was fair, with braided hair and a half-witted expression. The siblings slowed down as they neared the cars, looked at the men curiously, and then went on their way. Hussein didn't bother to hide the fact that they were utterly lost. A few lights appeared in the distance, and Hussein said they needed to stop and spend the night in the nearest village. Their nerves couldn't take any more.

They approached a weak light. A man similar to the men they had seen in the cars waved his flashlight at them to stop, and Hussein rolled down his window. The armed man beckoned at him to slowly approach what appeared to be yet another checkpoint. His accent was peculiar, certainly not Syrian. Hussein told his siblings that the man must be Chechen and added that he knew the type from having escorted so many Russian dancers. They reached the checkpoint and waited. Their hearts were thudding almost out of their chests, and Bolbol felt he could almost hear them. A sniper could easily pick them off here. The wait was enough to liquefy anyone's backbone. Who knew what they'd landed themselves in this time. After more than half an hour another vehicle straying through the night stopped behind them. They felt safer when they saw that the three young men inside were civilians like themselves. Hussein wanted to ask them where they were going; talking to strangers would be a good way to make them all feel calmer. Hussein lit his third cigarette and opened the door of the minibus and immediately a disembodied voice ordered him to get back in the vehicle. A few minutes later they were approached by a man wearing black clothes and a mask. He asked for their identity cards in faltering Arabic and caught sight of the body before they'd managed to describe the purpose of their journey. Hussein launched into a lengthy explanation at once. The man spoke into his hand-held radio, then pulled the blanket off the corpse. The body had changed again, was covered with lacerations and was oozing pus all over. Its stench billowed out and clogged every nose. Three armed men headed over, got in, and ordered Hussein to drive to the prince's villa at the edge of a nearby village, in the middle of a field, heavily guarded by more masked men. There, they all disembarked and went into the building.

The smell of incense wafted through the entrance hall where they stood, waiting for permission to meet with the prince. The masked guards didn't say a word, as if they were made of wood. Fatima asked them to show her where the bathroom was, and neither their faces nor their fingers, still resting on the triggers of their rifles, moved. Hussein tried to show off his military knowledge and said they were Dushka machine guns, but one glance from a guard was enough to shut him up. They heard a murmur behind a huge door. The only cheering thing about their situation was that the room was very well heated. Luxury was evident in every detail of the villa. Soon the murmurs got closer and a group of Bedouin men emerged from behind the door, thanking the prince and wishing him long life.

After a few more minutes a tall man opened the door for them. It was a kingdom of masks, no faces at all, no details, and no features. Fatima was the most afraid; she hastily adjusted her head covering so it concealed half her face as well as her hair. In her shabby clothes she looked like a poor woman. Exhaustion from the journey showed clearly on the siblings' faces, as if they had traveled five thousand kilometers rather than two hundred and fifty, a journey that ought to have taken two and a half hours at most.

Bolbol was astonished to see Fatima kneel down to greet the prince in imitation of the actresses in historical dramas. The prince, who was also masked and wearing an embroidered robe in a sort of Abbasid style, asked them their business. His tone betrayed his irritation, and from his ponderous accent they guessed he was Afghan or Chechen. One of the guards entered, gave them back their identity cards, whispered something in the commander's ear, and left. Nonchalantly, and in a stately formal Arabic that almost made Bolbol burst out laughing, Hussein stated briefly that they needed permission to proceed so they could get on with burying their father's body before it rotted away entirely. Hussein had been surprised at the prince's question; surely he must know the rules governing burial of the dead according to Sharia? Hussein looked at Bolbol for help, but Bolbol had nothing to say, only telling himself that the insults would never end; the children of the revolution weren't everywhere as his father had said. Here the three of them were, in a strange land, surrounded by foreigners, and they had no idea why they weren't being allowed to bury their father's body.

Hussein went on to mouth a few courtesies, resorting now to the sayings in his beloved almanacs. He spoke about honoring the dead through their burial, but all were astonished when the prince told the siblings, quietly but angrily, that it was suitable for a Muslim to be buried anywhere within the nation-spanning land of Islam, and last wishes like Abdel Latif's were tantamount to heretical innovation. Hussein heartily agreed with him; Bolbol knew Hussein's most fervent wish was to be rid of the corpse at any price. The prince went on to enumerate all the Companions of the Prophet who had been buried away from their homelands. Bolbol tried to speak, but the prince gestured to him to be quiet. Then he sprang a question on Hussein about the number of *rak'at* performed in the prayer for the dead; he asked them about their sect, and they explained that they were from Anabiya . . . then something unexpected occurred. Dozens of missiles thundered nearby. The prince rose and left quickly, leaving the family in his large hall. They wasted no time and hurried out behind him. Hussein waved at Bolbol to go back to the minibus with Fatima. An odd current was running through the people in the building. Hussein told the guards that the prince had given the family permission to leave; they raised no objection, indeed didn't seem to care one way or the other. The bombs were still falling nearby; one of them must even have hit near the villa, for they felt it quaking. The battle was right on the other side of the road but seemed just as likely to intensify and move even closer. The siblings quickly climbed into Hussein's minibus. In their hurry they barely noticed that the vehicle had been thoroughly searched, papers and CDs flung everywhere. They simply made sure their identity cards were safely with them and then sped off without turning on the headlights.

Yet Hussein slowed down again after only a few kilometers. He told the others he had lost the road. Raqqa was nearby, but he wasn't sure which junction would take them to Aleppo. The prince's villa and his village had disappeared from view, but they could still hear shooting and explosions. Hussein felt they should stop for the few hours left until dawn. They needed some sort of guide if they were going to find the road, and anyway—as they were all well aware— traveling with a corpse in the car at this time of night would just arouse more suspicion. He chose a spot near to a number of crossroads and turned off the engine, and silence reigned once more, broken only by the barking of a nearby dog.

It was midnight. Hussein lay down in his seat and closed his eyes. Fatima tried to cover her face. No one wanted to look at the corpse. It had become a plague upon them, nothing less. Bolbol could no longer object if Hussein suggested burying it here, by the side of this unknown road. He heard Hussein snoring for a short while and had no choice but to look out at the night. He tried to get some fresh air and opened the door to step outside, but the intense cold bit into his limbs, and he stayed inside the bus. Their heavy heads were the natural result of the stench that blew over them. They were breathing in death as no one had ever breathed in the death of a loved one; it permeated their skins and coursed through their blood, and Bolbol wondered idly if all three of them had gone completely moldy by now. This was all that remained of his father: decay and pus. Abdel Latif was done with dreams, and these thunderstorms were bidding him farewell on his final journey—a fitting tribute to a misguided warrior. Till his last moment, he had remained proud of all his defeats. He hadn't known a single moment of victory, but he had been intoxicated by it all the same, expecting it to come as inevitably as the fate that brought him to where he was now.

The three of them were unspeakably weary. None of them could bear to even look at the others. Fatima was lying on the floor, her face as blank and wide-eyed as a seal's. She was trying to piece together the fragments of their childhood that kept surfacing within her memory, but Hussein's voice interrupted her scattered thoughts. He asked Bolbol, "And afterward?"

It was true; Bolbol had no idea as to what would happen afterward and told Hussein as much. The drumming rain increased their desolation. Hussein said they had to put the body in the back of the bus. He couldn't quite manage to admit that the smell was making him dizzy. They prodded Fatima, who closed her eyes again after her few words were ignored. They arranged a space on the back seat, and when they began to move the body, they were astonished at how heavy it was, and how many more splits had appeared in its skin, all leaking yellow pus. They opened the door for a few seconds and immediately saw a pack of wild dogs rushing toward them. Howls filled the area, and they slammed the door to escape this almost unreal ferocity. The dogs leaped at the bus, attacking it from all sides. They bared their fangs, utterly enraged, and Bolbol had the feeling they would never leave them in peace again. He suggested to Hussein that they drive away and find somewhere safe and inhabited to take shelter. Hussein didn't reply. He was staring in fascination at the dog currently trying to scratch the windshield. Hussein laughed and began to tease the dog, which only became more furious. Bolbol was disgusted and frustrated. He knew that if the dogs reached the corpse they would tear it to pieces, and he began to feel genuine terror for his father, now reduced to little more than some carrion to be lusted after by wild animals. This was surely the utmost level of decay. After half an hour the dogs had only become more frantic, new ones had arrived, and now a whole pack was laying siege to the minibus.

Hussein began to take the matter seriously when three dogs began to hurl themselves at the windshield in frenzied concert. He started the engine, but the dogs didn't budge. The bus pulled away, and Fatima tried to cover the rear window to block their view, until Bolbol told her that it was the smell that had attracted the dogs when he'd opened the door. How and where would they flee? They chose a road that Hussein guessed would lead them back to the main route to Aleppo, leaving the junction for Raqqa behind them. Bolbol asked, "Why don't we go to Raqqa, and from there to Turkey? We could cross back over at Bab al-Salamah, near to Anabiya?" Hussein sneered at this bright idea, asking how they were going to get a body across the border without a passport.

The dogs were still chasing them. They were driving along a narrow road without any signposts, feeling well beyond lost. Hussein grumbled when Bolbol kept offering suggestions—for example, that they admit defeat for the time being and head back to the junction where they had stopped for the night, arguing that eventually the dogs would get bored and leave them alone. Bolbol saw Hussein scowling in the rearview mirror. It was far too late for them to be having any more adventures; a mistake at this point might cost them their lives.

It was still raining. They reached a junction with an old track that led through deserted fields to a distant village, drowning in darkness. Yes, they had no idea where they were. The dogs had fallen behind, but their distant barking wasn't exactly reassuring. The siblings were more than apprehensive. They were lost in the wilderness.

Hussein resolved to act on his own initiative, deaf to all entreaties. Fatima begged him to eat a morsel of the bread they still had, and he didn't reply. He sank down in his seat and stared at the rain, subsiding at times and intensifying at others. It would take perhaps ten minutes to reach the village, and being somewhere inhabited was preferable to staying in this wasteland. The dogs would inevitably come back; they knew their way to the prey, and unlike the siblings, they had noses that kept them from getting lost.

Bolbol recalled aloud how, in recent months, stray dogs had migrated from the towns surrounding Damascus to skulk in the city. They were not much like dogs anymore; their eyes were wolflike, and their jaws hung slack. Exhausted and not content with bones, they gnawed at the corpses that were too numerous for anyone to bury, especially after the larger battles. These dogs were no rumor but an established fact, confirmed by many. On the few occasions when he had gone out at night on some errand or other, Bolbol himself had seen them eating human flesh and wandering around the streets with a total lack of concern. Meeting a dog at night was horrifying now; it could be the end of you. When a dog's ferocity and hunger cause it to lose its gentleness, it will never again be content with merely barking. These dogs had tasted human flesh, and they couldn't forget it.

Hussein wasn't listening. He turned off the engine and began to smoke, reflecting on their ongoing disaster. These small unknown roads would get them even more lost. He was completely turned around. Suddenly, he told Bolbol that he was the one who had involved them all in this mess, and he had to take responsibility for it. If they didn't reach Anabiya by the afternoon, he would leave his siblings and the body by the roadside. He added that his father didn't deserve all this attention anyway; he had turned Hussein out of the house and never cared about him again. His voice was level and calm as he glared at Bolbol in the mirror. Bolbol surprised him by saying, "Why not just leave us now."

Hussein turned to his brother and then opened the side door of the bus and tried to drag the corpse outside on his own. While he worked, he made sure to say some horrible things to Fatima, who could still do nothing but cry. This labyrinth wasn't the place to settle scores, but Hussein was determined to throw the body out into the open air. Bolbol got out and was drenched by the rain within minutes, but he retained his self-possession. A strange force had sprouted in his heart, and he felt capable of murder. Yes, for the first time, he felt as though murder might, after all, be the best way to rid oneself of old grudges. He even caught himself thinking that either he or his brother would have to die: that neither Hussein nor he would ever feel safe so long as the other was alive.

Hussein's rage gave him strength. He held out against Fatima's pleading—she had thrown herself back on the bus's floor to kiss the feet of both brothers and was begging them to calm down. She spoke about the family, their father, their relationship, and their poverty, appealing to their noble-mindedness before she choked up entirely. Hussein cursed her and called her a whore, kicked her, and drove her out of the bus, where she fell to the ground. The sight of her, floundering in the mud, crying and unable to get up, was too much for Bolbol. He rushed at Hussein, grabbed him by the collar, and hauled him into the rain. The body, which Hussein had been trying to push and pull outside, fell over again, and their father's face got stuck in the narrow space between seats. Bolbol pushed Hussein onto the ground and kicked him, hard. He was crying now, too, and couldn't stop. Hussein got up and attacked Bolbol like a wild animal. He was solidly built and still fairly well muscled. The brothers struggled and fought for a few minutes before Hussein pinned Bolbol to the ground and punched him enough times to make Bolbol surrender. He let himself lie limp on the muddy ground, watching the overcast sky. He reflected that if his brother did manage to disappear, Hussein could at last distance himself from his childhood and invent the one he'd always wanted. And if Bolbol made it abroad and began a new life, he would be rid of his burdens forever.

The rain and the mud caused his body to lose all sensation. He licked the blood streaming down his face. He heard Hussein sobbing. Now all three siblings were crying. Bolbol wanted to get up but couldn't. With Fatima's help, he managed it after a few more tries. She led him back to the minibus, and Hussein followed them in silence. He started the engine and headed for the nearby village, still in total darkness.

The rain stopped, and the sky began to clear. When they reached the village, they realized it had been abandoned after some catastrophe. The houses were completely destroyed, obviously from aerial bombardment. The remains of furniture were strewn over the muddy roads. Everything was rubble. They proceeded slowly, seeking out anyone who might help them. The village had been small in any case, no more than forty houses lining a narrow paved road with a few other streets leading to a small square. Hussein stopped in this square and left the engine running. He honked the horn a few times in case anyone might still be around, but there was nothing here but desolation. Fatima mopped at Bolbol's wounds with her sweater, still crying silently. Hussein got out to explore. He didn't want to stay with the others; whatever little had remained between them was gone.

They had thought they would have a long time to talk during the journey. It would have been an appropriate occasion for reminiscence; after all, during his life, their father had only been able to gather his children on just such passing occasions, when a sense of duty, rather than desire, had been sufficient to corral them into the same place. Their father wouldn't hear of the seriousness of the rift between them, which grew daily, but this journey with his body hadn't offered either the time or the opportunity to voice their resentments of things that might have seemed small but, after many years, loomed large. Indeed, it had been a surprise to realize that it was four years since they had gathered together on any pretext at all, even for a special occasion. The general climate in the country gave them all an excuse. Families no longer braved checkpoints for gatherings. But the years before the revolution had been no better; none of them knew that they had all secretly wished to leave the family for good.

Bolbol believed, deep down, that Hussein was responsible for the first real crack in the edifice. That infamous night when he had picked up his suitcase and left the house had been a mortal blow to their stability, although later events may have seemed more catastrophic. At the same time, that departure had actually done

Bolbol some good; he felt that it had regained him his position in the house. When Hussein left, the clamor his presence always caused was over; it had been unbearable for a person as sensitive and weak as Bolbol. He had wanted to tell Hussein all the things he had smothered within himself for years, but there hadn't been a point during their journey when it wasn't either inappropriate or simply too dangerous to talk.

For one thing, Bolbol had also been astonished to see that Hussein really couldn't live at home anymore, after that night. And then the lack of anyone's interest or concern about Hussein came as another shock to Bolbol—until he stopped noticing it. Initially he'd believed it was all temporary, and that Hussein would return after a few days. But when Hussein was in prison, it was his friends who had followed up on his case and interceded as guarantors for his release; none of the family cared to do it. And despite all the intervening years, that night had stayed with everyone: never forgotten.

They had spent too long with the body. They were in no shape to continue. When they first set out from Damascus, they had been reasonably optimistic that they would eventually deliver their father's body as promised and were relatively united in their common goal to defend it. But after the first night, holding on to their own selves had become a goal that couldn't be ignored. The corpse was no more than a pretext. Deep down, all three thought that they couldn't sacrifice themselves for anyone. Holding on to their lives, despite the misery of them, was the real goal that everyone harbored.

Hussein walked off, down yet another empty road, and left the square. He came back a little later, climbed into the van, and took them to a house where a gaslight was burning and the door was open. Clearly he had spoken to its owners. He left his siblings in the vehicle and went into the single room left undamaged. An elderly woman came out and beckoned to Bolbol and Fatima to enter. Bolbol considered staying where he was, but Fatima took him by the hand and led him out. She kissed the old woman, thanking her for her generosity in hosting them.

Their father's body stayed alone in the minibus. Bolbol thought that if the dogs managed to find a way in they would tear it to shreds and that he wouldn't lift a finger to defend it; after it was over, he would pretend that he hadn't realized what was happening and that in any case protecting the corpse wasn't his responsibility alone. The others were also Abdel Latif's children and had an equal obligation to guard his remains.

The room was warm. The old woman's husband was inside. The old man and woman had to be about eighty. It was clear that they couldn't hear very well; they couldn't make out everything that the siblings were saying. Fatima behaved like the hostess, making tea and then warming some extra water in the kettle. She bathed her brothers' injuries, which had stopped bleeding. Bolbol saw that Hussein's eye was swollen, and in the large mirror hanging on the wall he saw his own face was full of bruises. They relaxed in the warmth and understood from the old woman that planes had bombed the village a dozen times. Its inhabitants had fled, and only two families remained. They had been waiting to die for many years now.

Gravely, Bolbol asked the old woman if it would be possible to bury their father in her village's graveyard. She was astonished at the question and said that there had been three hundred new graves in the graveyard in the past year alone. The Free Army had entered the village the year before, but hadn't been able to hold on to the territory for more than a year. Three of her grandchildren had fought alongside them, and after the great battle more than a hundred bodies had been strewn over the roads and fields. The villagers who were still alive had buried them before traveling to the camps in Turkey.

When the old woman mentioned the village's name, the siblings realized that they had gone in the wrong direction. The old couple was delighted they had come, however; it had been a long time since they'd spoken to anyone else. They told the story of death, bombardment, and battle with relish, before falling silent and asking the family about Anabiya. In his unadulterated country accent and using old-fashioned words, the man told stories about the time he went to northern Aleppo. He had bought straw there that day, but couldn't remember the name of the person who had sold it to him; the vendor had been determined to host him, as the hour had gotten very late. Although this had happened sixty years earlier, he spoke about his trip as if it had been yesterday and spent considerable time trying to remember the location of the house in case they knew the name of the person who had sold him the straw. The siblings couldn't bring themselves to care. Hussein stretched out on an ottoman and dozed off; when the old woman covered him with a worn blanket, he curled up like a child. The old woman led Fatima to a small larder to prepare some food for them. Bolbol felt warm and relaxed; there were only two hours until sunrise, and he spent them in a short, fitful sleep while their host went on trying to remember the name of the man who had sold him the straw.

They had to settle the matter. If they buried their father here, everything would be over. Fatima had regained some energy and, taking the kettle full of hot water, tried to clean her father's body. It was impossible to master the lethal smell, and the body's remaining fluids were oozing out of even more cracks in the form of diarrhea-like pus.

For the few hours they had spent in the warm room, Bolbol relaxed. Without preamble, he informed Fatima that their father had married Nevine and was shocked at her indifferent reaction, as if he hadn't said anything at all. She just laughed and carried on drinking tea. Hussein heard what Bolbol said but also made no comment. He reflected that the news given to him by his friend Hassan, who had been able to leave S during the siege, had been true. The marriage hadn't been a whim; it was the perfect story of a late love that had healed the wounds of his father's isolation and loneliness.

One day, Abdel Latif had gone with Lamia to the home of his old friend Najib, which was now the local field hospital. He was surprised to see Nevine with a strip of cloth bound around her head, and she seemed like a trained nurse as she cut and sterilized strips of muslin. She was assisting her first-born son, Haitham, the doctor, who was trying to save the wounded strewn throughout every room in the spacious house. Three other doctors, also from the town, had offered their help. The torpor of the mourners, of everyone, had transformed into inflexible rage.

Every family in the town had flocked to the field hospital after the Mukhabarat prevented the state clinics and hospitals from admitting any of the wounded. Everyone offered what they could: staggering quantities of medicines and muslin cloth were collected from houses and pharmacies, medical equipment was transferred in secret from the clinics, and a makeshift operating room was equipped in the basement after it had been cleared of provisions and the old dresses Nevine had carefully packed away ten years earlier after her husband died in a road accident on his way to Beirut.

Nevine was past sixty, still beautiful; there was a proud look in her eye that had sharpened during her marriage, which had been spent in never-ending battles with her husband's family. Haitham had graduated from medical college a few months before the revolution, and her younger son, Ramy, twenty-two years old, had graduated from business school the year before and gone straight into military service. Nevine couldn't bear the loss of Haitham after he was arrested at an air-force Mukhabarat checkpoint—they were notorious for their excessive cruelty—which had caught him leaving the town. When Nevine heard he had been arrested, she was struck with a terrible foreboding. Haitham hadn't known that treating the wounded was a grave crime in the eyes of the regime. In perfect innocence he acknowledged treating them in his family's house, and a week later a telephone call came for Nevine. A high-ranking Mukhabarat officer asked her to pick up her son's body from the military hospital in Mezzeh and then hung up on her.

No one slept in the small town that night. Police and Mukhabarat officers withdrew from the town, and the young people were ready to burn down any building belonging to the regime: the police station, the council building, the houses of informers who were individually known to them, supporters of the party. More than twenty thousand men, women, and children protested and raised their fists in the air in rage while they waited at the town gates for the bodies of Haitham and three of his friends, all murdered under torture in a Mukhabarat facility. One member from each family went to sign a receipt for the body of its son, who had officially died in a car accident or as a result of some mysterious illness.

The large car carrying the four bodies glided along in the

distance. Nevine was sitting in the front seat looking ahead at some invisible point, her face grim and unreadable. Abdel Latif was standing in the middle of the crowd, watching her. His tears streamed silently as his eyes, along with everyone else's, fixed on the bodies that the young men carried on their shoulders through every street, amid angry cries calling for the fall of the regime.

Nevine asked everyone carrying the bodies of Haitham and his friends to bring them to her house. They carried the three bodies and a black bag in which the dismembered lumps of her son's flesh were gathered. She coolly asked Haitham's doctor friends to reassemble his corpse. They tried to convince her that it would be useless. Why would a corpse care about that? Many people had buried whatever remained of their children when they hadn't received a complete corpse—but she was determined, and no one dared to dispute her. She waited for them by the door. The doctors worked for hours in a terrible state of mind. It wasn't easy to put their friend back together. Haitham's body didn't have any fingers, and the fate of those severed fingers remained a mystery, though his face and most of his other limbs had been returned. He had been shot in the back of the head before being cut up. When they were finished, the body was carried out in a shroud. Nevine lifted the shroud from his face and looked into his eyes for the last time, wanting her hatred to reach its fullest extent.

Abdel Latif's eyes didn't leave Nevine's face for a moment. He kept his distance to screen his anguish and didn't approach the mourners who stayed up with the four corpses all night. They put the bodies on a large wooden platform, surrounded them with flowers of every description, covered them with revolutionary flags, and left their faces uncovered. It was the utmost defiance. After the morning prayer, the bodies were buried in the new graveyard constructed on land Nevine had donated on the western side of her house. She now left that building so the whole house could be devoted to the field hospital and moved to her old small apartment close to Abdel Latif's house. She took very few things with her, just enough for a lonely widow in her sixties.

Over the following days, Abdel Latif spent hours every day managing the graveyard. He traced the outlines of walkways between the graves and left plenty of space to plant trees and flowers. He wanted it to be eternal, not just a simple cemetery. He hadn't expected that within two years it would be crowded by one thousand seven hundred graves. He arranged them in two sections: one for the young fighters, most of whom were no older than thirty-five, and another for the civilians killed by air raids, missile attacks, and every sort of heavy weapon used during the unceasing bombardment. Whole families were killed, including children and women and old people who couldn't get away. This territory of death became his whole life, and he spent most of his time looking after it.

At the time of Haitham's murder, when Abdel Latif was able to speak his few words of condolence, Nevine told him she was no longer afraid. Nothing in this life mattered to her anymore. He asked her to leave all the affairs of the graveyard to him and freed her from it completely. He spent his time arranging the paths, planting flowers everywhere, and distributing them over the graves. The graveyard acquired some narcissi, and every morning Nevine would watch Abdel Latif as he worked tirelessly. She expected him to invite her to join him in caring for the basil and rose seedlings. From the moment she had looked into the void, Abdel Latif also transformed and became like her. He no longer had anything to be frightened of. He was the bravest he had ever been. He would visit her in the evening and leave odd things by the door he said she had liked more than forty years before. He would remind her of moments so long past she couldn't remember if they had truly happened—had she really listened to those songs, smelled those roses? There wasn't much time left for the man granted inexhaustible energy by the revolution. He suffered from a surfeit of projects, discussed every detail pertaining to the town, joined every committee, swept the streets with young volunteers, filled placards with his beautiful calligraphy for the Friday protests.

Soon spontaneous protests were springing up almost daily, and in spring 2012 everyone was preparing to celebrate the revolution's first anniversary. The presence of armed men was nothing unusual by then, mostly defectors from the army, young men from the town, and other volunteers. They organized themselves and set up ambushes for vehicles belonging to the army and the Mukhabarat, who could no longer enter the town at will.

The battles intensified with each day. The angry debate between advocates of peaceful revolution and those of armed revolution was decided in favor of the armed faction, which possessed the force necessary to satiate everyone's hunger for revenge. Everything happened so quickly that Nevine couldn't believe armed fighters were wandering the streets at night in such numbers. The sounds of battle, which never stopped once they began, were all around her, and there was no longer any time for mourning. Whole families fled the town as the specter of death hovered over every house; university students left their studies, tradesmen and day laborers their work, and young men of every age and profession left their former lives, all to join the Free Army.

The city changed. Evenings were no longer safe. The columns of fleeing emigrants filled Nevine's heart with desolation. Her second son, Ramy, wouldn't listen to her pleas to leave the country after he defected from the regime army. At his first opportunity, he fled his barracks with some friends and joined a battalion in Deraa. They let him choose between crossing the border to Jordan, reaching the town of S, or fighting alongside them and sharing their fate. He chose the last option without hesitation, believing that every place was the land of the revolution, not just his home village. He was brave while he lived out his revolutionary dreams with his comrades. He didn't give much thought to what might happen to him; after all, everyone already despaired of their lives. Before joining the Free Army, he had seen everything; he needed no one to explain to him the principles of the regime and its army. He had already witnessed the looting and murder carried out by its penniless soldiers. Their orders were clear: kill indiscriminately, not excluding children, women, and the elderly. The last night before his defection, all his options seemed equally untenable. He wouldn't be a murderer of his own people, even if they shot him in the back of the head for refusing. On that great night when he finally escaped, more than forty soldiers defected all at once, and after they reached the other side, they split up, taking different routes and dispersing throughout the country. Some crossed the border into Jordan; others scattered among the armed battalions of the revolution; still others chose to go into hiding or to return to their families despite the difficulty of reaching them. Ramy fought until his last gasp. He was killed while liberating a military security facility in D, a battle that lasted more than twenty hours. Nevine was unsurprised when she heard the news of his death. She had known he wouldn't be able to live after his older brother's death. Their final conversation, three days before he died, had been upbeat. He told her about the comrades with whom he lived in a barren wasteland. He spoke loudly and boisterously, and she could tell he was frightened. He didn't tell her about the upcoming attack, which would most likely be a large battle, but reassured her and promised her he was trying to leave the country. She had been begging him with all her strength to do this; she didn't want him to die, she had already lost enough people, and she had no one left but him. But deep down she knew that death had him in its grip and wouldn't let him go. She was prepared to hear the news at any moment, and the grand words his comrade used to describe his sacrifice meant nothing to her. He had indeed been brave and had indeed fought fearlessly, but in the end he had died and left her alone. This was what she was thinking as she received condolences from the people of S; they had heard the news from their own contacts in the Free Army, which lamented him as a martyr and a hero.

Desolation gripped the land. As she wandered among the destroyed houses, Nevine reflected that she had nothing left to do in what remained of her life. Deep within, an inner void whistled with a cold breeze. She didn't care about the title "Mother of Martyrs" that was bestowed on women in her position. She sometimes wished her sons had been cowards and fled abroad as soon as possible, but at other moments she felt that everything had needed to happen as it did—that this was just another story of mass delusion. The shame and the silence they had lived through for years were exacting a price, and everyone would pay it, executioners and victims alike. Correcting hypocrisy may be hard, but it was inevitable in the end.

Before, she had loved life enough to want to live twice over, but there wasn't a lot left for her to see. She just wanted to see her sons' murderers cowering and afraid, to exchange her fear with theirs. Afterward she would close her eyes and die.

three

BOLBOL FLYING IN
A CONFINED SPACE

They left the village at dawn. The weak light revealed the extent
of the devastation. It seemed as if souls were still moaning under
the rubble, shreds of clothing and body parts strewn over the
abandoned fields and mixing with the skeletons of their goats and
mules. The dogs had scavenged what they could and left the rest
for the flies. It was complete and utter ruin. They had heard about
scenes like this, but here they were facing them and smelling them
for the first time in person, and it was quite a different thing. Bolbol
felt he should despise the foolishness of what had occurred between
himself and Hussein a few hours previously, but he wasn't ready to
comment or apologize, and believed that Hussein felt the same;

the grudges in their life had heaped up like worn-out clothes in a locked wardrobe.

The sky was still overcast and black. They regained the hope that the rotting body might eventually reach Anabiya. The grave, to be completed, needed a body. The shroud would give the body a new form, dignified and white. They guessed that it would take about two hours to travel the remaining distance, and then it would all be over. Their cousins would complete the task and bury their dead.

There had been no network coverage since the day before. Anyway, all their phone batteries had run out. Hussein had forgotten to bring his charger, but he hadn't regretted this when he saw that the towers along the road were all destroyed. They had no hope of calling ahead, and even if there had been a connection, it would have been no use. There was nothing to report. They were carrying the body and they were on their way to Anabiya. It was no longer important to get there at a particular time. They had lost their awe of death, and the body no longer meant anything to them—this morning they could have offered it to that pack of hungry dogs without a second thought.

They crossed a number of checkpoints held by the Free Army without difficulty. The fighters were good-natured and sympathized with their misery. They would uncover Abdel Latif's face and then cover it back up immediately, unable to bear the sight or stench. The siblings' identity cards came in handy here, at last; Anabiya was an influential region, and many of its sons were fighting in the Free Army, based in the countryside north of Aleppo.

When on rare occasions one of the local soldiers insisted on uncovering the entire body, he would see the scars and the splits and the marks on its face—the result of falling from the seat when

Hussein was trying to toss it in the mud—and assume Abdel Latif had been murdered under torture. No one would have believed this was the corpse of a man who had died peacefully in a hospital in the heart of the capital and that it was the neglect of his children and their utter lack of guile that had caused its current degradation.

In any case, carrying a health hazard that needed to be quarantined as soon as possible was a great help in speeding up their journey. Aleppo appeared in the distance, along with pistachio fields, traces of bombardment, and more widespread destruction. The sight of the ruined city revived their sense of connection to the region. They reached Aleppo just before ten. Fewer than seventy kilometers separated them from Anabiya. The closer they got, the stronger they felt; they were not strangers to these fields, their relatives were not far away, and here the family name was tantamount to an identity card in itself. Almost everyone was a relative under the pavilion of their clan, which always strove to uphold its connections—if little else.

Bolbol breathed a sigh of relief, opened his small window, and filled his lungs with the clean air of the countryside. The soldiers at the last checkpoint had urged them to take the outer road, which twisted and turned around the villages before it arrived at Anabiya; entering Aleppo itself would embroil them in another labyrinth they might not easily escape. They didn't know the road, but many travelers along the way helped them keep to it. They tried to hold off the feeling of power that comes from belonging to a herd; the closer they got to Anabiya, the more they tried to return to themselves, and reflected on their estrangement from this place that they didn't really know. And sure enough, Bolbol's eternal fear, that longtime companion, came back to him. He wished his own house were nearby; he would have bathed and purged his body of every stink that clung to him—from the body, the family, the revolution, and the regime—and gone back to his private peace and quiet. Fear might be his final haven, and it might even give him happiness. What had he cared about after he lost Lamia? He asked himself this, and his reply was: Nothing. The regime allowed him to eat and drink whatever he wanted, to spend his free time watching old Egyptian cinema. That little was enough for him; what would be gained by freedom? He had lost all his dreams, and it was difficult to break his cocoon and re-form himself. It was all too late. He was over forty, and all his dreams found expression in his own small house. His father had done a good thing by dying, Bolbol went on to reflect. They would sell his property—even if his big house was rubble now, the land was still worth something—and it would fetch enough for each of them to buy a small apartment in some poor area. Fatima would have to be content with a half-portion, as Sharia decreed; there was no way Hussein would allow her to dispute it. For some time now, Hussein had been dreaming of demolishing that hated house after his father's death. Since his expulsion from it, it held nothing for him but bad memories. He had never gone back.

Bolbol was sure he was overthinking everything, as usual. He told himself he was a spider dangling in a web of forgetfulness. His absence wouldn't cause pain to anyone; no one remembered him apart from Lamia, and even when she asked about him every now and then, it was a form of pity, nothing more. She needed him to prove to herself that she was still needed by others. The neighborhood vendors offered mute responses to his greetings; they might not hate him, but they had no affection for him either. He needed this web in order to be rid of the smell of his wife, the smell of the house they had shared that he hadn't ever wanted to live and die in. Of course he cared nothing about it and fled it very easily. He hadn't ventured any comment on it and spent seven years with his wife in a state of capitulation, raising no objection to the sofas she chose, the pictures she hung on the wall, or the plastic flowers she liberally distributed in every corner—though he found them strangely irritating and daydreamed about throwing them away. Their seven years together had been meaningless. Bolbol could now admit that he had been afraid of her, a peculiar kind of fear; he felt he didn't deserve her, even though she was exactly like most other women.

Within a few months of marrying, they had nothing to talk about other than television serials, which they both followed closely so as not to discover that they had been living in entirely different worlds from day one. They wanted to get the nuisance of living over and done with. His wife dreamed of the moment when she would lie on her deathbed, clasping Bolbol's hand: a rusty, sentimental image, and a common self-indulgence for people who worry that they might end up forgotten, that they're nothing more than an encumbrance to be tossed aside into oblivion. Bolbol's wife was prepared to sacrifice her entire life for this indispensable, dramatic image. She always said, with hope in her voice, "Goodness me, we're aging so quickly!" For her, life had three moments: birth, wedding, and death. What came in between was an isthmus that had to be crossed with a minimum of inconvenience. The only distinguishing characteristic Bolbol had liked about his wife was her lack of demands on his time and thoughts. She was content with not too much sex, considering it a method of communication at best, not a pleasure that should be experienced as fully as possible, at leisure and via all the senses.

The closer they got to Anabiya, the more oddly dejected Bolbol felt. A deep feeling of guilt weighed on him, although he didn't know why. Perhaps because of how he had distanced himself from Abdel Latif in his final years, and for no good reason. His father had suggested that Bolbol come back and live with him in the big house after his divorce, but Bolbol had made do with staying there for a few months before returning to his isolation. He had wanted to discover another self inside himself, the self he'd imagined throughout his life in his daydreams. He imagined himself brave like Zuhayr, worthy of a woman like Lamia, or foolish like Hussein, or a thinker like Sadiq Jalal al-Azm. He had adored the great man's books and way of life, a life Bolbol knew nothing about but still imagined, as he imagined so much else. He spent years alone in total isolation, drinking cheap booze on the weekend, eating cold, stale food, playing with himself, and getting more and more afraid. He couldn't drop down to earth, and he wasn't able to fly, as though he were hanging from a rusty nail in the sky.

Once, Bolbol hadn't enjoyed being alone, but he soon became more involved than he should have been in the search for his definitive form. Simply put, he hadn't done anything; his existence was tantamount to a vacuum. All he had done was observe other people's lives and discover they were like him: a collection of walking lumps taking up space, spending their lives striving to negate death. They repeated the same actions day in, day out, and when, like him, they noticed that time was passing, they made some futile gesture toward extricating themselves from their addiction to daydreaming instead of living—that ultimate human weakness. Faith was the path that came closest to providing some small comfort, but there, too, Bolbol didn't know how to take the first step. It would have taken a powerful faith to stave off the questions that kept him awake at night, not a half faith. He noticed the faces of his neighbors, when they returned from church every day, were more worried than they had been beforehand; even worship hadn't rescued them from their nagging questions, it seemed. It pleased Bolbol to affect a talent for reading human nature, but his lack of conviction in the truth of his intuitions always returned him to square one.

His daydreams became more and more all-encompassing. In them, his body was made anew; it was beautiful, slender, strong. In narrating his fantasies to himself he didn't mind one bit that he was borrowing clichés from the so-called plebs, especially because for the purposes of his daydreaming he had also purloined for his personal use a few of the gorgeous sculpted models appearing on the endless television commercials. Though sometimes, too, he imagined himself transported back to an earlier, more refined era, rather than indulging in the vulgarity of a modern-day setting, and considered himself outstandingly sophisticated for doing so— but manufacturing the past required an energy and imagination he had to admit he didn't possess. It is hard to discover that your self is nothing but a delusion. You consider yourself aloof from the oppression and power of the masses, but in the end you realize any individuality you might have perceived is a lie and that you're just one more worn-out pair of shoes walking the streets. Bolbol felt oddly comforted when his crowded daydreams finally spat out these conclusions shortly after he turned forty-two, and he realized all of a sudden that time had passed and he had never asked himself what he had been doing all these years.

For seven years, Bolbol had lived in the same alley where Lamia had lived as a student. Most of its residents were immigrants, penniless soldiers, public-sector employees, and *fellahin* who had migrated to the city from their distant villages. Most were Christian, but Druze and Muslims of all sects had moved in over the previous thirty years. Although the alley itself was no longer solely Christian, it had retained its churches and Christian graveyards.

When Bolbol went outside, he became a different person. He smiled at everyone walking on the street, didn't raise his voice to the grocers, averted his eyes when a woman passed him, and tried to help small children if he saw them stumble and fall. He thought that creating a good impression would help him to form friendships and forge a sense of belonging in his new neighborhood, but in his daydreams he lusted openly after all the women. He wished he were one of those men who chased every girl who dared to show her thighs to passersby. He would wait for an opportunity to take his neighbor Samar home after she finished work at the Post Institute so he could grope her under the stairs, bare her breasts, and bury his face in them—or, rather, he liked to pretend he might be the sort of reckless libertine who might do just that. But despite his kindness and his increasing flattery, his careful demeanor and his elevated morals, no one ever acknowledged him. They saw him as merely pathetic, another lost soul searching for some peace away from his rural family.

And yet, even still, he didn't know why his heart sank the closer they got to Anabiya. Maybe it was this: he didn't want to see his father's final defeat, returning after more than forty years to a home he had willingly left in search of himself—a self that was admittedly just a collection of slogans borrowed from a past era, but a self that his father had clung to nonetheless. It's hard to admit your emptiness after half a century of delusion, to be reduced to a suppurating mass giving out foul odors, with maggots sliding in and out of your sides ... Putrefaction is the real insult to the body, not death.

Now Bolbol understood why bodies are shrouded before burial. It is the last moment of dignity, the last image the deceased's loved ones should preserve before the body disappears from their eyes forever.

Bolbol looked at his watch; it was just after ten o'clock in the morning. The first opportunity he'd had in three days to indulge in one of his preferred imaginary scenarios—the ones in which he was handsome, reckless, and successful. Hussein's scowls in the rearview mirror were beside the point. Bolbol felt their task and their relationship would come to an end at the same time, as if their father had arranged it this way, giving them these three days to explore everything between them. And yet, contrary to this, he felt their relationship was the best it had ever been. Their fight had purified their souls of the residue of the past. Bolbol told himself that they had needed one last battle to go back to how they had been, two children who could erase a train from existence with the scribble of a pen or perhaps draw a calf on skis. People accepted all sorts of irrationality from children, as if respect for the imagination was bound to age alone. If they had remained children, neither would be afraid of the other.

Fatima closed her eyes and dozed for a few minutes. She, too, was afraid of reaching Anabiya. In a few hours she would be a true orphan. She couldn't rely on her brothers; they weren't selfish, just enormously weak. In fact, she thought, the presence of a single weak sister would have suited them perfectly, if they were strong. The strong always like to surround themselves with the weak, the better to demonstrate their strength.

Bolbol heard Hussein wake Fatima and ask her to get their identity cards ready; they were nearing a checkpoint. Bolbol opened his eyes and straightened up in his seat. He was happy to ignore

Hussein, who wasn't bothered by this and let him carry on daydreaming. Things went faster than expected. Hussein was smiling as he took the arm of a soldier, and they walked toward the minibus. The fighter was a relative on their mother's side, one of the many defectors from the regime's army in that area. He was a raw recruit, no more than twenty-two, and his strong rural accent reminded them of their father as he greeted them politely and introduced himself. Wisely, he ignored the deplorable corpse. He spoke into a radio to arrange a smooth and quick passage for them and told them about the upcoming checkpoint. He said that extremist fighters harassed travelers and advised the siblings to keep quiet and ignore any provocations. The villages they passed through were deserted. Most houses had been destroyed, and those that were left had been abandoned. They bore the marks of fierce battles. They could smell fresh death and saw clear signs of mass graves. Everyone wanted to forget and make the time pass quickly so this nightmare would be over. They easily passed the next checkpoint. By now they were very close to Anabiya, but they didn't recognize these villages or these roads. Nothing awoke any feeling in them, everything was the same, even the colors of the *fellahin*'s clothes were the same. Bolbol ignored Hussein's anxiety; they were lost, the road was almost empty, and he simply wanted to be rid of his burden and go back to his other life. Bolbol tried to scrutinize Hussein's face. He guessed that it was the last time he would see him. There was nothing between them anymore, but he was exhausted. He, too, wanted to be rid of the body, to be absolved of his promise to his father to bury him with his family, but he still felt moments of awful tenderness for their distant childhood. Images overlapped in a peculiar fashion; memories of his mother escaped him altogether, not wanting to keep still long enough to form a picture of them all as a family. Bolbol told himself that even mental pictures can be torn up: he couldn't get all of them into a single image. They had never been happy, and everything they'd revered was a fantasy. Hussein had rid himself of this delusion, only to exchange it for another. But the fact was that their father hadn't ever been as perfect as the image *he* had cared for more than the truth. He had been cruel; that was all. Burdened with constant fear of his past, present, and future.

In his later years, Abdel Latif had begun to renew his connections with Anabiya. He contacted his cousins, assured himself about his nephews and nieces. Abdel Latif felt a tenderness toward his hometown, but his pride prevented him from allowing himself the happiness of spending his last years near the graves of his loved ones: his wife, his sister Layla, his father, and his older brothers and sisters, of whom the only one still alive was Nayif.

At eighty years old, Nayif was still performing the same function, welcoming the prodigal sons of late family members. He would play this role dozens of times, sitting in the large room of his house, welcoming mourners and pointing out all the rules they would need to comply with, waiting for the relatives who lived far away and informing them of the necessity of undertaking their sacred duty. These were the only moments he could once again be the head of a family, venerated by all. He woke up at five every morning, ate breakfast, and walked to the graveyard to recite the Fatiha for everyone. He completed his promenade with a vain search for someone to talk to. Most of the young people had already abandoned the town for Aleppo. It was futility after futility for him. The days, all alike, accumulated, and he grew cynical while waiting to die. He retold the same stories he had already told thousands of times in the same words. And here he was now, waiting for the body of his last brother, so he could bury it. Abdel Latif would be the least painful, as Nayif's memories of the man didn't extend beyond childhood and youth. And, after the burial, Nayif would, as usual, disappear inside his house for a few months, waiting for his own death to arrive—a death that had already overlooked him so many times before. If he could only learn to forget, it might help him live longer; really, the best route for everyone would be to sweep away the dark rubble of memory and leave nothing behind but the clean white page Bolbol had spent his entire life trying to dream up for himself.

In these dreams, Bolbol once cast himself as part of another family—a family with a single, unified identity. In this family, Lamia was always mistress of his house and mother of his children. He even used to imagine it was Lamia in bed with him when he slept with his wife. But the more he repeated this dream, the more he summoned up her scent, the more it all lost its efficacy. Lamia, with her slim face, delicate lips, and slender body, became more like an affectionate mother than a sexy woman—useless for a man trying to get himself off on a lonely night.

The corpse was unbearable. It had endured three full days. The bloating was so bad now that the body looked as though it might burst at any moment. If it had been in the open air, the smell would have attracted every scavenger for kilometers around. Fatima held her nose, and Hussein opened the window to let out some of the intolerable stench. The body had turned into a putrid mass, no longer appropriate for a dignified farewell. It would be enough to recite a quick prayer over it and to throw a handful of earth into the grave and run.

They passed through more villages and were bewildered at seeing black flags raised over buildings both far away and nearby, along with the skeletons of tanks and burned-out military cars, all remnants of a battle that testified to its ferocity. For many of the dead, these desolate plains had been the last thing they had seen. Bolbol wasn't in a serene-enough mood to think about them. They arrived at the next-to-last checkpoint, where huge cement blocks distributed over the road were forcing the cars down to a crawl. Armed men appeared nearby and in the distance, aiming their rifles, all clothed and masked in black. Their headcloths indicated they belonged to an extremist group occupying much of the countryside to the north and east of Aleppo that was renowned for its terrifying ruthlessness.

The siblings waited their turn in silence. They no longer had anything to say; silence was the token of their desperation and fear. Hussein asked Fatima to cover up completely, and she wrapped her headscarf around her face. A masked man carrying a heavy gun opened the door of the minibus and immediately stepped backward, alarmed at the stink. He asked them to pull over and get out. He spoke with one of his comrades, and then three more armed men approached. Their accents revealed they weren't Syrian. One of them, a Tunisian, tried to speak in formal Arabic. The siblings explained again that they were on their way to Anabiya to bury their father's body, and they proffered their documents and identity cards. The Tunisian asked where in Damascus they lived, and they told him proudly that they lived in S, thinking the name would facilitate an easy passage through the checkpoint. He spoke with someone over the radio. He told Fatima to stay in the van and Hussein and Bolbol to follow him to a nearby building, where he asked them to wait.

Hussein and Bolbol sat down on a bare wooden sofa and proceeded to wait for more than five hours. Masked fighters passed back and forth, and while nothing about them pointed to their specific character or nationality, everything indicated their identity: their black clothes and masks, their long beards. They came and went from a large room in the heart of the building. Time passed with a peculiar slowness. No one spoke to the brothers. The building, which in the past had been some sort of governmental office, had been turned into the local headquarters of the extremist organization in control of the area. Guards emerged from the lower levels accompanied by blindfolded prisoners in chains, exhaustion clearly marked on their bodies and what was visible of their faces.

Hussein and Bolbol were more than ordinarily confused at this latest setback. Hussein tried to speak to one of the soldiers, but the man just glanced at Hussein in bemusement before continuing on his way. Later, this same man came back and beckoned them to follow him. They went into a small room containing a large table and a laptop and a single chair on which a masked man sat in full field uniform, turning over their identity cards. He spoke to them in a laughable attempt at formal Arabic, in an accent not too far away from their own, trying to enunciate each word properly. He said they would submit to being questioned about their religion and added that if they could simply answer a few questions correctly they would be allowed to pass. He didn't add anything else but waved at the masked fighter to take them to the Sharia judge's room for questioning. Before they left, he said that the organization was aware of their father's membership in the Baath Party fifty years earlier; equally, they knew they were also relatives of the late Lieutenant Colonel Jamil, who had been executed by the government forty years before. The past was catching up with them. Hussein now knew that their family name would hardly serve as a password among these people; it might even be a hindrance. They could be detained on account of the delusions of dead family members. He guessed at the identity of the man who'd ordered their transfer to the judge; Hussein was certain it was one of the three men from S who had joined this organization.

They left the room, trailing behind the fighter, who led them to another building. A large sign hanging on the door read SHARIA COURT. A group of women and men were waiting in a corridor, and despite the crowding, silence pervaded everywhere. The brothers moved through the crowd and, behind their escort, turned into a narrow passage that opened onto a large, dusty courtyard off which opened a number of doors, evidently locked. Huge men guarded these doors, their fingers on the triggers of their automatic rifles.

Bolbol entered the courtroom first; their escort asked Hussein to wait. Without preamble, the judge asked Bolbol simple questions about how many *rak'at* should be performed at each prayer time. Bolbol was taken aback. He counted and made a mistake in his answer. The judge asked him outright if he prayed and undertook all his religious duties, and Bolbol replied without fear that he did not, apart from fasting at Ramadan and giving alms. The judge asked him the extent of these alms, and Bolbol wasn't sure what to say. The judge then made him listen to a short recitation of the Qur'an and asked him which verse it was. Silence reigned as the judge waited for an answer. Finally, he asked Bolbol his opinion about this organization. Although Bolbol knew it would take all his courage to get out of this mess, he felt himself slipping into a deep, dark hole. Without a word, he allowed himself to creep slowly into this abyss. Speaking, he knew, would not be to his advantage. The judge directed a few more questions at Bolbol, who had no answer for any of them. He thought of saying something along the lines that, to him, religion meant good conduct, integrity, and devotion, but nothing came out. What he wanted was to slip back into his daydreams.

Bolbol's refusal to speak was irritating the judge. At last the accused summoned up all his energy and tried to explain about the body, about bringing it home to be buried, and Bolbol then affirmed that he would in future take care to carry out all his religious obligations; he would pray at every prayer time, he would listen to recitations of the Qur'an, and he would commit it to memory, as he had done when he was a child. The judge pointed. The fighter who had brought the brothers to court blindfolded Bolbol with a leather strip and took him through one of the rear doors and down a few steps. Bolbol heard a door clang and then felt a hand shoving him inside a cell.

Hussein passed his examination successfully. The judge asked him about how he performed his religious duties, and Hussein replied vehemently that he was a good Muslim and performed all his duties; he correctly explained the number of *rak'at* and the right way to perform ablutions, and thanked God fervently for the blessing of Islam. He was allowed to leave. As he left the court, the judge told Hussein to forget about his brother; he would be staying behind to complete a religious reeducation course.

Hussein left the building. When he reached the van he was astonished to find that Fatima had been struck mute. Five hours of waiting had paralyzed her vocal cords. She could only point to the corpse, from which dense clusters of maggots were slithering. Hussein set the minibus in motion and fled that horrifying place like a fugitive. He was afraid the maggots would soon be chewing on himself and his sister as well. He didn't much mind that Fatima was mute. He assumed it was only temporary, the result of too many shocks. At the next, "last," checkpoint, he asked one of the guards to help him call his family. There was only a short distance left to Anabiya. The maggots were multiplying uncontrollably, it seemed, climbing the windows of the bus and covering the seats. Fatima moved to the front, tried to speak, and couldn't. She knew she would never be as she was. She was mute, and that was that. She lost all desire to try speaking again and surrendered to her new world.

Hussein managed to get through to one of his cousins, who promised to come and meet him at the checkpoint. Hussein now disavowed all personal responsibility for the corpse. He couldn't wait for the dawn. He couldn't spend another night in a place where death was so rife, whose only inhabitants were widows and orphans. He felt every ounce of the idiocy of bringing his father's body all this distance. It was the same old story here: the houses on both sides of the road were utterly destroyed, all the villages were abandoned, the marks of aerial bombardment were clearly visible, and no one cared about the skeletons.

Hussein didn't have to wait at the checkpoint long. Car lights gleamed in the distance, and he felt oddly relieved when his cousin Qasim strode toward him, armed, with three other cousins. Hussein realized that his young cousin had grown up quite a bit in the past four years; he remembered a shy teenager trying to convince his family to let him finish his studies abroad. Now he wore a long beard. The cousins were shocked at the terrifying number of maggots crawling from the corpse and all over Fatima, who had given up and no longer bothered trying to brush off the ones clinging to her clothes. They wasted no time in asking for the details of the difficult journey. Qasim asked Fatima to switch to the other car; Hussein told his cousin that Bolbol had been arrested at the checkpoint of the Islamic extremists. The cousins exchanged glances and decided to handle the matter quietly, assuring Hussein everything would be fine, and there was no need to worry. The remainder of the trip took less than an hour. They didn't stop at the checkpoints along the way but made do with a quick greeting to Qasim's colleagues, also armed, who all exchanged a few words of condolence with him. There was a swift discussion in the other car about Bolbol and some ambiguous words about future interventions and threats should Bolbol continue to be detained. Fatima was afraid for Bolbol. She had surrendered to her own fate, but his rested in the hands of a family he didn't know and who didn't know him. Still, custom decreed that their northern bloodline, blighted since time immemorial, should be defended.

Hussein regained his equanimity. He tried unsuccessfully to forget about Bolbol. He kept thinking of how close they had been back in childhood, though there had also been all their petty fights as a result of Hussein constantly teasing his brother for his puny size, sage opinions, and perpetual good manners. It was in their childhood that they found safety and comfort—more so than in their present and future, anyway; it was the only thing they had, they thought, that others might envy them. But the truth was, that too had been an illusion; theirs had been no different from any other lower-middle-class childhood, with a mother darning their socks and letting out their clothes as they grew, and a father whose delusions dictated his life and made him overlook all sorts of telling details. He was sure that his children would become noted in society, but the time when that might still have been possible was definitively over. The only one left of Abdel Latif's generation was his brother Nayif, who had refused to leave his village. He cared for the graves of his siblings and friends, buried them quietly, and held one 'aza after another in the living room that hadn't changed since his youth.

The road was easy despite the winter storms and the rain that never stopped falling all night. Hussein relaxed. In the end, the body would be safely delivered to its rightful place after all. At midnight, when they reached Anabiya, the lights were on in Nayif's house. They heard the murmurings of the men who were waiting inside for the body and the sound of cups of tea being passed around. Qasim was strict and prevented anyone from seeing the body. He decided that the burial would take place at the morning prayer; they were used to burying the dead at dawn, as air raids rarely started before seven in the morning. Another young man went with him to the graveyard to dig the grave. Qasim paid no attention to his father Nayif's instructions, nor to his late uncle's wishes. Abdel Latif had chosen to be buried in his sister Layla's grave, or so Hussein had told them, whereas Nayif ordered his son to bury Abdel Latif next to their mother's grave, in accordance with their mother's wishes. She had died forty years before and had mentioned she wanted her children's graves to be near her own. But the armed young man considered such wishes an outrageous luxury. The grave Qasim dug for his uncle was distant from his other family members and easily lost among the profusion of graves. Layla stayed alone, aloof, and repudiated, surrounded by empty space on all sides. Every now and then, unknown young people would plant a rosebush on her grave, but it would soon wither and die. Her tale lived on despite the family's efforts to erase it. Stories here might change over time, might be told in new ways, but they never died. Hussein seemed content and basked in the praise for being so brave in carrying out his father's last wish. Nayif spoke briefly to Hussein and suggested he and Fatima sleep for a few hours; tomorrow would be a hard day. Most of the village's inhabitants had left, but they still had to hold an 'aza and wait for relatives and friends. Before Hussein fell asleep, he heard shots being fired in the air and movement in the next room where they were washing his father's body before shrouding it. He clearly heard his cousins say the maggots should be killed in boiling water. More bodies arrived, fighters from the village who had been killed on distant battlefronts. Hussein heard voices discussing the names of the new casualties, but he didn't care. He curled up like a hedgehog and tried to sleep. His body was exhausted and his soul perturbed, and a terrible estrangement from everything and everyone around him had taken root. He wished he could go right home in the morning. He didn't want to see Bolbol or Fatima ever again; he didn't want to know anything about his father's grave or to visit it and care for it. He slept and no longer heard the loud voices. The volleys of gunfire were repeated, announcing the arrival of more bodies; or maybe they were the same bodies and their comrades were chasing away their fears by putting new holes in the sky, Hussein reflected, without caring either way. He had a strange dream he wouldn't forget for a long while: Bolbol was floating, swimming in the sky and smiling, free as a bird. He was like an angel as he swam in space, scattering roses over the hordes of pedestrians in the Salhiya quarter of Damascus.

But at that very moment, Bolbol was convinced that his death was imminent. He had no hope of leaving this cell, which contained more than twenty prisoners who had committed terrible crimes indeed: One of them had been caught drinking in an olive grove— his breath had given him away at the checkpoint. Another had cursed God in the souk. The rest, like Bolbol, hadn't observed their religious duties, though they seemed less afraid than the other condemned and acted largely indifferent. Most of them had been here for some time, waiting for an end to the negotiations that might secure their freedom. Strangers lost on the road, sons from families who had tried to flee across the Turkish border, others accused of being agents of the regime: they all lined up every morning in the religious classes given by a sheikh who cursed them and called them "deviants from the true path." From his first moment in the cell, Bolbol's senses felt as though they had frozen solid. He couldn't sleep in such bitter cold.

In the early morning, the door was opened, and a huge prison guard ordered the prisoners to get up; it was time for ablutions and the dawn prayer. Everyone performed their ablutions, including Bolbol, who thought the icy water might end him entirely, but he endured the pain in silence and didn't exchange a word with anyone. He was deeply upset, paid no attention to what was happening around him, having surrendered to his fate. He reflected that he wouldn't feel too sad about it if he were killed.

It had been the winter of 2012 when, for the first time, he began to question the worth of what was happening throughout the country. The images of the young murdered protesters were engraved on his memory, and other pictures of crowds of mourners with bullets raining down on their heads. With equivalent hysteria, regime supporters called for even more brutality. On their websites, he read articles written by boys and young men who appeared to come from educated families, judging from their Facebook pictures. They castigated the regime for not having burned Deraa to the ground, adding sardonic recommendations about turning the city into potato fields. The majority of regime supporters approved the idea of burning the country from north to south, applauding the slaughter as if they had tremendous confidence in victory. This hope had been diminished four years later, but they still called for various cities to be pulled down on the heads of their inhabitants. On the opposite side, there were other groups undertaking the same actions, calling for regime supporters to be burned in their beds and cheering their murder. Bolbol would muse on this in silence and wonder what could be achieved by either side through a victory oozing with blood.

Bolbol reflected that when the walls of fear around you crumble, there's only a strange emptiness inside. Nothing can fill it but a new type of fear, perhaps. You don't know what to call it, but it's still fear, no different in flavor, really, than the old type. It makes you feel you're the only one afraid in a tide of humanity that regards dying as the ultimate solution to the enigma of living. And it was true, mass murder or suicide could be a kind of solution, Bolbol supposed. He often imagined whole communities committing suicide in protest against a life so soiled. He himself couldn't bear living among a human flood goaded to such massacres, who evoked old feuds from the depths of history to justify their own slaughtering. He was convinced this was his own personal problem, not the problem of humanity as a whole: each human losing themselves, then finding themselves again by banding together with the other humans who seemed to most resemble themselves, or else transforming themselves in order to resemble those groups . . . all drowning in emptiness.

He had watched his neighbors in the first days of the revolution and heard a large and astonishing collection of slogans it was impossible to believe, broadcast by all as if they were fact. His astonishment was redoubled when he saw men, whose names indicated they were members of the ulema, the religious authorities, appear on state television to analyze and confirm this propaganda to the delight of the heavily adorned female broadcasters who seemed confident of the upcoming victory. Bolbol couldn't bear the commentaries that stated that the protesters had taken to the streets purely under the influence of drugs. One analyst took two hours to explain how the government of an unnamed reactionary country had promised each protester five hundred liras and a kebab to take part in a conspiracy to overthrow the regime. It was easy enough to blindly direct the herd of supporters anywhere you wanted them to go. Questions almost choked Bolbol. For him, the most disturbing thing was the fear that grew and embedded itself in his depths. Several times, he felt a pressing need to speak to Lamia and admit that whenever he went outside, he worried his neighbors would rape him. He avoided even looking toward the windows, and the obsession with spying he had enjoyed for several years no longer interested him. It was fewer than fifty meters from his house to al-Harra Square, where he waited at the stop for the official bus to the institute, and where he returned after work on the same bus to the same spot. On weekends he shut himself away in his house, keeping the windows open so the neighbors could have no grounds for suspecting he was hatching some conspiracy. He was utterly exhausted by defending himself and imagined everyone was watching him, but at the same time he was incapable of moving elsewhere. Renting a house to a man with his identity card would be considered a crime, and he couldn't go back to S. He couldn't bear to look his wretched neighbors' victims in the eye as they were cursed so loudly and openly. Several times Bolbol hid his background, inventing stories about there being a mistake in his paperwork, how he wasn't born anywhere near S . . .

Now here he was, walking with a bowed head alongside twenty others to be taught how to pray at gunpoint. He performed his freezing ablutions, following the instructions of someone in a mask, and felt ridiculous as all the prisoners lined up behind another masked man who explained each step of the prayer. Everything was ridiculous . . . After prayers, what would these people do with them? Would they kill them? Would they exchange them for ransom? Would they make them into slaves? Bolbol didn't care in the slightest; to him, the imperative thing was that by now his father's body would be underground, embracing the bones of his beloved sister, whose burning image had given him sleepless nights till his dying day. Yes, surely not a day had passed without his being reminded of his cowardice. His failure to defend her made him complicit in her suicide, and her choice to burn on the roof on her wedding day was a clear message to everyone: she would never forgive them. She could have committed suicide in a myriad of ways, but she wanted her story to live. She wanted to die in flaming defiance of the lies that would be told about her; she had chosen to die rather than live with a man she didn't love.

Shortly after the sunset prayer, the guard came in and asked Bolbol to follow him. He walked behind the guard unquestioningly and was led to the room of a man who called himself a Sharia judge, where his uncle Nayif was waiting for him, having signed a pledge to instruct his nephew in his religious duties. His uncle kissed him and embraced him, offered his belated condolences, and took him by the hand, and they left. His cousin's car was waiting outside. Everyone called him by his original name, Nabil, which he had almost forgotten, it was used so rarely. He liked regaining his original name and resolved not to let anyone call him Bolbol anymore. A heavy silence settled in the car. No one asked Bolbol any questions, and they kept Fatima's muteness from him. His uncle exchanged a glance with his cousin; they were wondering about his sanity. His vacant eyes, trembling hands, and twitching body all indicated that something traumatic had happened to him overnight. Bolbol understood and assured them that the only reason for his appearance was the biting cold, saying that he would soon recover. When he reached the ʿaza, the women started crying again. Weeping, Fatima rushed toward him and embraced him. She tried for the last time to recover her voice, and her sobs grew louder when she realized she still couldn't speak. Muteness had taken total possession of her. Bolbol wished it had been him rather than Fatima; he envied her eternal silence. Still, he was moved at having finally arrived; he felt great gratitude for being among people who were able to protect him. It had been a long time since they had left Damascus.

Hussein was ignoring him, which hurt. He'd considered it sufficient to ask Bolbol briefly if the extremists had tortured or harassed him. All Bolbol could hear in these questions was his brother saying *I hate you*, so he made do with a brief gesture of dismissal and returned to gazing into a far corner of the spacious but cozy guest room.

Bolbol bathed in warm water, and his cousin gave him clean pajamas. He ate dinner with everyone but kept silent, surrounded by sympathy on every side. When he lay down in bed, he was assailed by nightmares; he felt he was hanging from the ceiling of a wide room, flying in a narrow space, crossing a nearby border, and beginning a new life. Despite the nightmares he was able to sleep for a few hours and woke up at dawn. He didn't yield to the temptation of remaining in the warm bed but got up at once and walked to the graveyard with his cousin. He stifled his anger when he saw his father's grave had been dug at a distance from all the others. He hadn't been buried beside his sister's grave, and so his last wish had not been carried out after all. Nor, indeed, had he been buried near his mother or his grandmother. The grave was isolated in a distant corner of the graveyard. He had lived at a distance and had to be buried at a distance—but in the end he had a grave, and that was no trivial thing. They didn't linger; Bolbol stayed just long enough to uproot some dead weeds from his mother's grave. He felt an overwhelming grief; perhaps she'd never known that she hadn't meant anything to his father, that she had been just a wife. Everything that had been said about their great love story had been a lie no one dared to refute even now; the living had to keep telling hypocritical stories about the dead. Bolbol didn't protest or wonder why they had buried him so far from his loved ones. He thought, later, that a distant grave was the truest, most appropriate one for his father. His aunt hadn't wanted anyone from her family to share her grave; she had wanted a solitary resting place, where no one would dare to sleep but her. Her legend grew day by day, exciting the imagination and widening the distance between herself and the living. Many had considered moving or even destroying her grave, but none of the living dared to raise a finger. Even her brother Nayif, the last witness, hadn't been brave enough; he asked everyone to be content to forget. The story would endure, and any attempt to erase it would only reignite it. Layla shouldn't be turned into the patron saint of lovers. She should be left to lie quietly in oblivion, without notice, in a neglected grave without a marker.

On the morning of their third day in Anabiya, Bolbol decided to cross the border to Turkey. One of his cousins drove with him in case he needed any help. The crowd at the Bab al-Salamah crossing was frighteningly large; thousands of people were waiting to cross. Bolbol thought then that his desire to start a new life was basically just another lie; he knew he was too weak to manage it.

A new life meant a new unknown, and that required strength. He missed his house, and the repetitive moments of his work and his office, his pickles, his fear of the fascists who raised their rifles and wanted to plow through Deraa and plant it over with potatoes. His cousin sensed his confusion; his expression changed, and he suggested they go back to Anabiya and think again. He took Bolbol by the arm and drew him away. He was starting to be convinced that Bolbol had lost his mind; he couldn't let him cross the border when his silent face showed plainly that he couldn't tolerate the consequences of such a decision. On their way back to Anabiya, Bolbol's cousin assured him that they could help him to cross into Turkey any time he liked.

At dawn on the fifth day, their cousins accompanied the three siblings to the outskirts of Aleppo. The checkpoints were all opened to them, and the journey was easy. They bid each other goodbye at the last checkpoint before his cousins turned around to go back. The siblings felt relieved and cheerful; they had carried out their father's last wish, and they weren't carrying a body with them. A long silence settled over the three of them. Fatima was content to sleep all the way back. No longer able to speak or nag, she, too, wanted to go back to her house. Hussein and Bolbol ignored each other.

When they reached Damascus in the evening, Bolbol got out of the minibus and raised his hand in a wordless farewell to Hussein. He had appreciated his silence. His neighborhood wasn't far, and he walked back through the shadows along the Corniche Highway. It was nine o'clock when he opened his front door. The smell of his father wafted through every nook of the house. Bolbol sat there in darkness. He felt more alone than he had ever felt. He resolved not to let anyone call him anything other than his original name, Nabil, from now on. He felt as though his head had been gnawed by the dogs that had attacked them and that he, too, was now just a cadaver. He got up and put his head under the hot-water tap. He wanted his features to melt and disappear. His silence would last all night. He walked to his bedroom, slipped into bed, and felt like a large rat returning to its cold burrow: a superfluous being, easily discarded.

A NOTE ABOUT THE AUTHOR

Khaled Khalifa was born in 1964 in a village close to Aleppo, Syria. As well as being a screenwriter, he is the author of four novels, including *In Praise of Hatred*, which was short-listed for the International Prize for Arabic Fiction, and *No Knives in the Kitchens of This City*, which won the Naguib Mahfouz Medal for Literature in 2013. He lives in Damascus, a city he has refused to abandon despite the danger posed by the ongoing Syrian civil war.

A NOTE ABOUT THE TRANSLATOR

Leri Price is a translator of contemporary Arabic fiction. Her translations include *In Praise of Hatred* and *No Knives in the Kitchens of This City*, by Khaled Khalifa, and *Sarab*, by Raja Alem. Her translation of *No Knives in the Kitchens of This City* was short-listed for the 2017 ALTA National Translation Award and the 2017 Saif Ghobash Banipal Prize for Arabic Literary Translation.

meditations for pregnancy

36 Weekly Practices for Bonding with Your Unborn Baby

Michelle Leclaire O'Neill, Ph.D., R.N.

Andrews McMeel Publishing

Kansas City

The material in this book is intended for education. It is not meant to take the place of treatment by a qualified medical practitioner or therapist. No expressed or implied guarantee as to the effects of the use of the recommendations can be given or liability taken.

04 05 06 07 08 RR2 10 9 8 7 6 5 4 3 2 1

Library of Congress Cataloging-in-Publication Data
O'Neill, Michelle LeClaire.
    Meditations for Pregnancy : 36 weekly practices for bonding with your unborn baby / Michelle LeClaire O'Neill.
        p. cm.
    Includes bibliographical references
    ISBN 0-7407-4711-8
      1. Pregnancy. 2. Meditation. I. Title.

    RG525.O43 2004
    618.2—dc22

RG
525
.043
2004

                                                                        2004055090

Book design by Desiree Mueller

For my children,
Brendan, Erin, and Maria,
and my granddaughter, Ava

Suddenly, as if without a reason,
Heart, Brain and Body and Imagination
All gather in tumultuous joy together.

—Harold Munro

contents

INTRODUCTION
The Experience of Expecting

Within this book, you'll discover simple weekly ways of connecting to your body, your emotions, and your yet-to-be-born baby. These connections will help to create the smartest, safest, most intelligent, and most valuable beginning for your uterine guest and yourself.

The experience of your baby growing inside becomes more available to you when you can feel her moving inside you. The purpose of this book is to help you to enhance this experience by becoming aware. By being aware, you share directly in the union between you and your baby, and you will experience the richness of your pregnancy. This book is not about the concept, the science, or the idea of pregnancy. It is about the loving relationship between you and your baby that begins at conception. You can become aware through your senses and through sensations from this new connection to your unborn baby and from your cellular memory of past connections in the world. You bring to this developing love your awareness of each moment and an awareness of thoughts and emotions that might otherwise remain dark and silent to your mind, thoughts, and emotions. These may affect your perceptions without your even realizing it. Your experience of this pregnancy, of this amazing connection between you and your baby, is not merely the result of your sensation of bodily changes such as your growing abdomen and your omnipresent uterine guest. It issues from all your past perceptions and your present realizations. The kind of prenatal mothering and nurturing that you do and the kind of mother you want to continue to be or become are established by your present relationship with your baby.

This book is about your consenting to accept your present feelings, both physical and emotional, and to change those feelings, thoughts, and perceptions that you feel will not benefit your growth and development as well as the growth of your baby and your evolving interaction. This *umbilical code*, which is what I call it when I work with pregnant women like you, is about the meaning of this relationship for you, your intuitive and concrete connections to your baby, both conscious and unconscious. The true awareness of the umbilical code comes about through your stillness, your mindfulness, your willingness, to feel all that is revealed to you. To fully develop the expression of meaning behind this code you need to take time for reflection of this experience, time to courageously connect spirit to spirit with this new reality in your life, in your body, in your mind, in your heart, and in your soul. The essence of your pregnancy is not your baby growing inside you or your growing belly; it is the umbilical connection, the flow, the unique reality of the two of you as one and as two separate yet equal beings. It is the vital union of love between you.

Only you can choose to participate as fully as possible with the umbilical code. You may keep silent your feelings from the world but there are no secrets between you and your baby. The umbilical code is a wordless yet direct message, a direct line that is easily deciphered by your baby. This connection will frame his perceptions, his emotions, his intellect, his mind, his body, and his spirit. The secret of the umbilical code is that nothing is disregarded by your fetus. Yes, your emotions and the food you eat translate into chemicals that are passed on directly to your baby, who is formed by them and affected by them long after your physical separation at birth.

Pregnancy presents a time of possibility for an amazing transformation for yourself limited only by your lack of desire to participate or by fear. I hope you are able to detach from your past so that you may fully experience the drama of the now of your pregnancy. I hope that you will be able to listen to your bodily sensations and to your emotions. I hope you will give yourself permission to feel them so that you are not limited by them. The umbilical code allows the possibility of your own rebirth. You deserve to become all of who you are, as does your baby.

Through this union of love, all things are possible.

MEDITATIONS for pregnancy

HOW TO USE THIS BOOK and CD

Choose a time each week to read your meditation; they are numbered by the week of your pregnancy to make it easy to keep track. The purpose of each weekly meditation is to help you understand what is going on in your body and to help you be aware of your baby's presence and of your feelings. The meditations are simple and efficient ways of getting you to be present in the now and in touch with this special time in your life and your baby's life.

After reading the meditation, read the affirmation and suggestions. Make a decision to do at least one of the suggestions each week. It is best to make your goal attainable and measurable, for it is better to make a goal easy and meet it than not to meet it and feel like a failure.

Your participation will enhance your peace of mind, your baby's growth and development, and the peace and serenity of your baby. The bonding between you and your baby will also be improved.

Take time once a week to rest and listen to the CD that is included with this book. It will calm your emotions, help you to carry your healthy baby to full term, and relax your nervous system. It will also prepare you for the relaxation that is imperative for a calm, centered, and safe birth, whether it is natural, induced, medicated, or a C-section.

Have fun, and "begin with the magic"!

SECOND MONTH

WEEK 5

Peach blossoms fallen on running stream pass by;
This is an earthly paradise beneath the sky.
—Li Bai

This week your backbone is forming. Some of your vertebrae are in place, and somehow my body knows how to care for and develop this wonder that you are. I hope that my strength and your strength will give you the emotional support to one day stand up for what you believe.

Your brain is more developed now. You are a living being within me, one who can now sense and feel. My thoughts, I realize, become feelings that I send to you. I must take care of what I think and send you nurturing thoughts. I shall relax as much as I can and send soothing messages to you as you float peacefully within me.

You now have buds for your arms and legs. I visualize them forming and wish them well in their growth. One day I'll kiss your tiny toes and feet; you'll grasp my finger and I'll let you hold on for as long as you want. You're receiving so many wondrous gifts in such a short period of time and I bet you're accepting them with ease.

> **Like my own miraculous spine, I can be flexible yet strong. I can accept the changes in my body and rejoice in the new life that grows through these changes. Today I ask for the flexibility to allow this miracle.**

In the broad daylight
Thou art unseen,
but yet I hear thy shrill delight.

—Percy Bysshe Shelley

This week, I will:

- Take my prenatal vitamins daily to help your growing body and find at least one day to practice a few of my stretching exercises to keep my spine flexible.

- Sip miso soup or ginger or peppermint tea if I'm having nausea or morning sickness to calm my stomach and to provide hydration. (I won't use ginger or ginger tea after the first trimester, however, because it may cause miscarriage.)

To make miso soup, take 1 tablespoon fresh yellow or white miso paste and dissolve in 1 cup boiling water. Drink warm. This is also good to sip throughout labor because it helps maintain proper pH balance in the body. Fresh miso is sold in many supermarkets and most health-food or natural-food stores.

week 6

That's the wise thrush; he sings each song twice over
Lest you should think he never could recapture
That first fine careless rapture.

—Robert Browning

You have two folds of tissue that will grow to be your sweet ears. The magical convolutions of your ears are taking place inside of me. May you hear the sounds of love and equality and peace and serenity and joy. The lenses of your eyes are now appearing and—guess what?— there is a tail apparent at the end of your spinal cord, a remnant that connects us to our primal ancestors. This tail will disappear with time, yet may the spirit of freedom, of swinging from tree to tree or walking with tail erect and proud or wagging with delight, remain with you.

You're getting so many wondrous gifts in such a short period of time and I bet you're accepting them with ease. I wish I could say the same. Sometimes I feel a bit anxious about being a mother. In fact, I'm not sure I have even come to terms with being a daughter yet, or a partner. Maybe I can learn from you and just grow and develop in new ways along with you. Perhaps I need to see through new lenses in my own eyes. Perhaps I ought to look differently at some things.

With my own eyes I can see that change can be good: change from winter to spring, when birds gather twigs for their own babies. And the changes that seem bad, perhaps they will slowly evolve into something else, disappearing like the remnant of the tail we all once had. I can become the mother you deserve, accepting change with grace and ease, and welcoming the new into my life.

Your clear eye is the one absolutely beautiful thing
I want to fill it with color and ducks
The zoo of the new.

—Sylvia Plath

This week, I will:

- Choose vibrantly colored foods to enjoy the vitamins they bring you and me: bright orange carrots, green and red cabbage, purple eggplant, white cauliflower, and bright red beets. They will be a feast for my eyes while they help yours grow!

- Observe my own reactions, trying to accept changes with grace and ease: the roundness of my belly and the extra sleep I need.

KITCHARI RECIPE

This is a healing food for pregnancy and is especially good postpartum. Make this ahead and keep it in the freezer or refrigerator to reheat when you're too tired to cook.

1.5-inch piece of fresh ginger, cut into pieces (fresh ginger can be used up until week 10 of pregnancy and during postpartum; *do not use fresh ginger* during the second and third trimesters of pregnancy)
2 tablespoons unsweetened shredded coconut

1/2 cup chopped fresh cilantro
1/2 cup water
3 tablespoons ghee (clarified butter; can be purchased at Indian food stores or natural-food stores)
1/2 teaspoon ground turmeric
1/4 teaspoon sea salt, or 1 tablespoon fresh miso paste (yellow or white miso is best)
1 cup yellow mung dahl (mung dahl can be purchased at Indian food stores or natural-food stores; mung dahl nourishes all the tissues of the body and is a healing food; it detoxifies cells)
1 cup basmati rice
6 cups water

Put ginger, coconut, cilantro, and 1/2 cup water into blender and liquefy. Heat ghee over medium heat in large saucepan and add the blended mixture, turmeric, and salt or miso. Stir to mix well and then add mung dahl, rice, and 6 cups water. Bring to a boil and boil uncovered for 5 minutes. Cover, but leave lid slightly ajar to allow steam to escape. Turn heat to simmer and cook for 25 to 30 minutes, until rice and dahl are tender. Makes six servings.

week 7

To see a world in a grain of sand,
And a heaven in a wild flower,
Hold infinity in the palm of your hand,
And eternity in an hour.

—William Blake

You are growing inside me, and by the end of this week you'll be a half-inch long. I'll help you this week in your big stretch by eating well and taking prenatal vitamins. By this week, your heart has started to beat inside your tiny chest. It is now truly yours. Our heart rates are different and yet in many ways I am responsible for the way yours beats, as my rhythm affects your rhythm. To help create a peaceful environment for you, I'll walk mindfully and do some stretches to soothe and calm myself.

Right now, your sweet face is forming. This week it flattens and you get little openings for your nose. I wonder whose nose you will have, and whose would I like you to have. Of course, it doesn't really matter as long as you can inhale and exhale easily through your nasal passages and as long as you can appreciate and differentiate smells. This week, I'm going to have fun smelling all the different spices in the pantry. Maybe I'll even take you to the woods or a garden so I can send you the excitement of other scents. I know the smell I'm looking forward to the most, though: your sweet, new baby scent.

This week you also begin to grow muscle fibers. Maybe you can even make micromovements. How interesting it must be to move a muscle for the first time. What a busy week you're having, and I thought I had a lot to do!

As I breathe through my nose, I think of the miracle of your growth. I realize that each fiber of my being is influencing each fiber of your new body, and I take the time to calm myself to observe what makes me angry or sad or joyous. I can observe my feelings and find positive ways to surround you.

Let even obstetricians fall quiet,
For Chloë is on her latest diet
So rapidly our Chloë passes
From bananas to wheat germ and molasses.
First she will eat but chops and cheese
Next only things that grow in trees.

—Ogden Nash

This week, I will:

- Choose foods to help you grow. I'll eat whole grains, leafy green spinach and kale, arugula or Swiss chard. Maybe I'll even try sea vegetables or explore the scents of fresh herbs as I shop, celebrating your new nose.

- Allow any feelings of mine that arise. If they are upsetting, I will be gentle with myself as I try to observe the feelings and understand them.

WEEK 8

Each cell has a life
There is enough here to please a nation.
—Anne Sexton

Well, you are no longer an embryo. You have now graduated to a fetus and by the end of this week you'll be all of an inch long. You still don't look like the final you, but by now you have a jawline and your facial features are becoming clearer.

Your head is about half your size. May your head continue to be strong and full, and your thinking be healthy and creative and adventurous. I hope I can guide you that way, and with such a good start in life, who is to say what your limits and what your potential might be?

You are also developing your tooth formation. One by one they align above the smooth skin of your gums. You were once just a gleam in my heart's desire, and now you have tooth buds secreting enamel and dentin. Some months after you are born, they will break through your gums and then you'll have twenty magnificent baby teeth.

Although I can't see you, I can feel the surge of your presence within me. What a wonderful thing you are: bit by bit you're coming together and becoming you. The surge of you fills me and makes my heart sing. Happy growth spurt, little one!

Your arms are now long enough so that you can touch your own face. For now, until I can touch you, feel the growth and grace of your head for me. Your larynx has begun to develop. One day you'll have a voice of your own, but until then, I'll listen with my being to the song of your being within me and that will help calm and center me.

Give to these children new
from the world,
Rest far from men!
—William Butler Yeats

This week, I will:

- Eat foods high in calcium to help you grow strong, even teeth: turnip greens, kale, watercress, and whole grains.

- Eat alone and in silence one day, and I'll chew each bite until it becomes liquid in my mouth, meditating on how this food will travel through me to nourish you.

THIrD MOnTH

week 9

Invisible, visible, the world
Does not work without both.
—Rumi

This week, we share our new organ together—our placenta. It produces hormones and nurtures you. How efficient it is, connecting us now, manufacturing the estrogen that helps my uterus develop blood vessels for your present home. The progesterone it produces prevents my uterus from contracting strongly until you've reached full term, until you're ready to come out into the world on your own. It is also our fluid poem, our pathway for communication. We send blood and love back and forth, back and forth.

The milk glands in my breasts are beginning to develop. I can remember when my breasts first began to swell and grow and even before then, when I wanted them so that I could look like a woman instead of a girl. Now I'm a bit ambivalent about their growth. I don't want to look like one big mammary gland, but I want to provide your milk, your nourishment. I close my eyes and I'm a little sad, a bit scared, and rather excited.

For the time being, you're drawing your food through your umbilical cord, your connection to the placenta. I close my eyes and wonder if this flow makes a sound, or a vibration, and if you feel it on its way to you.

My skin is a little softer now and I even look a bit younger. Maybe I'm too young to be a mother, or am I too old, or does age have anything to do with it?

My body is anticipating your arrival in this world and you still have quite a long way to go. The feast is being prepared long ahead of your arrival. Perhaps, in the same way my body knows what to do, and your cells know how to grow, I'll grow more and more naturally into motherhood along with each of your growth spurts. May we both progress smoothly and with grace into our new roles, our new bodies.

Maples swell with sap a-syruping!
Nature is spreading herself today!
—Ogden Nash

This week, I will:

- Periodically spend five minutes contemplating the environment I've created for you. With my hands lightly on my growing belly, I'll breathe in and out slowly, sending you warm messages of love.

- Massage my breasts with sesame oil, ghee, or coconut oil, using the oil on my breasts and around them to soothe discomfort. After you're born, I'll use only ghee. That way, if even a tiny bit remains on my breast, it is safe for your digestive system.

week 10

My two breasts that were fine and as
White as are mushrooms
Are now covered with honey, and fingers of moon
Have rounded them as with the pulp of a fruit.

—Helen Wolfert

Now you are about one and three-quarter inches long—not
even two inches, yet so much activity! Hard to believe that I was
once that size, carried in my mother's womb, and now I am big
enough to carry you. My mother, too, was once that size. Someday,
you'll think about it, too, perhaps, if you're a girl. Your uterine
home has expanded to the size of an orange. How interesting to

have a home that grows with you. Still, you and your house are hidden deep within my pelvis. Enjoy your solitude in your custom home. It can get hectic out here.

My breasts are getting heavier. They are a good reminder of what is going on in my body. Sometimes I forget until I'm getting dressed, or I'm working out, or I move too quickly, and then I realize that I need a lot more support. I really am manufacturing milk. How astounding!

Your ankles have formed. I hope the strong connection they form between your feet and your legs will help you walk, run, and jump with pleasure. May you move lightly through life and may your gait be easy and strong.

Your wrists, too, are formed, and your fingers and toes are clearly visible. Years from now, we'll circle them with ribbons and garlands of flowers, and I'll tell you how I dreamed of your bones, of your five perfect fingers fluttering in sacred exhalations of touch like a silk worm's gentle spinning. May you reach out to the world with great wonder and joy. May you nurture and caress well. May you give freely and receive graciously.

Today I relax a bit as your rate of growth slows down. I stop all outward motion and feel the magnificence of my own breath. Then, I think of you and your new limbs. I open my palms and spread my fingers softly. I cannot embrace your touch or count your toes, but I will. Still, I do not quite realize you.

And I will make thee beds of roses,
And a thousand fragrant posies,
A cup of flowers and a kirtle
Embroidered all with leaves of myrtle.
—Christopher Marlowe

This week, I will:

- Choose a new bra to provide more support and perhaps a bra to wear when walking or working out.

- Hold in my palm an orange, thinking of the size of my womb and your tiny form, growing there.

WEEK 11

Let me believe in the clean faith in the body,
The sweet glowing vigour
And the gestures of unageing love.
—Dylan Thomas

The amount of blood circulating throughout my body has begun to increase. I am filled with the energy of an emerging life force within me, red and glowing. The chambers of your heart are forming. May each one of them know love and understanding, and rapture and harmony. Your liver and spleen have matured and are now producing red blood cells. Radiant with the element of life, they march in honorable procession.

Your lymph nodes and thymus are forming white blood cells. These amazing cells know exactly how to keep you free from all sorts of poisons. Today we are responsive to all the healing emissions from the sun and the sky and the air and the moon and the earth and the stars. Now you have testicles or ovaries. Testicles: a sign of male strength, a witness of virility. Ovaries: the exaltation of fruit in female animals and in plants. I have always had ovaries. Is it possible that I now have testicles within me, too, or do I have a whole new cascade of eggs whirling within my womb?

> Today, I honor my strength and remember my body's healing power. I breathe in oxygen, swelling the blood cells with life. Today, and all the days to come, I send my loving strength through my blood to yours, helping you grow and thrive.

When you begin, begin at the beginning.
Begin with the magic, begin with the sun,
Begin with the grass.
—Helen Wolfert

This week, I will:

- Imagine us as one: a single cord stretched between the heavens and the earth. I'll stretch my arms around my growing belly and hug your growing life and breathe in the fresh oxygen on a morning or evening walk, thinking of how the oxygen goes from my nose to my lungs, then to my blood, and then travels through the umbilical cord to your blood.

- Research childbirth classes and perhaps find other expectant mothers to share ideas and information.

WEEK 12

Sleep, my babe; thy food and raiment,
House and home, thy friends provide;
All without thy care or payment:
All thy wants are well supplied.

—Isaac Watts

Now you are about three inches long. I think of you as a leaf: translucent, illuminated, leaning toward the sun. Like the leaf, you turn to forces I don't understand, to spirit and matter, your internal intelligence. Your tiny body knows how to expel what doesn't belong, and your immune system adjusts to my activities and the foods I eat, harmonizing them and using them as you develop. Your mouth opens to swallow amniotic fluid, and it is absorbed into your bloodstream through your very own digestive tract. You then excrete some of it through your kidneys, taking in what is desired, absorbing what is necessary, and letting go of the rest. You're learning the process of life.

Now your face is well defined, and you can move those muscles. I move my hands across my belly, trying to outline your visage, thinking of your features. Your eyes are fused together while mine are gently closed, thinking of you. What color will you be? The color of me? Are you trying these new movements? Are your eyes squinting now? Are you opening and closing your mouth?

I open and close my mouth, and think of yours, opening and closing, and your eyes, opening and closing. I let my body's own wisdom help me to use what I need, and to let go of the rest. I can let the bad moments wash over me, like fluid, and absorb the good moments into my very pores, like the sun on a warm day.

So far from sweet real things my thoughts had strayed,
I had forgot wide fields and clear broad streams,
The perfect loveliness that God has made,
Wild violets shy and heaven-mounting dreams
And now, unwittingly, you've made me dream
Of violets, and my souls forgotten gleam.

—Alice Dunbar Nelson

This week, I will:

- Gently close my eyes in concentration of you. What will you look like? What will you see?

- Eat plenty of green, leafy vegetables, yellow vegetables, and fruit to enhance your immune system. I'll also take my prenatal vitamins with folic acid and iron.

week 13

From a dark and narrow street
Into a world of love.
A child was born, speak low,
Speak reverent.
—Dora Greenwell

Well, my sweet, we're in this together, you and I. I do hope you like the environment that I've created, both physically and emotionally. I do hope that you are comfortable and content. This week my uterus has risen above my pelvis. The doctor and midwife can feel it on external examination and now we'll be checked at least once a month. It's nice to be taken care of by people who know what's happening to us both.

Of course, I have little daily worries—bills and nourishing you and gaining weight. These might be considered minimum concerns, so I try not to focus on them as problems. I'll try to deal with things as they arise and not let them build up into troubles, because you cannot take a continual assault of anxiety hormones. By dealing with issues as they arise, I try to set your emotional thermostat at a healthy level. I really want to do that for you. What a tremendous responsibility! Is this possible?

Your growth and development have become much more subtle. My behavior, however, needs to be explicit, as you are so fine-tuned to my every move. Smoking can cut your oxygen supply. Alcohol can maim or even kill you. No wild nights for me now, just sweet guitars and abstinence.

Of course, you are also very resilient. Occasionally I do ignore your physical needs. What you need is not unreasonable, but I just find discipline difficult at times. I'll continue to do my best, and we'll support each other—sometimes I'll be able to do for you what I might not be able to do for myself.

When I rub my belly, I sometimes feel a surge of love, and I think you feel my touch, my love through the rubbing. Perhaps by thinking of your needs I can acknowledge my own, and honor them. We both deserve love and attention. I send you love now.

She knew this instant would remain
A sacrament not touched again.

—Robert P. Tristram Coffin

This week, I will:

- Rub my belly and chat with you so you can enjoy a tranquil swim and feel protected and nurtured.

- Respect our needs for nurturance and do something special for myself. What should it be? A massage, a facial, a walk in the park, a book I've waited to read, an extra meditation, a nap?

FOURTH MONTH

WEEK 14

The pattern of the atmosphere is spherical
A bubble is the silence of the sun,
Blown thinner by the very breath of miracle
Around a core of loud confusion.

—Elinor Wylie

Now you have clear patterns of movement. You are beginning to move your limbs, making fists and kicking. Though I can't yet feel those tiny movements, sometimes I think I have vague sensations of you. Soon you'll be communicating to me through your arms and your legs, your hands and your feet, your elbows and your knees, and I will do my best to pay attention. You have also established a resting rhythm. I'm not quite aware of that yet, either. I look forward to understanding your communications.

What is it like to move for the first time? You are stretching and thrusting your tiny arms and legs outward. I bet your motions are as gentle as a cloud floating across the sky.

These periods of movement alternate with periods of quiet, motionless sleep. Like a soft breeze you move inside me and then like a quiet mist you hush and rest deeply. One day, you'll watch your hand move for the first time. I recall once seeing a ring of mountains and a layer of whispering clouds hovering in their center, silently protecting all below. In that stillness there was great peace. I'll think of that when I'm restless, or uncomfortable, and need to find stillness and quiet within. I hope you will always keep a space inside you for that grand silence.

And soon you will rise up again, little tai chi movements, wondrous thrusts and stirrings, and I still am unable to really feel that it is you. I admit I am impatient.

I'm waiting in anticipation for a definite movement, some awareness of you. I await your touch.

I offer thanks to the miracle of movement and rest, and stretch my fingers and toes, sensing touch and precision, and my legs and arms, feeling strength and flexibility. You're doing the same now, testing these miraculous movements, and I marvel at what is to come.

> *To and fro we leap*
> *And chase the frothy bubbles,*
> *While the world is full of troubles*
> *And is anxious in its sleep.*
>
> —William Butler Yeats

This week, I will:

- Be very open in my stillness, with my eyes closed and my hands on my belly, listening for you.

- Do at least one thing to maybe make our environment more peaceful. If I get upset, I'll breathe deeply and gently and focus only on my breath.

week 15

On clear quiet days,
        when mind and body
        are still,
I sense her presence
        within me.

—Helen Whitaker

Flutterings! I am told that's what you will feel like. If I am still, I may perceive you. I shall lie here as motionless as I can, attentive only to the tiny flutterings inside. I have discovered that I like being still with you. In fact, in some ways, you have become my good little teacher.

I realize that often I move about too much. I'm busy, but

many of my doings are routine and habitual, with little purpose. Sometimes I go and go and go until I think I'll collapse. As I look at some of the trivial things that make me worry, or the many unimportant things I let take over my days, I realize I can choose to keep things simple and to focus on the stillness, learning from you that in this stillness is peace and contentment. By watching the sun, and how a plant will follow the sun, I realize that nature has a rhythm, just as you have a rhythm and I have a rhythm.

Today I'll watch the light. When light grandly moves to dark or when a cloud unveils the sun abruptly, my mood alters drastically. I wonder how my brash movements affect you. I'll do things evenly and with grace. I'll try to move like gradients of light bending throughout the day. Such a peaceful way to be: quiet and illuminated. I wonder if the great sun herself can penetrate my belly. Does she light your way? Do you glisten in delight and ride the bright amniotic waves?

At night, the mesmerizing moon shines through all the blackness. Sometimes she is round and large and full, much like my belly. Her light softly sighs through the night. When I introduce you to her spell, you'll be chirruping in delight, and all the nights of your life she will call to you.

I can allow the rhythms of nature to guide me. My movements will be even and graceful, and I'll accept what unfolds with calm.

"Come here" she said "I'll teach you a poem
I see the moon
The moon sees me
God bless the moon
And God bless me."

—Nikki Giovanni

This week, I will:

- Watch the light at least one day, paying attention throughout the day and evening.

- Honor my body's rhythms and rest when I am tired.

week 16

Beauty never slumbers;
All is in her name;
But the rose remembers
The dust from which it came.

— Edna St. Vincent Millay

Last month, you tripled in size; this month, you will only double. I hope that I don't mimic you. Getting used to my new body is difficult. I love the soft curves that you give me, yet sometimes I feel a bit anxious when I think about the changes as distortion rather than a swell of new life. Is it in this quiet month of being that your soul begins to form? Is there a place inside of you that remains apart, a place that reaches for the absolute, a place where you extend into infinity?

There is a place inside of me where my heart aligns with yours, a place that has nothing to do with our genes or my egg or your bloodline. It is an ancient place, where we meet in the darkness of all there is, a place where I unite with you in utter silence.

There will be many moments of speaking and touching and listening. Today, in the deep, restful quiet of my body, and in the imponderable formation of your soul, I rest at peace with you.

There is still a sacred hush about you. Your movements, like a distant rustle in a far-off bush, still elude me. I am content.

I enjoy the bond we share. You have helped to turn my focus from the outer world to a place much deeper and richer, a place I had forgotten for a while. I honor that inner place today.

Something austere hides, something uncertain
Beneath the deep bank calls and makes quiet music.

— Dylan Thomas

This week, I will:

- Slow my world to keep time with yours.

- Practice being fully present in the moment. When I am experiencing our connection, that is all I will do. I will do one thing at a time.

week 17

And sleep as I in childhood sweetly slept:
Untroubling and untroubled where I lie—
The grass below; above the vaulted sky.
—John Clare

Well, little cherub, this month seems to be about layers and coverings. My nails and hair are growing rapidly. I even have a visible line down my abdomen; *linea nigra* is its official name. I can no longer comfortably sprawl on my back in wild abandon. Soon it won't be good for our circulation. Left side, pillow between my knees, will be our sleep position. I'm feeling a bit restricted. Your presence is influencing every aspect of my being.

Your skin, delicate and translucent, is becoming thicker, hiding your blood vessels. I imagine your veins and their colorful rich lines like sea kelp, exquisite and just barely visible through a protective, sunbathed golden layer.

New cells are forming in the layers of your skin. One morning we'll collect the dew from the clover; close to the earth we'll bend. Later on we'll run by the sea and you'll feel the sand between your toes and the salty breeze on your flesh, and your skin wet from the water will greet the sun.

You waste nothing. Your dead skin cells are continually sloughing off and mixing with the oil from your skin glands. This great recipe becomes your *vernix caseosa*, a substance composed of downlike hair, scaly cells, and fatty gland secretions that gently coats your skin while you float in your amniotic fluid. How self-sufficient to manufacture your own little wet suit. Surf well in your watery world.

I trace the line on my abdomen with my finger, feeling the pressure of my skin and its flexible strength. I think of your skin growing strong and translucent, and then thickening, protecting your inner organs. I hope your skin is thick yet soft and pliable, wonderfully protective and ever so gently receptive.

I feel the warmth of air exhaled by coming Spring
As through my window screen I hear the insects sing.

—Liu Fang-Ping

This week, I will:

- Spend some time listening and feeling you, paying careful attention to your movements, your unique way of communicating with me.

- Seek a certain amount of expansion now other than in my belly. I'll keep up my regular daily exercise.

Daily exercise can be as easy as half an hour of movement such as stretching, walking, or rhythmic movements. This is great for you and the baby; he gets more oxygen and nutrients transported to him and you decrease fluid retention and facilitate his easy passage.

FIFTH MONTH

week 18

Child, thou bringest to my heart
the babble of the wind and water,
the flower's speechless secrets, the cloud's dreams,
the mute gaze of wonder of the morning sky.

—Rabindranath Tagore

The skin on your palms and the soles of your feet is becoming thicker. With your bare hands and bare feet you can touch and explore and feel your world. Your life line is developing on your palm, reflecting the formation of your digestive and respiratory systems. I hope your life line will be long, deep, clean, and unbroken.

The middle line on your palm reflects the development of your nervous system. I wish you a strong and balanced constitution and a deep, intuitive awareness of yourself and others. Another palm line, the uppermost, is also developing, which reflects the development of your circulatory and excretory systems. May you let wisdom and joy flow through you, and may you excrete all that is evil and negative.

I hope that the lines of your palms and the major systems of your body that they represent coordinate smoothly, integrate easily, and reflect a genuine clarity and strength of being. According to Chinese medicine, your right palm reflects all my heritage. Your maternal grandmother, my mother, influences your digestive and respiratory line. I haven't the vaguest idea of what kind of eating binges she indulged in. Let's hope she liked grains and nuts and that she craved an occasional carrot for good luck. Your maternal grandfather, according to this tradition, influences your nervous system, and I hope he sent you peace and serenity.

I focus on your right palm and imagine the intricate development there and inside your body. I think of all the people who have come before you and how their genes are within you, yet you will thrive in your own way, and in your own time. With the choices I make now, I can do my best to help you thrive.

No need of motion or of strength,
Or even the breathing air:
I thought of Nature's loveliest scenes;
And with memory I was there.

—Dorothy Wordsworth

This week, I will:

- Think of the good things that I have received from my ancestors and let go of the rest.

- Enhance your nervous system by doing things to relax myself, perhaps a yoga video and my *Guided Meditation for a Healthy, Calm Pregnancy* CD that came with this book.

week 19

I am gone into the fields
To take what this sweet hour yields.
—Percy Bysshe Shelley

Let's consider your left palm. I'm grateful that it reflects your father's heritage. Sometimes I feel responsible for everything that comes along, and I'm pleased that this one palm shows that it isn't just you and me alone in this. When I feel overwhelmed, I remember that I'll do what I can but other things I can let go.

Your little hands are amazing; they tell so very much about you. May they reflect the constitutional strength I so desire for you. I can't wait to kiss each finger, each line. My wish for your palms is that they know love and healing and discretion.

You have been taking in proteins, fats, and minerals, and you are now discharging them in the form of fine hair. You are in balance. What an amazing little system you have. Spirals are developing on your skull, and the main one is at the crown of your head, to draw in the heavenly forces. May your body be filled with a divine energy, your own true self. You also have soft, fine hair on your back and arms and legs; you are gently furry. Your soft covering of hair is called lanugo. You'll probably shed this soft, downy covering during your first week after birth.

Now and then you're swallowing bits of your hair and a little of your *vernix caseosa*, all contained in your amniotic fluid. Some of this you can absorb through your digestive tract. It doesn't sound too palatable, but then again, neither do some of the foods I eat or that have been offered to me.

> **From the lines on each of your palms, to the swirls of fuzzy hair on your head, to the tiny lines on your toes, I imagine each cell of your new body holds promise and receives love. I send them both to you and receive them in my own new and changing body.**

He that question would anew
What fair Eden was of old,
Let him rightly study you,
And a brief of that behold.
Welcome, welcome, then . . .

—Robert Herrick

This week, I will:

- Eat one meal in silence, meditating on the taste, texture, and color of the food. I will eat slowly and chew many times before I swallow.

- Remain aware of my nutrition. I will also become aware of the environment in which I eat, always sitting quietly and never eating on the run.

WEEK 20

No puddings just shouldings
No chocolate and goodings
Just raisins and kumquats
And spinach and green squash.

—Corinne Roussie

This is our halfway point. If you go to full term, you will be born forty weeks from day one of my last menstrual period. May your body, well dressed in an amniotic veil, continue to thrive.

I must continue to ensure that you get all the ingredients you need. It's difficult to drink eight glasses of water, eight ounces each, daily. That water is necessary to support the increased volume of blood in my body and to maintain your amniotic fluid. Freshly squeezed juice or milk is okay, too, but no soda, tea, coffee, or alcohol. Now and then, I find a cup of hot water soothing.

This halfway mark is reminding me of all I have to do. Sometimes I forget to exercise the muscle between my pubic bone in front and my tailbone (coccyx) in the back, sometimes called the Kegel muscle. If my Kegel is weak, it can't support your uterine home. If it's strong, it helps my bowel and bladder control.

> **Rest well beneath my heart chamber, little one. You have spent half your time within me, and you'll be in my arms when you've rested there just that much time again. I can be patient until that day arrives.**

The whole world is here on my body
Multiple coloralities bursting into spirit
Which is me.

—Ruth Lerner

This week, I will:

- Exercise my Kegel muscle.

- Continue to exercise daily, yet now I will choose less strenuous methods, such as prenatal yoga and walking or swimming.

Prenatal yoga classes are an excellent way to prepare for birthing, but *never* do any inverted poses (with feet above your head) during pregnancy.

Kegel muscle exercise: To tighten the Kegel muscle, squeeze the pelvic floor muscles as if you are preventing urination. Do this in sets of five at least ten times each day.

week 21

Like all vessels, fragile
Like all vessels too small
for the destiny poured into it.

—Rosario Castellanos

Some of what you take into your tiny body is indigestible, and your large intestine accumulates your waste in the form of a watery feces known as meconium. Such delicate waste, your meconium. The secretion of your bile into your intestinal tract causes it to take on a dark green color. All of this usually stays in your intestine until shortly after birth, when you discharge your uterine feedings. Will I get to change your first diaper?

By now you weigh practically two pounds. I'm a little ahead

of you in gaining weight. Right now, of course, I'm focusing on my nutrition and not on weight gain. Cheers to a bit of maternal fat.

My, how you are growing. The average length at this stage is thirteen inches long. That means you're a tad longer than a ruler. Do you ever stretch to your full length?

Even though it has been thickening, your skin is still thin, and you are so very fragile. I'm glad that you are well cushioned. I close my eyes and breathe a gentle caress across your flesh. I understand that your new skin is shiny, which makes me think it is pulled taut across your being. I wonder what you feel and whether you are comfortable in your commencement suit.

> I think of your tiny form, and how your fingers and toes are printed as yours. You are developing your own fine definition. I pledge to guide you in placing your finger-prints with care and grace as you journey with your hands.

As a sweet organ harmony strikes the ear
So, for the primal mind, my eyes receive
A vision of your future drawing near.

—Dante Alighieri

This week, I will:

- Look around at all the varieties of noses and faces waiting in line at the bank or grocery store, and express gratitude for the differences and similarities that make us human.

- List the gifts my hands and feet have brought me, and think of how yours will serve you. As I walk, I'll think of my toes and how they help hold me erect and guide me, and my ankles and how they flex and bend yet hold me straight.

week 22

Here are threads, my true love, as fine as silk,
To knit thee, to knit thee,
A pair of stockings white as milk.

—Anonymous

Your eyelids are beginning to part. Take a peek at your surroundings and let your eyes be flooded by the rich fluid of your drift. Right now, you have barely any fat under your glistening skin. You do, however, have much protection and other kinds of coats and layers.

I don't know why, but when I think of you without any underlying fat, I want to protect you even more. I think I'll buy you a beautiful shawl today: warm, softly textured, and white.

You are sipping amniotic fluid daily. It's rather salty, as I recall. (It was once my liquid diet, too.) Let's drink to your health!

You have fluttering eyelashes now, all wet and beautiful, and eyebrows to go with them. You're becoming more and more complete day by day. There is certainly nothing routine about your days!

We couldn't be closer than we are now, and yet I long for the ability to caress you and cradle you in my arms. Somehow, close as you are, you feel a bit far away, as the constancy of my own heart does.

> As I close my eyes and feel my lashes brush my skin, I think of you and wonder what color your lashes will be, and how they will curl below your arching brows. I think of cradling you in my arms, wrapped in a snow-white shawl, and I smile with delight and joy.

Everyone suddenly burst out singing;
And I was filled with such delight.

—Siegfried Sassoon

This week, I will:

- Protect you by keeping your amnion strong when I eat well. I'll choose something dark green and leafy for lunch. Perhaps cooked spinach, chard, escarole, or bok choy, perhaps with a mound of tofu or cottage cheese for protein.

- Sip celery-and-beet juice. It's a great energizer!

- Listen to some joyous music.

A Perfectly Balanced Meal

1/2 cup almonds, or 1/4 cup sesame tahini or almond butter
1 cup cottage cheese, milk, or yogurt
1/2 cup brown rice, or 1/2 bagel
3/4 cup spinach, asparagus, kale, or mustard greens
3/4 cup yellow squash or carrots
1/2 cup cantaloupe or watermelon

SIXTH MONTH

week 23

Let the dark walls that enclose you
tumble down!
Receive the lap of your mother the earth.
—Rosario Castellanos

Your lips are distinct this month. I'd love to see you grin from ear to ear! May your mouth be generous, loving, warm, and expressive. At this stage of your life, you are well proportioned, and I hope that continues into old age. I feel a bit out of proportion myself right now, so I'm glad one of us is in balance.

When I feel a bit out of balance or out of proportion, I meditate on the perfection of you. When I do this, my enthusiasm soars and I feel at one with your limitless potential.

Your eyes are developed, but your iris still lacks pigment. At birth, your eyes will be similar to those of the other "neonates" (that's what they'll call you at the hospital, you know). Their color will not be as sharp or clear as they will be when you are a bit older. With your eyes barely open, you experience the nature surrounding you. One day, we shall look at the stars together and laugh with the new moon.

> You are growing and are enclosed in my womb, yet you know no limitations. I will balance fear of my own physical limitations with the knowledge that my limitations arise from your boundless potential and meditate on the perfection of you.

That then, is loveliness,
we said,
Children in wonder watching
the stars,
Is the aim at the end.
—Dylan Thomas

This week, I will:

- Send you my unbounded love and energy. I am here for you. You're so calm inside me. You bring me a deep sense of inner peace, and I send it back to you in loving reciprocity.

- Continue to eat foods rich in vitamins, especially vitamin A for your eyes. Perhaps I'll have a glass of carrot juice balanced with a handful of nuts for protein.

week 24

A measure of holiness a measure of power
A measure of fearfulness a measure of terror
A measure of trembling a measure of shaking
A measure of awe.

—Hebrew, third century A.D.

Sometimes I feel as though I need more support than I am receiving right now. I know this feeling is normal, but knowing that doesn't always help me feel better. Sometimes I feel very alone. No one can participate as I really want them to, because only I am carrying you. I wish your father would reassure me that he feels as deep a bond with you as I do. I need more physical involvement with your daddy, but some of my desires may be overwhelming to him right now.

Can I ever feel totally independent? I move from needing my mother to needing my husband. Now is not the time for distance. It is a time for forgiveness and closeness. I desire connection: physical, spiritual, and emotional.

I will honor my connection to you, my new child, and I will ask for the connection I need with others. I will surround you with love yet honor my own needs and desires.

To look at you gives joy;
your eyes are like honey,
Love flows over your gentle face.

—Sappho

This week, I will:

- Find a way to see some friends or spend time with my family, since social support is important to me right now.

- Ask my partner to cuddle for at least five minutes: no talking, just being happily together, caressing.

- Take a walk in the park with a friend or with my partner.

WEEK 25

Heart to heart as we lay
In the dawning of the day.
—Robert Bridges

Your world is shifting now to one of sound. You can hear all the rumblings going on in your womb palace and even now and then outside voices. I try to stay calm and centered in hopes that my heart beats rhythmically and makes you feel safe.

The path between you and me is alive. You are the expansive bridge between mind and spirit. I hear the ring of your being inside me with great clarity. As you gestate within my womb, you make me know that all things are possible. You seem like the largo, or slow, movements of most baroque music. Surrounded by such beauty, our hearts beat restfully.

According to most studies, you and your unborn friends have a preference for Vivaldi, a baroque composer. Your fetal heart becomes steady, and your kicking declines when you listen to his music.

> My heart calms with my breathing as I listen to soft music and align my breath into calmness. Like the soft rhythm of a cello, my breath is even and my heartbeat is soothing and sure.

Mingling me and thee,
When the light of eyes
Flashed through thee and me
Trust shall make us free
Liberty make wise.

—Algernon Charles Swinburne

This week, I will:

- Read aloud to you. I understand that you like repetition. I'll pick out a few books today and begin to read to you daily. Then, when you're born and I read to you, you'll remember and you'll be comforted.

- Find a comfortable place to rest and close my eyes. We will listen to Vivaldi, Handel, or another baroque composer.

week 26

O world invisible,
*   we view thee,*
O world intangible,
*   we touch thee,*
O world unknowable,
*   we know thee,*
Inapprehensible,
*   we clutch thee!*

—Francis Thompson

Now your brain is becoming mature enough that my
behavior can be experienced by you emotionally. This is a new

71

responsibility. Now I must deal with any ambivalence that I have about being a mother so I can send you all the warmth and love you deserve. Your daddy also has a big responsibility now. If his voice is any less than loving to me, you are annoyed by its sound but also you experience the result of my feelings. We both need to be surrounded by peaceful, loving, and supportive people.

I'll do my best to make certain that you know I love you. I'll continue to stroke my abdomen often because you like that.

You're now sending me messages by the way you kick and move about. Loud voices agitate you and even a bright light on my abdomen can stress you. If I sunbathe, I'll cover you gently. I'll demonstrate my love by heeding your gentle communications. Sometimes my emotions are so muted that I'm not quite aware of them. Our connection amazes me, and sometimes I wonder what you feel when I'm happy, or when I sing or hum or laugh.

Here we are sending messages back and forth to each other. The more I understand my own feelings, the more I can understand and respect yours. We're in this together, after all!

I can't be perfect. There will be times when I am upset and when certain events cause me stress. However, I make this commitment to you, little one: I shall not ignore you physically or psychologically on a consistent basis. I'll do the best I can to give you a healthy environment. Peaceful floatings.

We dance round in a ring and suppose,
But the secret sits in the middle and knows.

—Robert Frost

This week, I will:

- Listen to my dreams and work to understand them, thinking about them so that I understand how those messages and emotions affect you.

- Remember that silence is important. I'll be quiet and sit absolutely still for at least five minutes. I'll focus on my breath.

seventh month

week 27

Sweet babe, in thy face
Soft desires I can trace,
Secret jobs and secret smiles,
Little pretty infant wiles.

—William Blake

We are repeating evolution, you and I. Since your conception, your nervous system and your brain have become increasingly complex. In this process you are repeating, and in you lie the origins of society. Our relationship affects all our attitudes toward life. Your arms, legs, eyes, ears, and blood vessels are partially a result of the environment we create together.

This channel filled with reassurance that we have flowing between us is another part of protecting you from all the uncertainties that you will encounter in your lifetime. The work we do in our silent time together is more important than all the politicians realize. Perhaps they could learn from us, from our bond.

I love that you reverberate like an endless hymn. My being hums with your being, and together we can make this world better, simply by our awareness and love, our combined humming.

> In some sense, my brain regulates yours, and your brain regulates the functioning of your organs. I offer you social awareness and centered emotional responses, as you have offered me a connection to the universal cosmic consciousness.

A heart as soft, a heart as kind,
A heart as sound and free
As in the whole world thou canst find,
That heart I'll give to thee.

—Robert Herrick

This week, I will:

- Listen again to our baroque music and let go of all thoughts. Resting with my eyes closed, I let the music flood my being.

- Do something to bring peace to this planet, recognizing our oneness.

week 28

Deep, deep our love, too deep to show.
Deep, deep we drink, silent we grow.

—Du Mu

You reach and grasp with every bit of your being. I imagine and focus and push into what I think is infinite capacity, where at last I have grasped the endless—and then there you go again, taking boundless leaps.

We play together in the night. You kick and crawl in wondrous ceremony. Then you turn inside me. You magnetically draw me forward, then you leap and bound once more. I know that I shall silently meet you again today or tonight and that I shall feel you circulate and frolic in the splendor of your play. I shall feel you dance and swim and leap inside my womb. You are an endless stretch of wondrous breath, a rising hush of all there is. I delight in you.

You playfully flip and kick once more, making way for your independence. I look directly at you, and you kiss me softly with your knee.

> I caress my belly and you float and rise in me. You whisper fathomless invitations, and I hear the echo of your form, sweet and ancient in the night. I relish our oneness and send you my joy to permeate every cell of your being.

Surely, I said
Now will the poets sing.
But they have raised no cry
I wonder why.

—Countee Cullen

This week, I will:

- Continue to eat and drink healthfully. I will recognize one unhealthy thought when it comes and transform it to a healthier belief.

- Contemplate all that I am consciously contributing to your growth and development. I shall be both accepting and willing to change what I can if it is important for our well-being.

WEEK 29

Give to these children new from the world,
Silence and love
And the long dew-dropping hours of the night,
And the stars above.

—William Butler Yeats

Well, our good nutrition is paying off. You are beginning to have some fat deposited under your skin, making you just a bit more cuddly. I'm growing rounder, too, of course. Sometimes, I wish I were eating chips and salsa, or maybe just chocolate, relaxing by the pool. Then I realize my choices today will help you grow, and I eat brown rice and steamed kale, perhaps spinach or lentil soup, and we both thrive. Your blood, cells, tissues, organs, and amniotic fluid are renewed by the foods I eat, after all.

When I feel fat and tired of being pregnant, I look forward to feeding you, to holding you in my arms and letting you suckle. I've seen pictures of babies in the womb, babies your age, sucking their thumbs. Have you found your thumb to suck, to comfort yourself? Soon you'll have other choices. My breasts are full and ready for you. Sometimes I feel you hiccup. Just because the volume of your amniotic fluid is diminishing doesn't mean you have to gulp it. Relax, little wonder. Soon you'll taste the sweet milk of my breast instead of the salty fluid of your amniotic ocean.

Right now, I feel full, full like a soft but firm pillow with all that is needed to nourish you: My heart swells with love as my belly swells with your growth and my breasts will swell with milk. I sense the fullness of this world I live in and the completeness of our love together.

Dear little saint of my life,
Deep in my breasts I feel
The warm milk come to birth.
—Federico García Lorca

This week, I will:

- Recall a time when I believed my intuition and followed it with good results, and I'll try to listen to my intuition. If I *know* something, with my strong inner *knowing*, I'll do my best to act on it, but I'll be careful to sort those things I fear, or worry about, from things I strongly "know."

- Practice letting go of at least one thing that is unnecessary to my well-being so that I can maintain my peace and happiness.

Dear little child of mine, I picture your hands and your mouth meeting in your watery world as you float and explore. I think of the changes in my own body as there to help you, and I massage my swollen belly with love. Most days, I choose healthy foods to feed you, and healthy thoughts to comfort you. We grow closer as we come nearer the time when I will rub your belly, and I will talk while seeing your face, and kiss you, yet we already talk, and my kisses are the thoughts I send you.

Week 30

My heart is high above,
my body is full of bliss,
For I am set in luve as well
as I would wiss.

—Anonymous

Now you weigh about three pounds and you are about seventeen inches long. You still have a lot of growing to do, with only ten weeks left until your debut. I feel you kicking within me. Sometimes your movements are soft and gentle like the flutter of miniature angel wings, and I smile and touch you. Can you feel me? Other times, you seem rather playful and frisky; at other moments you seem to be trying to find the best and most comfortable position, squirming. I hope your umbilical cord doesn't get in your way.

I feel you again deep within me, and suddenly a wave of you ripples across the space. Like a barefoot gypsy beckoning the flamenco dancer from the cobblestone path to the soft-soled plains, you listen to the song I sing to you and roll and tumble quietly and rhythmically.

Sometimes, I picture how it will be when you are in my arms, not in my womb. I think of the night high in the vastness of the sky; the night soothes and rocks her midnight world. In a bassinet, wrapped in the soft cotton robes of a cloud, you are soothed in this veil of darkness and sleep, at peace.

> I feel you, and I am at times overwhelmed, and I feel unable and perhaps a bit unwilling to fathom you and me and our connection. Yet as I calm myself with my breathing, I know I can love you enough and nurture you enough.

Dance upon the shore;
What need have you of care
For wind or water's roar?
And tumble out your hair.

—William Butler Yeats

This week, I will:

- Choose a song that is ours. I'll sit peacefully with my hands on my belly and sing it to you. One day soon it will be one of your first memories.

- Relax more frequently, exercise more gently, and drink plenty of water.

week 31

And I am free to know
That you are bound to
me only by choice,
that you are bound
to me by love,
And I am finally
Out of control.

—Helen Whitaker

You must stay in my womb for now. This is a crucial time and we must prevent the possibility of your being born prematurely. It's safe in there, I hope. I listen carefully for your subtle communications.

Amazing nuances of development are occurring. The muscles of your chest wall and diaphragm, enabling you to expand and contract during breathing, are being fine-tuned.

The reflex centers of your brain, which coordinate your muscles for breathing and for swallowing, are beginning to function. Again I'm reminded how important my diet is in providing the optimum development of your nervous system and the many dimensions of your body and mind. I try not to worry, since that is not healthy for either of us, but nutrition is so important, especially iron and vitamin B_{12} to prevent anemia.

> You are well cushioned by your amniotic fluid, and I send my voice rippling across your waters. What name shall I call to you, child of mine? Whatever name we choose I shall sing to your ears and look on you, sweet child of mine, and try to allay all your fears.

This week, I will:

- Try pumpkin seeds, sesame seeds, and sunflower seeds. I'm doing my best to eat whole grains like millet and buckwheat, sea vegetables, and soybeans. I've learned that sea vegetables provide calcium and other nutrients, so I'm going to shop for hijiki, wakame, and arame, and though I don't always find the taste appealing, I can make a powder to sprinkle on soups, salads, and other foods.

- Sit quietly and say the names we're thinking of naming you aloud. Those names will be my meditation.

EIGHTH MONTH

WEEK 32

A fire-mist and a planet
A crystal and a cell,
A jelly fish and a saurian,
And caves where the
cave-men dwell;
Then a sense of law and beauty,
And a face turned from the clod;
Some call it evolution
And others call it God.

—William Herbert Carruta

    I found out that you have a new trick. You can now turn your head from side to side. I just turned mine, realizing how amazing that must be when you do it for the first time. You're a bit more rounded this week, and I'm so happy you're still inside me. Please stay until you've reached term. It's a lot safer that way.

Your skin is now covered with white grease, your own little intrauterine outfit. I hope your worldly sense of fashion will be as natural and creative.

Right now, cotton seems to be my fashion statement. It's comfortable and allows my body energy to circulate freely. It keeps me warm or cool, whichever I need at the time.

For me, it's also important to massage my skin all over, especially my perineum and breasts. Sesame oil is so soothing, and ghee on my breasts will help prevent my nipples cracking. I'm preparing for you to stretch me vastly and for you to eat.

> **Everything I see vibrates within me and has the potential to nourish you. Every day until you're born will be a treasure hunt. We're both preparing for our new roles now, and as I await your debut I do what I can to prepare my body and my mind for the next phase of our life together.**

Given conditions
As they be,
Desire no thing
Beyond what is
Now.
—Jack Crimmins

This week, I will:

- Acknowledge my yearning for harmony, peace, and serenity.

- Stroll one day with you in some beautiful spot, not waiting until you arrive "in person." It will be a mindful walk; I will be only in the moment, with no thoughts of past or future.

week 33

I'm on the shore and thou on the sea,
All of thy wanderings far and near,
Bring thee at last to shore and me.

—Bret Harte

After you arrive, you'll teach me many things. Each moment for you will be new, filled with all possibilities. Just contemplating you has enlightened me. Each moment for me is new also, but I don't often realize that. Thank you, baby guru.

I'm continuing to nourish us both. Frequent small meals are easier and more comfortable than three large ones. You take up a lot of space!

I know our prenatal vitamins, rich in iron and folic acid, are no substitute for food, but they are important as a supplement. I must remember to take them every day. I'm learning about continuity, order, routine, and responsibility—good lessons to learn before you are born.

Your daddy has a strong influence on my feelings and emotions. This is a time when we need to encourage and support each other more than usual. There is so much to talk about.

Our intimate connection is still intact. I have begun to think about the change in our relationship that will take place after you are born. There is a part of me that wants to hold you inside. I feel a bit anxious about severing our tie when you've reached term. I know it's important for you not to be forever attached to me. After all, this life you are now living inside of me is yours. I am here only to nurture and support you.

> At times, my realizations sometimes border on being overwhelming. When that happens, I breathe quietly and try to let go of expectation and worry, and simply feel. I feel my breath, my heartbeat, your gentle movements. I release worry and instead embrace love.

Come, for the soul is free!
In all the vast dreamland
There is no lock for thee,
Each door awaits thy hand.

—Bliss Corman

This week, I will:

- Discover how meditation is another important facet of simple vaginal birth, as is an acceptance of our impending new and different relationship.

- Begin to discuss parenting philosophy and practices with my partner.

week 34

The mulberry is a double tree.
Mulberry, shade me, shade me awhile,
It is a shape of life described
By another shape without a word
Mulberry, shade me, shade me awhile.
—Wallace Stevens

This week will be one of meditation. I will sit in a chair with my feet on the floor and my hands open in my lap. I'll close my eyes and focus on my exhalations for about five minutes. That's just the beginning. By the time you're born, we'll be seasoned meditators, you and I.

Another way I'll meditate is to sit for five minutes actively listening. I'll be listening to the silence of you within me, and you'll be listening to my heartbeat. A time of sitting perfectly still is such luxury. Peaceful floatings for you, peaceful sitting for me.

Meditation is good for my heart rate and my blood pressure. Even my digestion is affected positively. We're off to a deeper state of relaxation. This is a good way to prepare for labor, and it's a process where your participation is helpful.

When you are ready to be born, I want to be ready to open my cervix and my mind. I continue to take time to focus on my exhalations. I automatically inhale, as you will when you take your first breath. Now I'll practice alternating sending my exhalations down my right and left legs. Concentrating and focusing are important preparations for bringing you into the world.

Pregnancy, labor, and birth are natural. Women have been doing this for ages. I celebrate our silence in other ways of knowing, and the resonating harmony we share.

My mantra for labor will be: "All I have to do is keep my mind out of my body's way of the work it knows so well how to do." I will repeat this to myself now, relaxing and exhaling into the thought, letting it fill my mind and body, knowing that it is true.

And so in mountain
    Solitudes—o'ertaken as
    by some spell divine—
Their cares dropped from
    them like the needles shaken
From out the gusty pine.

—Bret Harte

This week, I will:

- Observe my thoughts. I will not cling to them; I will not judge them; I will not push them away. I shall only observe them. It is a good way of letting go of what isn't necessary.

- Play my *Guided Meditation for a Healthy, Calm Pregnancy* CD.

week 35

At times a fragrant breeze comes floating by,
And brings, you know not why,
A feeling as when eager crowds await
Before a palace gate.

—Henry Timrod

Since I don't want anything to interrupt the course of your vital flow, I think it's important to be aware of the seven energy centers in our bodies. One is at the base of my spine (and yours, too, of course), and one is below my navel; that one is important during labor. I'll focus on these two places now, while sending my breath to free the energy that might need unhinging with focused breathing. I'm getting better at this. It may seem strange, but it's actually rather fun.

A third energy center is right around my navel; if it is blocked, it can interfere with my digestion. Energy center number four is right in the center of my chest, between my two nipples; this is the heart center, and from it flows love to you. The fifth is in my throat and has to do with communication and creativity. You and I are doing pretty well in that area, I think. Just to make sure these three areas are functioning as well as possible, I'll focus my exhalations on them. No kicking for a moment or two, please.

The sixth energy center is located between my eyebrows (something you recently grew). This is the area on which yogis focus when they walk on fire so they feel no pain. I wonder how painful contractions are. On a scale of one to ten, I think they're a ten or maybe even off the scale. If the yogis can do it, I can at least imagine being able to attain a pain scale of three. Now, I will focus on the point between my eyebrows and imagine an easy, pain-free birth.

Energy center number seven is located at the top of my head. I think about your magical head and how your bone plates slide together to safely reduce the diameter of your skull as you pass through me on your way out and into my arms. The thought of your descent at once thrills me and makes me a bit anxious. I hope there is room for you as you wend your way through the birth canal. I worry about it sometimes. Now I send my breath to protect your crowning soft spot. Your body is so flexible. May your spirit be the same.

> Could it be true that you are wiggling your way downward? I feel a bit more room in my upper abdomen and I can breathe freely again. My lungs are expanding with great joy at each inhalation. I had forgotten how pleasurable a long, deep inhalation can be. I look forward to your first breath and hope it will be as wondrous to you as it will be to me.

Still there's a sense of
blossoms yet unborn
In the sweet airs of morn.

—Henry Timrod

This week, I will:

- Read about the energy centers and focus where indicated for a few moments at a time.

- Continue my peaceful birth preparation by listening to my *Guided Meditation for a Healthy, Calm Pregnancy* CD.

Ninth Month

Week 36

I never saw a moon,
I never saw the sea;
Yet know I how the heather looks,
And what a wave must be.

—Emily Dickinson

What is it like to breathe for the first time? Is it like inhaling the first scent of spring that arrives on a gentle breeze, or is it like a thrust of a cold winter's gale, harsh and penetrating upon your entire being?

Oh, you are so safe, so protected! I don't care that you are now perched in such a fashion that there is more pressure on my bladder and my rectum. I am getting tired of being pregnant, and yet the thought of you floating inside of me is more soothing than considering your sliding forth into this vast world. It's difficult for me to feel comfortable at all now. Lying on my left side gives some relief. What about you? Can you feel my mounting excitement? Do you know it's getting close to your arrival? Are you ready? Actually, this is a delightful place. You won't be cramped anymore, yet you'll feel safe. I'll protect you.

Very soon you'll be making a journey all by yourself into this world, through the birth canal. As I breathe quietly now, I think that will be a joyous ride, if scary, but we'll both be filled with love and wonder at the end, and that will be only the beginning of the life we'll share. Rest for the journey, little one.

I think a lot about my participation in your outbound journey. I promise to make it as short and easy as possible. To prepare, I'm listening to my *Guided Meditation for a Healthy, Calm Pregnancy* CD. I'm taking my birthing classes and learning to relax my jaw and my hands as I visualize sending my breath all the way through my body and out through my vagina.

Hug me round
In your solitude
Profound.
—Georgia Douglas Johnson

This week, I will:

- Give you my undivided attention for twenty minutes daily from now on. We shall meditate together and visualize your passage.

- Use my breathing to practice focusing as I'll do during labor. I will also pick out the music I'll use in the birthing room.

Repeat this simple meditation aloud to yourself, using the
"so hum" phrase to stretch out your breath and make it
vibrate through your body, relaxing and releasing tension.
So. I breathe in the healing forces of the universe
and, *hum,* I exhale my ego-bound limitations. *So hum. So
hum. So hum. So hum. So hum. So hum.*

week 37

High between dream and
day and think how there
The soul might rise visible
as a flower.

—E. J. Scovell

My body, in its great archetypal wisdom, knows exactly how to give birth to you just as the earth knows how to give blossom to the flowers.

Sometimes I wonder if I can birth you vaginally. I really don't want a C-section. I close my eyes, and I visualize you and me at term. I have a lot of tension in my body when I think of birthing you. I increase the tension in my feet, legs, chest, arms, and hands; then I release it. I inhale through my nose and breathe in the healing forces from the universe as my abdomen rises with my breath. I then slowly release my breath through my mouth, sending it deep into my perineum. I focus on the peacefulness of you within me.

I sit here quieting my anxious mind by focusing on my breath. As I breathe in and breathe out, as I focus on each inhalation and exhalation, I am almost in a trance. This week, you receive your own breath. Your lungs mature, which means that when you are born your respirations will be as easy and as natural as mine are now. I imagine you here, fresh and new and wet on my abdomen, your breath and my breath rising and falling in unison. One day, we'll go to the headlands high above the ocean; the seagulls will soar and ride the wind while you and I fill our lungs with the clear air. We'll laugh and shout with glee as we breathe without a thought and look together at the colors of the wildflowers and the sky. Develop, little lungs, make yourselves complete! It's not long before your first respiration.

Each day I think gratefully of how our bodies, yours and mine, know what to do. Our wisdom comes from a greater wisdom, and as the seagulls know how to swoop and soar, we also know how to be. I sit as comfortably as I can in a chair with my feet flat on the floor. I focus on the perfection of you, and I send a healing white light from the center of my two brows to the center of yours. A brilliant white umbilicus of light flowing from me to you and from you to me.

Mother and child,
*   lover and lover mated,*
Are wound and bound
*   together and enflowing*
What has been plaited
*   cannot be unplaited.*

—May Sarton

This week, I will:

- Close my eyes and relax my jaw whenever I remember to. I will practice sending every other inhalation deep into my uterus and out through my cervix and my vagina.

- Prepare with gentle stretches, gentle thoughts, plenty of water, and rest, and listen to my meditation CD.

Dear Baby: if you stay within a bit longer, I will rest peacefully so that you can reap more of the benefits from your uterine hideaway. Gather all the immunities you can; eat and drink of me, supping to your heart's delight. My body is still your home for now. I have done my best for it so I can carry you to term. Love, Mommy.

week 38

Let love embrace the ten thousand things;
Heaven and earth are a simple body.
—Hai Shih

My abdomen is grand with the size of you. I want you to stay, yet I'm feeling uncomfortable. Now for a moment I rest in silence. I send my thoughts out to sea. I let go of my fear and tension. I breathe in the serenity of a vast blue sky, and I send that calm throughout my body. I float on the fluffy cumulus clouds, and my body feels free and weightless. I am at peace as we journey together, abandoning ourselves in silence.

I've heard that formula is easier than breast-feeding. I still have some reservations about the process of nursing you. The way I see it, my milk is ready to flow for you. It would be a shame to deprive you of that wonderful bond that we can continue to develop. Its temperature is perfect for you. It has all the nutrients you need. You are less likely to get sick if I suckle you. When I think of all the chores of life I must deal with after you are born, I can't think of any more delightful respite than to sit with you as a life force from my breast trickles into your eager mouth.

Again I contemplate relaxing and feeding you. I shall make the time to nurse you for at least three to six months. It's also good for my uterus. Nursing you reduces the risk of hemorrhage and causes my uterus to return to its normal size quickly and naturally. That's certainly a plus. It also helps me get back in shape.

If I breast-feed you, you will have a much smaller chance of having upper respiratory infections, ear infections, and colon infections. You'll be less likely to have allergies, and you'll be calmer. All of this also means that I'll have more time to do what I need and want to do. If I feel anxious or uncomfortable or feel as though I don't know what I'm doing, I'll ask for help.

When you arrive, I'll massage you with sesame oil. Until

then, I'll pay special attention to you through my enormous belly. Every time I touch my abdomen, you seem to answer with a gesture: your first game.

As your debut approaches, I remind myself that when I stay in the present moment, in the now, I feel safe. I can trust my relaxed body, and I can trust you to find your way into this world from your peaceful floatings.

Sing when you're happy
and from worries keep away!

—Luo Yin

This week, I will:

- Practice this labor meditation: You are still growing, and I'm curious how you will manage to squeeze through your birthing passage. I send to you a white light of love and lubrication. I imagine you, at term, being guided down through my body on this path of light, surrounded by it and filled with it. The same light softens, ripens, and easily dilates my cervix and pushes you out into the baby catcher's hands. It is with great ease that we perform this miracle.

- Take a warm bath before sleep, a practice first-stage-of-labor bath. I'll add two to three drops of rose water to the water, then I'll relax, soak, empty my mind, and focus on the rise and fall of my abdomen for ten minutes. I'll climb into bed totally relaxed and I'll sleep peacefully.

Rose water can be purchased in the baking aisle of most grocery stores and is better than scented oils for labor.

week 39

*Days and months appear
long in the fairyland halls.*

—Bai Ju-Yi

I plan to relax with you daily this week. Soon our labor will begin. I know whatever I think and feel and hear affects you. I know whatever drugs I take during labor will also affect you. I'll do my best to give you a drug-free beginning. I want to have an alternative to drugs.

I wonder if you somehow sense that you will soon be moving from your warm and dark fluid habitat to a very bright and spacious world. I'm feeling all sorts of different physical sensations, which I'm certain you must be experiencing also. You don't have very much space in there anymore. I feel excited, a little impatient, and somewhat uncertain.

> Now that the time is near, I visualize myself strong and physically ready for the transition from prenatal mothering to accepting you into my arms and life and knowing that my strength will rise to meet the challenges. Just as my mind-body has let you grow and thrive within, so my mind-body will help you grow and thrive in life, and we'll learn together, you and I, seeking and finding help when we need it.

Ah! When will this long
weary day have end,
And lende me leave to come unto my love?
How slowly do the houres
theyr numbers spend!

—Edmund Spenser

THE INVITATION

Dear Baby: Today I send you an invitation. You have been a most welcome resident, although I hope that you don't stay inside for too much longer. Outside, the sun shines, the flowers bloom and toss scents of pleasure in the air, the clouds play tag, and the butterflies do the same. Rain falls and rivers flow, trees grow high in the sky, vegetables grow from the earth; gentle breezes will kiss your face, and stems of nipples with streams of milk are waiting for your wanting mouth. Last, but not least, I cannot possibly grow another inch. Do come soon. Love, Mommy.

The rising sun appears
sublime
But O! 'Tis near your
birthing time.

—Anonymous

This week, I will:

- Prepare us nutritionally for this labor. I need to eat several small meals a day, as there seems to be very little room for anything more. Oatmeal, cottage cheese, nuts, seeds, soy milk, warm miso soup, vegetables, egg whites, and some apples—simple, nourishing, and fresh, similar to a marathon runner's diet.

- Soak again in a warm bath with some lavender if my bag of waters has not yet broken when the first stage of labor arrives. This will help my uterus contract more efficiently and will reduce the pressure I feel from inside of me.

week 40

*Last night, I pulled the
moon down
out of the sky and onto my
waiting belly.*

—Ruth Lerner

We are a team, you and I, a unique collaborative system. Let
me explain how it will work, and how our bodies will work together.
There are molecules that regulate the production of progesterone in
your fetal membranes, in my placenta, in the lining of my uterus,
and in the muscle cells of my uterus. When the prostaglandin-
regulating molecules inhibit the progesterone production, the

process of birth begins. As the time approaches, I visualize the progesterone decreasing and the prostaglandin increasing.

I visualize the molecules as friendly and competent. They aid my cervix in softening and dilating. Let the process of birth begin! I hope that my pituitary gland soon secretes oxytocin, a hormone that is another factor in the contracting of my uterus. I visualize all of the secretions effectively causing the muscles of the wall around you, my uterine wall, to contract. This gentle momentum is how birthing begins and proceeds until you and your placenta have arrived.

Come, my wonderful child, let my uterus usher you down the birth canal! I realize that you begin the process of birth and that I must be ready in order to complete it. I am ready. I await you.

So waste not thou; but come for all the vales
Await thee; azure pillows of the hearth
Arise to thee; the children call, and I
Thy shepherd pipe, and sweet is every sound
Sweeter thy voice, but every sound is sweet;
Myriads of rivulets hurrying thro' the lawn,
The moan of doves in immemorial elms
And murmuring of innumerable bees.

—Alfred, Lord Tennyson

This week, I will:

- Not sit and wait for you. I'll go to the garden or to the park. I'll walk and admire other creations. I'll listen to music and do anything I can to keep my mind out of my body's way.

- Imagine my contractions as coordinated and efficient. Enjoy the full massage as your head and body easily move through the gentle stimulation of your first passage.

Moon of the Ninth Month
Cast its shadow.
How weary is the life within
When it sees its dark prison
It struggles to be free
And make its camp on earth.

—Native American birthing song

THINGS TO TAKE TO THE BIRTHING ROOM

- Cotton clothes to wear

- Cotton socks

- CD player

- Gregorian chant or baroque music CD

- Warm miso soup in a thermos to sip during labor

- Rolling pin in case of back labor

- Rose water

- Something beautiful to look at, perhaps a photo from a magazine

- Bubbles for blowing to enhance relaxation during labor

- Phone number for the local La Leche League for breast-feeding support

- A support person, either family, friend, or professional

- Birthing ball (if not already available in the birthing room)

OTHer resources BY
MICHeLLe LeCLaIre O'NeILL

*Hypnobirthing Bundle for Happy Hypnomoms
and Blissful Hypnobabies*

Creative Childbirth

CD 1: *Hypnosis for Pregnancy*

CD 2: *Hypnosis for Labor*

CD 3: *Music for Pregnancy, Labor, and Breast-Feeding*

Hypnobirthing: The Leclaire Method

Twelve Weeks to Fertility

Meditation and Healing CD

Healing from Stress and Trauma (Six CDs)

Michelle Leclaire O'Neill, Ph.D., R.N.,
is available for consultation by telephone.

For details visit www.leclairemethod.com or call 310-454-0920.

ABOUT THE AUTHOR

Michelle Leclaire O'Neill, Ph.D., R.N., has worked in the field of psycho-neuroimmunology for the past sixteen years. She was on the staff of the Simonton Cancer Center in southern California for ten years. While there, she taught meditation, imagery, their two-year health plan, dealing with death and dying as part of life, and getting well again. As a balance to her work with cancer patients, Dr. O'Neill began working with reproductive health and preventive medicine.

She developed the Leclaire Childbirth Method, the first childbirth method developed by a woman; coined the word *hypnobirthing* and created the Hypnobirthing Method; and created the Mind Body Fertility Program, which she teaches at various locales and expects to write about in her next book. She lectures and speaks extensively on her program. She counsels and works from her Mind Body Center in Pacific Palisades, California. She is the mother of three children. Her Web site is www.leclairemethod.com.